THRESHOLD

TRANSFORMATIONAL PRAYER

TRANSFORMATIONAL PRAYER LEADERSHIP

Paul Covert

To my three boys—Ben, Joel, and Daniel—
and their families,
who are making the world a better place,
by serving the Lord.

Contents

Acknowledgements

I must begin by thanking my wonderful wife, Annie, for all her help and unflagging encouragement. This project would have died long ago if she had not challenged me to continue and provided amazing clarity to the material. She believes in me and in this message, and for her support I will always be grateful.

I also wish to thank Cathy Cryer, who was the associate prayer pastor at Central and has worked alongside me for seven years. Although she was only paid for part-time work, she has worked much more, all because of her love for people and for connecting them to prayer. Her insights, loyalty, and editing skills were a blessing.

Also, thanks go to my longtime friend Rob Harris; without his keen eye and writing skill, this book would not have seen the light of day. Thank you, man!

Finally, I want to thank my readers and advisors, who helped clean this manual up so that you could enjoy it: Wanda Hall, Patti Vernon, Don and Denise Sherman, Lori Grogg, Mike Fleming, Bill Sweitzer, Dean Trune, and David Butts.

THRESHOLD

Introduction

*Delight yourself in the LORD and he will give you
the desires of your heart. Commit your way to the LORD;
trust in him and he will do this.*
(Psalm 37:4-5)

It is Sunday morning at nine o'clock, and services will start at Catalyst Community Church in thirty minutes. Catalyst is a multiracial church in one of the roughest neighborhoods in Phoenix. And the place is exploding.

A year earlier, Samson Dunn, senior pastor of Catalyst, and his staff had come to Central Christian Church along with some students from a Bible college to attend our Threshold Intensive. This is a four-day intensive training on prayer, presented along with practical experiences to bring the teachings alive. Not only did Dunn and his staff attend; they bought in. They completely bought in to the idea that getting their church founded on prayer takes it across the threshold into everything else God wants to do there in the church and through the church in the community.

Since then, the Catalyst church has experienced hundreds of baptisms and has grown from 900 to more than 1,300 weekly. *The only change they made was their commitment to prayer and prayer ministry in the church.* They began a weekly prayer meeting and have been enjoying a spirit of unity they had never known before. And there's another change: since the church was started, they had averaged eighty decisions for Christ per year; in the year since the Threshold Intensive, they saw 388 come to Christ. Samson and I have talked about it many times: the decision to become committed to prayer is the reason for all God is doing in that church, in a place *where these kinds of things should not be happening.*

But I digress. It was 9:00 a.m. when one of the elders escorted me to the prayer room. (Let me digress again: the senior pastor had *given up his office* so that the church would have a prime location for a prayer room to use for service intercession during all three services. How many senior pastors do you know who would be willing to give up their office so that the church could have a crucial space for prayer?) Several men joined us, and together we called out to God for the three services that were to take place that day.

Then, as the first service was about to begin, one of the men went to the front of the auditorium, and I watched with interest as all the other men who had come for the service gathered with him. I had never seen anything like that before, so before the second service I slipped up to the front to see what was going on as the men in that service did the same thing. Philippe, one of the elders, was leading the men in a time of prayer, saying:

> God, help us to be the fathers, husbands, and protectors of our homes you intended us to be. Help us to be the pastor and warrior of our address. We pray for this service this day and we are not content with just another service. Join us, Lord! Break us, Lord! Show up so you will be made known and worshiped by all who attend today.

I was dumbfounded. No wonder this place was exploding with growth, and no wonder it felt so alive! Prayer had become truly central here, not just something to say to start a service or to move from one element in the service to another. Prayer was now the very bedrock of this assembly. They got it; they had crossed the prayer threshold into an incredible journey with God as a church.

This book is intended to inspire Christians. I hope and I pray that it will help move those of you who already believe in prayer to *actually pray* fervently and consistently, and that it will begin to equip you to motivate fellow believers in your local church to do the same. My greatest joy would be to help many Christians to become true leaders in prayer ministry, and then to hear back from across the country the stories of their churches exploding with prayer ministry and the overwhelming blessing of God.

Do you, and does your church, have the guts to be remade through prayer? You and your church stand at the threshold with a choice.

Not About Me

Perhaps you have read books that contain too much material about the author and his or her work. As you work through this book, you may note that it also has much of my own life and ministry experience wrapped up in it. At times "I" bleed through more than I would like. Efforts have been made to remove as much personal material as possible and to include excellent thoughts from a variety of other sources. Much of what I have learned about prayer and practical prayer ministry has come, quite frankly, from the experiences that I have enjoyed in prayer and in years of prayer ministry. But please be sure to see and evaluate these personal stories and prayer ministry ideas as examples to fuel your thinking. You need to make your own experiences with the God of prayer. That being said, allow me to jump right into my story! (That's supposed to be funny.)

One Man's History with Prayer

I am one of those people who won't believe anything you tell them. You know people like me; we're the ones who refuse to take things at face value and who insist on having things proved to us before we will believe. I have been this way my whole life, as far back as I can remember.

One of my earliest memories of being this way centers on Santa Claus and my need as a serious-minded five year-old to authenticate his existence. My troubling suspicions about Santa had arisen through my observation of our Christmas stockings. Each year my mom would lovingly go to the store to buy fine foods we did not have at other times of the year. She would return with large navel oranges—the fancy ones, along with a selection of nuts, hard peppermint candies, and candy orange slices. But what seemed odd to me was that these same items would end up in my stocking on Christmas morning. So I pondered, is Santa bringing his own treats and oranges from the North Pole, or is he using ours? If he is using ours, why is he doing so? Is it because he has some kind of shortage at the North Pole? Or is it maybe even possible he is *not real*? To get answers to my questions, I hatched a devious plan. I took a ballpoint pen and marked each orange in the fruit bowl with a small dot. Then on Christmas day I could check to see if these were our oranges or if Santa had brought his own, and then I would decide if he was real or make-believe. The dots proved he was using our oranges, and my experiment led to Santa's demise.

You can probably imagine the problems a mind like mine has had with prayer.

Beyond regular doubts about supernatural topics of all kinds, a skepticism that can probably be viewed as completely normal, a more unusual struggle manifested itself during my childhood prayer times themselves. From around age five on, when I began to pray, it was as if someone was swearing in my ears. This continued for some years, and it evolved from a whispering of swear words to a loud screaming of filthy words in my ears. Obviously, this had a dramatically negative impact on my desire to pray and on the content of the prayers themselves. The profanity caused anxiety, uncertainty, and fear, and I can remember feeling guilty and very puzzled by it all. This torture went on for five years or so. I can't tell you exactly when it all went away, or how, but I was so grateful when it did.

From my perspective, there can be only one explanation for this kind of bizarre experience: yes, Satan. He was, I'm convinced, already working hard to discourage me from praying and attempting to keep me from developing a prayer life. (Isn't it interesting that later in life I should become a prayer pastor? Satan can't read our minds, but one of his strategies may well be to analyze us and then to attempt to block God's purposes in our gifts and lives. And I'm pretty sure he has never been happy about my praying.)

Another prayer problem cropped up when I was at college, studying for ministry, where we were told to pray and to have our devotions regularly. This is excellent advice, of course, but we were given so much homework that personal time with God most often got crowded out by other daily demands. Frustrated by the inability to pray as I was being taught to pray, and always feeling like it would be a good idea to pray more, I made up my mind to conduct another experiment to test the value of prayer just as soon as I graduated from college.

My first ministry after graduation was in Lawton, Oklahoma, where my role was to serve with the youth in a great midsized church of five hundred or so. Western Hills was one of the most dynamic churches in Oklahoma at that time, and I was thrilled to be on the staff.

Soon after arriving in Lawton I put my experiment into action. For the first thirty days I did not pray about anything we did in the youth ministry. I didn't pray for the weekly meetings, the special events, the church services, or even the people in the ministry. Then, at the end of thirty days, I switched my methods and began to pray for everything. My goal was to pray over each event, meeting, and opportunity for a full thirty days before it occurred. The intention was to determine the difference between prayer-backed ministry and personality-backed ministry (ministry done in our own strength and talents).

After the allotted time was up, I made an assessment of the value of my prayers. I noted that the ministry we'd conducted without prayer seemed flat and lifeless; not much of significance had resulted from it. We had our appointed meetings and did our studies, but to little avail. But the prayed-for ministry seemed to be filled with life and purpose.

I distinctly remember one prayer-backed Saturday night when my wife and I decided to have the youth group over for a movie. It wasn't the most creative event we had ever planned, but we decided to open up our home and just see what would happen. The kids showed up late as usual and hung out. Then, in the course of the evening, one girl opened up about her parents' struggles and her inability to cope with their fights. She revealed the significant fears their conflicts stirred up deep inside her. One of the younger boys revealed some of the issues he was having with a friend. At the end of the night I was astounded at what had transpired. That simple movie night had become one of the most fulfilling and meaningful youth events we experienced during our time in Oklahoma. So why was our ministry so much better? (And "better" is the only word that fits.) I concluded, somewhat subjectively I realize, that *the only possible reason was that God had moved in response to all that prayer, and had shown abundant grace* to a twenty-two year-old youth pastor who didn't have much experience.

I became personally convinced that prayer-backed ministry and life are much more effective than personality-backed ministry and life. Again, I realize this conclusion was based on my subjective observation, but it has proved true over the thirty years of ministry I have experienced since then. From that time on, I have been a believer in covering ministry and life in prayer, preferably at least thirty days of it.

And I'm convinced that by backing *your life and ministry* with thirty days of prayer you can have a confidence that is extraordinary when you go into a difficult meeting or event. Thirty days of prayer will make a vast difference when you preach, teach, and encourage people, or when you do whatever work you normally do. You may not have thirty days to work with, and that's of course not the point. God has obviously not laid down any legalistic lines here. The principle is to consistently back what you are doing with prayer. In fact, instead of saying we should "back" our ministry with prayer, it might be better to say we want to "front" it with prayer. Thirty days of fronting all we do by speaking to God about every aspect of it, asking Him to move through it, humbling yourself before Him about your role in it, and turning it completely over to Him.

If I wanted to build an effective ministry of any kind, I knew that prayer must be at the foundation of my work. Oh, I could get a crowd without prayer; just give away something electronic (today it would be an iPod or an iPad), and they'd come out in droves. But it goes without saying that lasting impact and life change are connected with paying due attention to the most important things. True ministry has always required time and energy and getting your hands dirty, so it follows that true ministry should also require a foundation of *time and energy in prayer*, investing in the spiritual elements of ministry. Unfortunately, because of the difficulty and time demands involved in covering events and life in prayer, few are willing to make the investment. Many try the shortcut that leaves the prayer foundation out, but I am convinced this will never produce all God intended. See Matthew 7:24-29.

Now back to my personal prayer history. After becoming convinced of the power of prayer and of praying for thirty days over events, meetings, and other ministry items, I tried yet another experiment. I decided to make a detailed record of my prayers in a journal. I am not referring to my daily prayers, the general requests I made for my family and our personal needs each day, at mealtimes, for example. I recorded what I would call "measurable prayers" that could be tracked and that were about more specific needs and requests. These needs were expressed in prayers such as, "Lord, we need ten more people to serve in the youth ministry as group leaders. Would you please draw people with the right passions and gifts to begin to work in this area?" On the personal side, a measurable prayer would have been something like, "Lord, I need some extra money to help with the car repairs. Would you please open a door for me to make some extra money or provide in another way?"

I entered the date I began to pray and what I was asking for, and then I left some space for what I called the "calendar of encouragement." For example, I was praying for the neighbors across the street to come to faith in Jesus. One day, after I had been praying for them for a while, I noticed the neighbor lady out in front of their house watering the grass, and I felt prompted to walk across the street to visit with her for a few minutes. If she was warm and pleasant and it felt like some of the walls were coming down in the relationship between our family and hers, I would note the date in the "calendar of encouragement" section of my journal for that prayer request. That prayer was not yet answered, but it seemed that God was preparing the way for the answer to arrive. Then, when it was answered, I would note the date of God's answer and thank Him for it.

I kept that particular prayer journal for five full years and recorded in it faithfully the whole time, and at the end of the fifth year I had literally thousands of answered prayers. The entries were things that only He and I knew anything about. Today that first prayer journal rests on one of the shelves of my office, and occasionally I pick it up and just read through it to remember what God has done. I cannot say this more emphatically: *Nothing has strengthened my prayer life more than keeping this prayer journal. Nothing!* Not Bible college classes or graduate study, not sermons or testimonies, not conferences, or slick video teaching I've seen; nothing has strengthened my faith more than keeping a prayer journal and watching God work in it. Psalm 66:5 says, "Come and see what God has done, how awesome his works in man's behalf!"[1]

Let me again pause in my story for a moment to more directly address this topic of recording our prayers. Many people pray but never record anything. Then, when the answer to a particular prayer comes, they have already moved on to something else and don't notice God's movement or thank Him for His involvement. Not saying thank you to God is wrong, *biblically* wrong. It is also at the very least remarkably disrespectful of Him, and it may be even deeply offensive to Him. Jesus was disappointed when only one of the ten lepers He healed returned to say thank you in Luke 17:11-19. Psalm 100:4 instructs us to "enter His gates with thanksgiving." It seems to me we're constantly trying to enter with a whining attitude and not a hint of thanksgiving to be found anywhere in our lives! If we have asked God for something, we should at least thank Him when our request is granted. So let's come back to the prayer journal for a moment: recording our prayers affords us the opportunity to watch the hand of God orchestrating our lives. And as we look back over the answered prayers, we will see His work and involvement in our lives, and that observation will serve to stimulate more thoughts of thanksgiving and a deep, heartfelt gratitude. These are gravely missing in the prayer lives of most American Christians.

Even though I knew I was on to something with recording my prayers, I still got it wrong at first.

Once I had seen such clear evidence of the power of prayer, of *my prayers*, I began to pray for all kinds of things. Sure, I prayed for ministry items and growth for our ministries, but I also prayed for more, you know, *personal* things: "God, I would like a newer, bigger TV and some better furniture in the living room." To my amazement, we wound up with a bigger TV and nicer furniture for the living room. Eventually, I began to view prayer wrongly, almost as if I were rubbing the bottle of a genie. I asked for too many personal things and thought—self-righteously, I am ashamed to say— that the reason others lacked God's blessing was because of their unwillingness to pray systematically and to put in the time as I was doing.

Some have observed that when a believer begins to get serious about prayer, God may answer a number of requests of all kinds to help him comprehend the power and importance of prayer. It's impossible to estimate a number of requests He might answer for a new prayer practitioner, and we can't begin to prove this statement; rather, it is simply an observation that I have also made. However, I am convinced His desire is to help us see the value and power of prayer, especially when we are new at it.

I eventually began, at least some of the time, to want something else when I came to God in prayer, and that was His presence. When we genuinely experience His presence, we find it so incredible that everything else seems empty and meaningless by comparison. I would love to be able to say that I live only in and for God's presence, but that wouldn't be true. I strive to, but I don't. It may not even be possible for most human beings to live in that state all the time, but I have tasted His presence, and it makes me desire heaven profoundly.

To be clear, God continues to answer the prayers and petitions I bring to Him. Some are answered quite quickly, while others take a long time. On the other hand, prayer for some requests seems to bring no movement whatsoever. But because He has been so faithful, and because I have a record of His faithfulness, it has become easier for me to trust Him with the ones that take longer.

And I am learning to become content with what He provides. Overemphasizing prayer for personal needs is an easy trap to fall into, once you begin recording your prayers and note with amazement all He does when you ask Him. I do still pray for personal material needs and blessings, but I am learning more and more to long for Him and His kingdom.

Sometimes people ask me, "How did you move from selfish praying to longing for His presence?" They want to know the steps, but I don't have any to offer. I believe that this maturation, if that's what it is, is something God performs in us as we enter His presence repeatedly. His presence is so good that everything else just starts to seem like garbage in comparison, and the sometimes-painful work of prayer becomes a true joy. C.S. Lewis wrote about this in his *Letters to Malcolm*:

> We shrink from too naked a contact (with God) because we are afraid of the divine demands on us that it makes too audible. As some old writer says, "Many a Christian prays faintly lest God might really hear him, which he, poor man, never intended." The painful effort that prayer involves is no proof that we are doing something we were not created to do. If we were perfected it would not be a duty; it would be delight.[2]

Are you as interested as I am in that kind of delight in your time with God? And do you think it would also represent a God-glorifying and tremendous blessing for every member of a church body?

Ten Reasons to Keep Reading

1. You are a church member or leader who is beginning a prayer ministry, and you need some help getting started.
2. You have started a church prayer ministry, but it is not going very well, and you want to make it vibrant.
3. You are leading a church prayer ministry, and you find yourself discouraged and beaten down.
4. You need a few practical ideas to build into your church's existing prayer ministry.
5. You need help seeing the big picture of prayer ministry and casting a vision for prayer in your church.

6. You are looking for current thinking on prayer from someone who is doing prayer ministry in a real church today (and maybe you're not so interested in stories from long ago).

7. You lead a small group, and you have trouble getting those in your study to pray.

8. You are not yet laying a foundation of prayer for the special events already on your church's calendar, nor are you taking advantage of these events to recruit and train up pray-ers.

9. You are responsible for prayer on more than one church campus.

10. You want to teach people to pray but are not sure how to go about it.

CHAPTER 1

The Mystery and Value of Prayer

And as he [Jesus] was praying, heaven was opened.
(Luke 3:21b)

You have to love this verse! And if you're at all like me, you also have to wonder if it applies to us, and for today. Would God open the heavens to us as we pray? I think He just might.

Have you noticed that the heavens are not necessarily opened after every prayer? Part of the reason for that may be that people actually pray for all sorts of strange reasons, with all sorts of motivations, for all sorts of things, and some of those people may unfortunately be us.

Just recently I was in a Middle Eastern country on a prayer journey with a team. We were praying for the nation and the persecuted believers who live there, interceding against the oppression of Christians and asking God to open the nation to the gospel. But while we were there, we noticed an unusual custom among some of the locals. The men attempt to mark or bruise themselves on the forehead to show their faithfulness in prayer. They do this by placing a little pebble on the concrete to ensure they get a bruise on their forehead as they bow into it. The larger the mark, the better and more spiritual that man is perceived to be.

We may view the idea of bruising ourselves physically to appear spiritual as strangely self-centered for something like prayer, which should so obviously be centered on God. But we are kidding ourselves if we believe we Christians don't do and say things to make ourselves appear more spiritual than we really are.

Moreover, are we fooling ourselves if we contend that we never pray for some reasons or motiviations that God may consider less than ideal? A seemingly innocuous example of a less-than-ideal reason to pray may be to make a smooth transition from one element to another during a worship service. Although smooth transitions are helpful to keep us on track in worship, I cringe to think we pray here just because it makes the service flow better. Doesn't God deserve more than that?

Why do we pray? One perfectly understandable reason people all around the world pray is that they want to "be more spiritual" in their lives, to somehow turn up the volume of their personal spirituality. Yes, many may be sorely misguided in their efforts, but it is impossible to deny that theirs is an admirable and reasonable desire for a connection with the supernatural, whether that means with their false god or gods, or maybe even with the one true God whom I have followed for forty-five years. Perhaps this is just evidence of the so-called "God-shaped hole" that, it is said, every person possesses. Wherever that motivation comes from originally, people of all kinds and cultures are praying with great earnestness, and some may pray with much more passion than we Christians do, employing varying memorized or spontaneous phrases, and even physical actions. The prayers of the world are expressed in many styles and formats, but this one desire behind all our words and gyrations is probably roughly the same. And for those of us who are blessed to know of and believe in the true God of heaven, perhaps we are going to these lengths in prayer to bond with Him spiritually and to have peace with Him. People do pray for these reasons.

And, of course, people of various faiths continue to pray because they want certain things, whether that's a healing for a loved one or their own personal private island, whether it's for effectiveness in their ministry or for some relief from the nagging guilt they feel because of a past sin or a broken relationship. People who want something tend to pray; what could be more natural?

But without denying the validity of these reasons we have just mentioned, let's begin to answer a second, more important, question, which is, why *should* we pray? Consider as an introduction to this question the strange events recorded in Ezekiel 37. We read that the Spirit of the Lord brought Ezekiel out into a valley of very dry bones. God posed Ezekiel an obvious trick question, "Can these bones live?" (v. 3). Ezekiel was too frightened to attempt an answer, so he dodged it: "O Sovereign LORD, you alone know!" he said. God then commanded Ezekiel to preach to the bones, so he did, and the bones began to rattle and make noise.

Bob Bakke, founder of the Global Day of Prayer, has said in a message about this, "We preachers like it when we preach and things begin to happen and make noise." But the passage shows us that even in the noise there was no life. So then God told Ezekiel to preach to the breath, saying, "Come from the four winds, O breath, and breathe into these slain, that they may live" (v. 18). Bakke says about this, "Now the life of God is invading these dry bones."

The application is certainly clear enough: without God, we are dead, lifeless, dry bones. But when we connect with Him, the sustainer and creator of life, the God of all, we receive life from Him, and we begin to truly live. So we pray—we *should* pray—in part because it is the way we bond with God and hear His voice, and also because it is the way we appropriate His *life and power* into our lives and into our churches.

The promise of an increase in life and power for myself and the ministry of my church appeals to me deeply, and it motivates me to pray. In the next couple of pages I list some other appealing and motivating reasons to pray. I realize that much has been written about prayer, including about this particular question: why pray? So I have chosen here to emphasize a few reasons that should be particularly appealing to *Christians in churches*, and to the *leaders of those churches* who are considering increasing their focus on prayer ministry.

We Should Pray Because God Increases Lasting Fruit Through It. Life operated without prayer is missing the power and increase that God intends for us to experience. In my years of ministry, I have consistently observed this simple principle in action:

No prayer ➜ little lasting fruit

Prayer ➜ increased fruit and lasting blessing

In conjunction with my first youth work in Lawton we started a second youth ministry to a little town known as Cache, located ten miles west of the city. This was a dying town where not much was going on for the kids, so we began reaching out to the community there. We called the ministry "Cache Bash," and we held events once a quarter or so for several years. It worked well, and many of those kids came over to our youth activities in Lawton and started to participate there as well. I am still in contact with some of them.

Now, this particular work was deeply immersed in prayer, not just "prayed for" a few times. After I left that Oklahoma church to start one here in Arizona, I looked back over what was happening in the Lawton church and the ministries of the past several years, and I noticed something very interesting. The ministries that had been heavily prayed over continued on long after I was gone. And not only did they continue, they produced. I think it is extremely safe to say, as a general rule, that prayer increases fruit; that is, God increases and multiplies the fruit of our ministry when we pray. There may be times when God withholds fruit to teach us something, or He may not bless us in some way when we are in sin. But these exceptions do not negate the principle: God responds to our prayer by increasing lasting fruit.

We Should Pray Because It Replaces Conflict and Anxiety with Peace. Anyone with any ministry experience whatsoever knows that it can often be plagued by conflict (the opposite of interpersonal peace), and by anxiety in the heart and mind of the one or ones doing the ministry (the opposite of personal peace). Prayer is real, practical help for both problems.

Satan wants us to live in troubling, water-muddying, time-wasting conflict with each other, especially in our churches and ministries, but God wants us to work in peace and unity with one another. By joining together in prayer with the other believers with whom we serve, we are injecting our relationships with strong preventive medicine, relationally and supernaturally. It is very difficult to be at war with a person you are agreeing with in prayer, and the Spirit's bond that connects you is strengthened as well.

Anxiety, the absence of personal peace, and its solution through prayer are directly addressed in Philippians 4:6-7:

> Do not be anxious about anything, but in everything,
> by prayer and petition, with thanksgiving, present
> your requests to God. And the peace of God, which
> transcends all understanding, will guard your hearts
> and your minds in Christ Jesus.

Paul is really talking about a prayer of surrender, and an unconditional surrender to God will most often result in an increase in peace. In fact, when we pray, peace rises in and flows through any given situation, no matter what it is or how deep the trouble may be.

We Should Pray Because It Opens the Door to the Supernatural: God Makes Connections and Coincidences Commonplace. Bible reading gives us the mind of a supernatural God; meditation helps us sound the depth of God and apply His truths to our lives; prayer seems to activate His power to flow through us and over us.

I first learned this principle one Christmas season many years ago. Annie and I moved to Arizona in 1984 and started a church in our living room on December 15 of that year. The following year around Christmastime, a family who had attended our church but had moved to the other side of town ran into some hard times. As a new church seeking meaningful ministry opportunities, we were looking for a need we could meet at Christmas, so we decided to help this family. Our first step was to send a reconnaissance team over to where they were living to see what their greatest needs were. When the team returned with their observations, the report was disturbing.

This family had moved into a very low-end apartment complex with twenty-five other families. Many of those living in the apartments were refugees from a country that was undergoing a period of political and social unrest. Our team felt pretty certain that, if we helped just this one family, some of the others might harm our family out of jealousy, need, or both. So the suggestion was made that we should help all twenty-five families in the apartments instead of just the one family we knew. This would be a fine idea for most churches, but we were still very small, around one hundred members at that time. Being the spiritual giant that I am, I made a quick and sweeping proclamation. "There is no way one small church can help twenty-five families," I said. "This is out of our reach." But our team would not let it go. And then we began praying! One man stepped forward with a bread truck and offered to transport all the items we were able to gather. Food, clothes and toys began to pour in. Finally, and very reluctantly, I agreed that we should try to do what we could, knowing this was going to be a mistake in leadership but feeling quite trapped. Still, we all moved together in prayer and action.

I was astounded at what transpired. We received massive donations of clothes, toys, and personal hygiene items. Household items like toasters and blenders tumbled in. There were more objects donated than seemed possible from a church our size. But we were still short on one thing, food. I distinctly remember sitting in my office and praying about all this when the phone rang. The person on the other end identified herself: "This is Maggie from Fry's Food Stores headquarters." Now, we were meeting in rented space along with a Fry's grocery store, so there were already some points of contact, and this didn't seem too out of the ordinary until she continued, "I am the president's administrative assistant, and we are looking for churches that are helping families at Christmas. We have two pickup loads of canned goods that we would like to donate to a church that is helping others at Christmas. Do you all have a use for the food?"

I was dumbstruck and actually dropped the phone. That was pretty embarrassing. Eventually I gained my composure and assured her that we had just the place for the food. Our team took it all over to the apartment complex, and we had enough for everyone. I learned a great lesson that day: prayer opens the door to the supernatural. Some may say that it was a coincidence that I was praying about that very situation when that call came, but I know better, and our ministry history is full of such supernatural connections and coincidences. Praying believers experience more of them.

We Should Pray Because It Changes the Course of Human History. Too often, our churches are unhealthy little microcosms unto themselves, pulling back into ourselves for protection against the seemingly overwhelming pressures put upon us by the ungodly culture that surrounds us. But praying Christians have power available to them that can dynamically affect the broader communities in which they live, and a praying church can be used by God to quite literally change an entire city or region, and can dramatically alter the daily experience of life for large numbers of people, which is nothing less than a page of human history itself.

I'll share just one example, a story about one community you may have heard of that experienced significant change at a key moment in its past. This account of a phenomenon that occurred in

New York City in the 1850s is taken from J. Edwin Orr's *The Light of the Nations*:

> Secular and religious conditions combined to bring about a crash. The third great panic in American history swept the giddy structure of speculative wealth away. Thousands of merchants were forced to the wall as banks failed, and railroads went into bankruptcy. Factories were shut down and vast numbers thrown out of employment, New York City alone having 30,000 idle men. In October 1857, the hearts of the people were thoroughly weaned from speculation and uncertain gain, while hunger and despair stared them in the face.
>
> On July 1st, 1857, a quiet and zealous business man named Jeremiah Lanphier took up an appointment as a City Missionary in down-town New York. Lanphier was appointed by the North Church of the Dutch Reformed denomination. This church was suffering from depletion of membership due to the removal of the population from down-town to the better residential quarters, and the new City Missionary was engaged to make diligent visitation in the immediate neighborhood with a view to enlisting church attendance among the floating population of the lower city. The Dutch Consistory felt that it had appointed an ideal layman for the task in hand and so it was.
>
> Burdened so by the need, Jeremiah Lanphier decided to invite others to join him in a noonday prayer meeting, to be held on Wednesdays. He therefore distributed a handbill:

How Often Shall I Pray?

As often as the language of prayer is in my heart; as often as I see my need of help; as often as I feel the power of temptation; as often as I am made sensible of any spiritual declension or feel the aggression of a worldly spirit.

In prayer we leave the business of time for that of eternity, and intercourse with men for intercourse with God.

A day Prayer Meeting is held every Wednesday from 12 to 1 o'clock, in the Consistory building in the rear of the North Dutch Church, corner of Fulton and Williams streets (entrance from Fulton and Ann Streets).

This meeting is intended to give merchants, mechanics, clerks, strangers, business men generally an opportunity to stop and call upon God amid the perplexities incident to their respective avocations. It will continue for one hour, but it is also designed for those who may find it inconvenient to remain more than five or ten minutes, as well as for those who can spare the whole hour.

Accordingly at twelve noon, 23rd of September 1857 the door opened and the faithful Lanphier took his seat to await the response to his invitation. Five minutes went by. No one appeared. The missionary paced the room in a conflict of fear and faith. Ten minutes elapsed. Still no one came. Fifteen minutes passed. Lanphier was yet alone.

Twenty minutes; twenty-five; thirty; and at 12:30 p.m., a step was heard on the stairs, and the first person appeared, then another, and another, and another, until six people were present and the prayer meeting began. On the following Wednesday, . . . there were forty intercessors.

Thus in the first week of October 1857, it was decided to hold a meeting daily instead of weekly. . . . Within six months, *ten thousand business men* were gathering daily for prayer in New York, and within two years, a million converts were added to the American churches. . . .

Undoubtedly the greatest revival in New York's colorful history was sweeping the city, and it was of such an order to make the whole nation curious. There was no fanaticism, no hysteria, simply an incredible movement of people to prayer.[3]

This is just one of hundreds of documented occasions of prayer changing a community or city and even changing a period of time for many people. In fact, even today the stories seem to be multiplying of groups of people who have taken prayer seriously and begun to pray transformationally for a city, a state, or a nation. George Otis Jr. has done a masterful job in his *Transformation* DVDs to illuminate places around the globe where prayer has either brought in a whole new regime or a change in a sitting government that gives it a new openness to the things of God.

We Should Pray Because of God's Wonderful Reserve of Resources. Matthew 19:26 says it clearly enough: "With God all things are possible."

If someone could give you access to the riches of Warren Buffett, would you be interested? Sure you would, even if you had to go through some serious paperwork to get at it. If someone promised you a thousand dollars for every hour you prayed, would it increase your prayer life? For most of us it would. But think about this, please, even if it is derived from a slightly overused platitude: God has the cattle on a thousand hills at His disposal, and He can put them at our disposal if He wills it. He framed the earth and the universe. He separated the darkness from the light and created the sun and the moon and the stars. The oceans are kept in their boundaries by His power. With the number of sheer *options* that His wealth of material and dynamic resources represents, all available to us, we are simply crazy if we do not invite Him into our lives or ask His help with our resourcing challenges.

It has become great fun for me to invite God into resourcing situations that seem impossible, and then to wait and watch Him work. A couple of years ago Annie and I began to pray for one of our sons to be able to afford a house for his family. Frankly, the chances did not look very good that he and his wife would be able to pull the finances together. But in time, and after much prayer, God opened His hand of blessings and provided them a great house.

One principle I've begun watching for in Scripture and in everyday life and ministry concerns God's supernatural multiplication of power and resources. Biblical characters such as Gideon and Joshua used small, ragtag armies (in battle, we could call that a serious *human* resources problem!), and yet these men experienced unbelievable victories.

Several Bible passages seem to directly address this multiplication principle. For example, Deuteronomy 32:30 asks, "How could one man chase a thousand, or two put ten thousand to flight . . . ?" Leviticus 26:8 says, "Five of you will chase a hundred, and a hundred of you will chase ten thousand, and your enemies will fall by the sword before you." And probably the most famous examples are the accounts of Jesus' multiplication of fish and bread to feed thousands, recorded in several places in the gospels.

I have to wonder how many resource problems go unresolved because we do not take time to pray. I want to say it forcefully here:

we should pray thoroughly and consistently about every resourcing hurdle we face.

We Should Pray Because It Causes Satan to Tremble. It would be very helpful if we could listen in on Satan sometime, or if we could get some clear video of him going about his work. Maybe we could learn something about where his weaknesses lie and what really upsets him—you know, his deepest fears. Honestly, I don't know what Satan fears, but it is my strong suspicion that he fears the prayers of humble saints. Samuel Chadwick came to that conclusion, stating it even more categorically:

> Satan dreads *nothing but prayer* [emphasis added]. The church that has lost its Christ was full of good works. Activities are multiplied that meditation may be ousted, and organizations are increased that prayer may have no chance. Souls may be lost in good works, as surely as in evil ways. The one concern of the devil is to keep the saints from praying. He fears nothing from prayerless studies, prayerless work, prayerless religion. He laughs at our toil, mocks our wisdom, but trembles when we pray.[4]

There is a spiritual battle going on in the invisible realms with regard to the prayers of God's people. Daniel chapter 10 makes this point fairly clearly. In that passage, we notice that the moment Daniel set out to fast and pray to gain insight, God began to respond, but the answer was delayed for twenty-one days by the "prince of the Persian Kingdom" (verse 13), a character and title many commentators have associated with Satan. The idea that our prayers play a large and significant role in a much more complex supernatural battle will be developed more when we talk about perseverance in prayer and spiritual warfare.

Expanding upon what Mahesh and Bonnie Chavda have written, prayers "are not toys for the spiritual playpen; they are weapons for the battlefield." The authors go on to say, "Healing, deliverance and miracles . . . flow from the anointing of the Holy Spirit as we step into the arena of prayer."[5] Solid Christians and truly healthy churches find their richest blessings in the victories won on that battlefield, where Satan is hindered in his efforts to obstruct what God is doing in and for us.

We Should Pray Because It Helps Protect Our Leaders from Leading in the Flesh. Leaders who do not pray lead from the flesh; what else can they do? Meanwhile, praying leaders can lead with the peace and confidence that come from knowing they have God's guidance for the issues or situations they are facing. Flesh-based leaders fall too easily into traps of insecurity and emotional reaction to all sorts of situations. These leaders are prone to errors such as moving too slowly or too rashly on a decision or action, or worse yet, missing God's leadership altogether.

For these reasons and more, we should pray for our church and ministry leaders to be guided and fueled by the Spirit. And if the leader in question is me, it is no selfish prayer to protect the church or ministry I lead by asking Him to guide and fuel me.

We Should Pray Because Prayer Is Intriguingly Mysterious. One final characteristic of prayer that both attracts me to it and frustrates me at the same time is the utter sense of mystery that surrounds every aspect of it. What spiritual mechanisms and dynamics are at work when we pray? How does God hear or receive my prayer, as acoustic words in the room where I speak or think them, or as some kind of reminder, because He already knew what I was going to pray anyway? Or is it both, or neither?

Even more confounding and interesting to me is the complete mystery concerning which prayers God will answer in the affirmative and which will be denied. Because I have been praying extensively for years now, I sometimes get a sense about which way God will decide with regard to certain requests. But I am frequently wrong. Some requests I think are a slam dunk for God's approval and outpoured blessing are apparently not granted at all, while other prayers I believe to be long shots are often blessed by God with amazing results. The truth is, we can evaluate and speculate all day long about what God is up to, but none of us knows the mind of God. He alone determines His responses to our prayers, and it is dangerous to think and pray otherwise, as some teachers would have us do. We will not trap God into responding in our favor by the manner in which we pray, or by framing the prayer a certain way.

Several years ago a man came up to me after a church service and asked me if I would pray for his upcoming ocean cruise. He and his wife were celebrating their twenty-fifth wedding anniversary and they wanted me to pray that they would have a good time on their trip.

People often approach me like this, or they e-mail me to ask me to pray for something. And there are some who seem to think that since I am the prayer pastor, I have a red phone in my office that connects me directly to God. Obviously, I have no such phone, and I do everything in my power to help people see they have all the same access to God in prayer that I do. But some prayer requests do catch my heart, and I genuinely want to pray for them. Other requests, like this one about the cruise, well, not so much. But it is hard to say, "No, I won't pray about that with you!" when you are the prayer pastor. This request was certainly one of those I did not have a passion for, but felt I ought to say yes, and so I prayed.

Later that same day another man came up to me and asked me to pray for his mother, who was dying of cancer and was suffering greatly. This was an easy request for me to bring to the Father, and I prayed hard for her in faith.

About a month later I saw the couple, the ones who had gone on the cruise. They had an amazing tale to tell about how the cruise line had overbooked their cruise and had given their room to someone else. So the only room left was the Presidential Suite. Our anniversary couple got this upgrade at no extra charge and had the time of their lives. Can you believe that?

The woman who had cancer continued to suffer, and later died.

Now, I did not want the couple to have a bad anniversary cruise experience! I wanted them to have a good time. But couldn't God have arranged for them to receive only a small upgrade, and given the rest of the blessing to the man whose mother was so ill? His need and request seemed more important to me. But that was not the way the Lord responded.

Prayer is nearly as mysterious as the eternal and almighty God behind it; like Him, it can never be calculated or manipulated. This both fascinates me about God and attracts me to prayer. The Bible tells us we will never understand completely the depths of these mysteries and many others until heaven, when we will see "face to face" instead of "in a mirror, darkly" (1 Corinthians 13:12, American Standard Version). And frankly, I'm glad our God is too complicated for me to be able to completely understand Him here and now. "The secret things belong to the LORD our God, but the things revealed belong to us and to our children forever, that we may follow all the words of this law" (Deuteronomy 29:29).

Instead of becoming frustrated by what you do not yet know or understand about prayer, allow yourself to be motivated by its mystery and the sheer joy of watching in amazement as God moves in ways you can't predict. By praying, allow Him to open the heavens to bless you, inspire you, and amaze you in any way He chooses.

Allow me to sum up this chapter by saying *we should pray because we want to,* because we want to speak to our Lord and our God about life, and to give Him free rein in our lives and churches. It would be most healthy if we American Christians could each move away from a sense of duty and the expectations of others as our primary motivations for prayer, and instead build in ourselves a heartfelt ache for Him and His rule in us. We decide what we want, and then we want it. We can therefore also *decide to want to simply be with Him* in prayer, enjoying His presence, telling Him what troubles us or overjoys us.

Our goal as praying believers is to want Him more than anything else.

CHAPTER 2

The Case for Prayer Ministry

Prayer does not change the purpose of God.
But prayer does change the action of God.
—Chuck Smith

A good friend of mine is the senior pastor of a strong church in our area. I have preached to his congregation for him when he needed to be out of town, and we have worked together at different times. His congregation built a new building a couple of years ago, and they have already filled it up. Not long ago he invited us to visit their new facilities, so Annie, my wife, and I went to see the building and share in their services. We had arranged to meet my friend backstage so that he could show us around, and the first thing he showed us was their prayer room. They had created a nice room, but it had a problem that became obvious to them only after construction, something they'd missed in the blueprints. His first words were, "This is our prayer room, but it isn't usable. This is the only way to get backstage, so people are always coming and going through this area. You would have thought someone would have picked up on this, but we just missed it."

This benign little example points out one of the weaknesses of one church, and there are obviously plenty of those stories to go around; there's nothing really exciting to be gained from focusing on yet another one. But if we will ponder for just a moment the gravity of this particular kind of oversight—and the church in the example above is certainly not the worst offender—we might think more aggressively about what to do about it. Because, you see, *this oversight, the thing we're consistently overlooking, is God's power and leading in our churches.*

The case for increasing the emphasis on prayer ministry in churches is based on this simple set of observations:

♦ Prayer makes a tremendous difference.
♦ God's people aren't praying as they could be.
♦ Each Christian and each church need to be systematically and clearly taught and led to pray.

I've already discussed some of the tremendous difference prayer makes, so let's look briefly at the second observation, which is all about prayerlessness.

The Biggest Prayer Problem: People Aren't Praying Much.
The impact of prayer in the lives of the early church and saints is undeniable. But over the centuries, and maybe especially over the past century or so, prayer has drifted or been downgraded from its place in the center of the life of the church to its current position as a sort of unspoken value. It may, in fact, sometimes still be *said to be important*, if you corner a leader and ask about it, and yet it is somehow not talked about very much in the day-to-day life of the church. In more recent years, prayer has been even more starkly de-emphasized in some circles and churches, and is frequently no longer even an unspoken value, but rather something many believers are downright uncomfortable with. And this is mostly because they have not done much of it.

We, the American Church, have plenty of fine minds thinking about the church all the time. They are reflecting not only on theology, but also on scientific elements of church work such as cultural trends and community demographics. They ponder best leadership practices and contextualized outreach methodologies. You would think that more great minds would have noticed the lack of emphasis on prayer and initiated a movement to correct it.

Look at the Numbers. I would estimate that the average American prays about thirty-two seconds a day and the average pastor prays somewhere around four minutes and thirty seconds daily. I haven't personally performed a scientific study to arrive at this conclusion, but there are a number of excellent studies and surveys out there, some of which helped me come to this estimate. Here's just a sampling of some of those studies and some other observations, in no particular order.

- According to a significant Gallup poll and study from 1996, "More Americans will pray this week than will: exercise; drive a car; have sex, or go to work."[6]
- Philip Yancey writes that nine out of ten of us pray regularly and that three out of four claim to pray every day.[7]
- C. Peter Wagner, in his now somewhat dated book from 1992, *The Prayer Shield*, observed slightly longer average times for prayer. He describes the parameters of his study in this way:

I personally conducted a survey of 572 pastors across regional, age and denominational lines. I wanted to find out just how much time a day pastors spend in actual prayer. In this survey I was not counting Bible study, reading devotional books, listening to worship tapes or other components of a fully rounded devotional life. I was dealing only with prayer.

Wagner concluded that the average pastor prayed twenty-two minutes per day.[8]

◆ The results of a more recent study were reported in the 2009 book *The Seven Great Prayers* by Paul and Tracey McManus. The question was asked, "When and how much do people pray?" Here are their findings:

◊ An average prayer lasts just under five minutes.
◊ Fifty-two percent of those who pray do so several times a day.
◊ Thirty-seven percent of people say they pray once a day.
◊ Thirty-three percent of these adults regularly participate in a prayer group or prayer-focused meeting.
◊ Twenty-one percent have extended prayer time with other family members (twenty-five percent among Protestants and thirteen percent among Catholics).[9]

◆ In the devotional thought for Day 8 of the *80 Days of Discipleship* by the Navigators, in an article entitled "Communion with God," Rusty Rustenbach writes, "It is estimated that a typical Christian spends about three-and-a-half minutes each day in prayer." (This number may be the one we should find most disturbing.)[10]

◆ Another survey was conducted by Evangelical Missions Quarterly, which reported that of 390 missionaries surveyed, eleven percent spent less than an average of five minutes per day in prayer. Sixty percent spent between eleven and thirty minutes daily in prayer.[11]

Although exact numbers are admittedly difficult to nail down, there is enough material out there to make a sound case that we are not overexerting ourselves in prayer.

One more statistic is worth noting: I recently heard that only one in ten thousand of us prays an hour a day. Do you know anyone who prays an hour a day? I do, and I find all of them to be amazing people. You can tell just by being around them that something deep is going on inside as they walk with God.

To help us visualize that one-in-ten-thousand number, let's consider the greater Phoenix area where I live, which has a population of roughly five million. That would mean, if this statistic is accurate, that we have only about five hundred people in our enormous (and very church-saturated, I might add) city who pray one hour a day. Is it any wonder we are not seeing the power of God as we would like to? Neither a deep understanding of God's will nor His intimate acquaintance can be packaged in one-minute, bullet-point conversations. Genuine and meaningful connection with God is not made hastily or without investment. To be alone with God is an honor and a privilege too few take advantage of.

To summarize, it is clear that Americans are doing a bit of praying, but our concern, as leaders, should be that we are a long way from being "devoted . . . to prayer" as Christians are described in Acts 2:42.

Let's look at a couple of scriptures that show the early church's commitment to prayer.

Acts 2:42 is a summary statement of the life of the New Testament church: "They devoted themselves to the apostles' teaching and to fellowship, to the breaking of bread and to prayer." Notice that one of the core elements of their devotion was prayer. What do you think the devotion to prayer meant to them? Do you think our churches in America today could be described as devoted to prayer?

Now take a look at Acts 6:2-4 and observe the reason for selecting the men whom many see as the first deacons of the Jerusalem church. It says:

> So the Twelve gathered all the disciples together and said, 'It would not be right for us to neglect the ministry of the word of God in order to wait on tables. Brothers, choose seven men from among you

who are known to be full of the Spirit and wisdom. We will turn this responsibility over to them *and will give our attention to prayer and the ministry of the word'* [emphasis added].

These first deacons were chosen so that the apostles/elders would not be distracted from their primary functions as spiritual leaders, which were to teach and to pray.

The sad truth is we have nearly lost prayer as a focus of the American church and even among the leadership of the American church. In his book *These Are The Generations*, Rev. Eric Foley gives this account:

> When my wife and I speak about North Korea at events in the West, people always ask us, "How can we pray for North Korean Christians?" So we asked a group of North Korean underground Christians that question. They answered, "Pray for us? We pray for you!" When asked why, they replied, "Because Christians in the West still have some wealth and freedom and power. Most have not experienced what it is like when all you have in life is God."[12]

North Korean believers are not the only people who observe the weakness in American Christians. Brothers and sisters in many countries know that our American freedom, wealth, and power create a comfortable mind-set among believers in this country. Despite the challenges we face, we still have enough power, freedom, and wealth most of the time to live somewhat independently of God. And so we don't pray.

One last sorrowful observation: I've noticed that in most churches, the prayer ministry is the smallest ministry with the fewest participants and the smallest allocation of resources, and many churches have no dedicated prayer ministry whatsoever. American

Christians as a whole, including avid churchgoers, cannot be described as devoted pray-ers.

If you look at it too long, all this information comes together to paint a rather depressing picture. Helping the church rediscover prayer has become my sincere passion and the true reason for writing this book.

So What Do We Do About This?

This is the question the rest of this book seeks to answer in some detail. As we begin to move toward an answer, please pause to ponder this thought:

Is prayerlessness a weakness or a sin?

Flesh, by scriptural definition, goes its own way instead of God's. The born again, or redeemed, part of us wants God and His way. Times of prayerlessness reflect our times of independence and of the flesh. Look at this comparison.

Prayerlessness	Devotion to Prayer
Is a declaration that not much stirs the heart of God, that He doesn't care.	Is a declaration that God cares for His people and hears their prayers.
Is a declaration of our independence from God.	Is a declaration of our need for God, our utter dependence upon Him.
Effectively minimizes God's power and His active influence in our lives.	Seeks to maximize His active role in our lives.
Says, "I'm just fine living without Him."	Says, "I will never be OK without God."

In short, as you may have surmised, I don't believe prayerlessness is primarily a weakness, though there's plenty of weakness associated with it. Prayerlessness is a sin, and beyond that it is a reflection of wrong, sin-derived attitudes that run much deeper than a simple scheduling failure to plan some quiet time into my day. There can be no effective move to rectify the problem of prayerlessness in myself or in my church until I and my fellow believers have identified the sin in it and confessed that sin. Only then can we hope to have some success in ridding ourselves of it.

Some, many even, of the roots of the prayerlessness of the American church are to be found in *wrong teaching* that has left us feeling that *prayer is another duty* Christians ought to fulfill rather than a pure and joyful relationship activity we enter into with the God of the universe. Yet another direct result of poor teaching and modeling in our churches, *plain old unbelief* can be singled out as another primary root of prayerlessness. These two biggest roots would probably be followed by *laziness, spiritual battles* going on in and around our lives, and our own *confusion regarding our motives*. It is worth some time in prayerful meditation to consider what the roots of my personal prayerlessness are.

We're conflicted and confused about prayer, and we compound our sin further by not even praying about that! It seems obvious that we need dynamic prayer ministry in the church to combat this sin, to teach right attitudes about prayer, to encourage the body, and to hold up high the value of prayer and the power of God for everyone who enters a church service or meeting.

Please go back one more time to that question about prayerlessness being a sin or a weakness, and consider it very, very personally. If, in fact, my prayerlessness is a sin, then I must do the gritty spiritual work of repenting of my prayerlessness, then I must confess it to God and ask Him to forgive and to cleanse me of that sin through the power of the Holy Spirit, who lives within me. Probably almost everyone in every US church should be doing this.

How Do We Begin to Embrace Prayer and Prayer Ministry?

Assuming for a moment that I have recognized that prayerlessness is a pervasive sin, and assuming I've taken the first personal step of acknowledging and repenting of that sin, I may very well find myself in a good position to begin helping myself and my family, my church, my church's sister churches and even the whole ship, meaning our American church and Christian culture, to move forward. It's a tall order, to be sure, but movements start with a few people. Here's a list of actions we can take, both personally and as churches, to begin to create change in favor of prayer. You may notice that some of these suggested actions are within your power personally, while others require the aid or cooperation of others.

- Ask God to guide our steps and lead us deeper into prayer. We need to continue to ask until He gives us a strategy for our church and her prayer life. (That's right, the primary practical step in developing a prayer ministry strategy is to pray.)
- Schools of Prayer should be scheduled regularly for churches to teach couples to pray together to help protect marriages, to teach everyone joint prayer to help members become comfortable with praying out loud together, and to teach all believers to pray for more than just health needs.
- Regular courses in the subjects of prayer and prayer ministry need to be added to the ministry degree programs in our colleges and seminaries.
- We need to hire prayer pastors for our churches. Their role is not to pray for us but to help us stay on the right path to prayerfulness.

    (If you are old enough you will recall the '60s and the crisis our youth culture went through. One of the things the church did in response to the struggle of our youth was to hire youth pastors. They did not take the place of parents, but were in positions designed to aid the parents in planting and nurturing spiritual seeds. This movement clearly gave American young people some help in navigating troubled times. Now nearly every church has some kind of student ministry team.

But in comparison, consider that I am one of only two full-time prayer pastors in the Phoenix area, with its population of roughly five million and hundreds of churches. I don't know of more than ten prayer pastors in the United States. Considering the struggle the church is having with prayer, it only makes sense to invest in prayer in the direct and practical manner of staffing for it.)

♦ Ask God to forgive us for the desire to go our own way instead of depending upon Him in prayer. Ask God to give you a desire to be with Him in prayer and to remind you to do it.

♦ Pray for the transformation of the American church at large in the area of prayer. Transformation in each church and life is easier if there is a movement.

♦ Create or join some type of accountability group to help keep your need for God before you. (Please also see the section on accountability groups in chapter 6.) Proverbs 27:17 instructs us, "As iron sharpens iron, so one man sharpens another." If this group prays together for the specific needs of the members, doing so should be considered an excellent second part of the group's purpose.

♦ Remember and rehearse the New Testament exhortations to pray, both in your personal devotions and in your church. Luke 18:1 tells us, "Then Jesus told his disciples a parable to show them that they should always pray and not give up." And in 1 Thessalonians 5:17 Paul instructs the believers to "pray continually."

♦ Remember and rehearse what the Bible says about the results of prayer. We will conclude this chapter shortly with a few of these passages.

Prayer Is the Foundation of the Church's Ministry. After myself, the next easiest entity for me to influence may be my own church. Alistair Begg, senior pastor of the Parkside Church in Chagrin Falls, Ohio, has summed up the churchwide need for prayer this way:

> If our prayer is meager, it is because we believe prayer to be supplemental and not fundamental [emphasis added]. When I don't pray, deep down inside, it is because I believe it doesn't really matter. When I do everything else except pray, it is because I'm suspicious of the possibility that all these other things matter more than prayer. When churches have everything in their church calendar and prayer is somehow an addendum somewhere, then it says about the church that they regard prayer as being supplemental and not fundamental to what's going on.[13]

When we emphasize prayer ministry in a church, we are not doing so at the *expense* of other ministry or other time concerns. We are doing so for the *benefit* of the general ministry of the church and because prayer is easily the best way to spend time on the improvement and general health of all ministries.

A church that wishes to step across the threshold into what God wants to orchestrate in and around it must lay a solid prayer foundation. Otherwise, like too many churches, that church will probably continue to linger, holding its breath, treading water, passing time just short of the explosion of God's blessing.

Finally, Remember What the Bible Says About Results. It seems an obvious choice to close this section about the case for prayer ministry with at least a brief reminder of the Bible's overwhelming testimony about the efficacy of prayer. This is why we need prayer, this is why we need prayer ministry, and this is why you and every Christian you serve with should be a part of a movement to raise the value of prayer in homes and churches. Quite simply, we need what our God gives to those who pray. Here is just a small sampling of the direct results of prayer in Scripture:

- In Exodus chapters 7 through 10, Moses prayed, and the plagues over all Egypt were reversed: frogs, flies, hail, locusts, and more.
- Elijah prayed, and fire came from heaven, and 450 false prophets were destroyed. See 1 Kings 18:36-40.
- When Elisha prays in 2 Kings 6:16, God opens Elisha's servant's eyes, permitting him to see the hills full of horses and chariots of fire ready to come to his and Elisha's aid. Notice it is after prayer that the servant's eyes are opened.
- In 2 Chronicles 7:1, when Solomon prayed, "fire came down from heaven and . . . the glory of the LORD filled the temple." Why did the glory come after his prayer?
- In Acts 12:1-18, Peter's jailbreak comes while the church is holding a prayer service for him.
- In Acts 16:25-26, Paul's miraculous escape from jail happened during a time of worship and prayer. "About midnight Paul and Silas were praying and singing hymns to God, and the other prisoners were listening to them. Suddenly there was such a violent earthquake that the foundations of the prison were shaken. At once all the prison doors flew open, and everybody's chains came loose."

Many of the believers we read about in Scripture lived perpetually on the other side of the threshold. Let's do what it takes to join them and to help our churches go with us.

CHAPTER 3

Prayer Philosophy and Ministry

"My house will be called a house of prayer."
(Isaiah 56:7b)

What Are We Thinking? This question, when applied to any project, will tell us volumes about where we're going to wind up. For a church to progress to a point where it has a thriving prayer ministry and to cross the threshold into truly remarkable change and God's greatest glorification, somebody in a key role has to think very clearly about prayer, formulating the philosophy that guides it.

For example, what we think about what a commitment to prayer can be *expected* to accomplish will, to a large extent, determine whether or not we do accomplish it. Dee Duke, in his speaking about prayer, has explored the roles prayer plays and the effects it has in the church. This list is intended here to provide both motivation and a sort of checklist so that you can be sure you are expecting enough. Duke says, the more praying a church does:

- the more unity and singleness of purpose will exist in the body;
- the more genuine love for God the people will possess;

- ♦ the more the people in the church will "know" God personally, and the greater sense of His presence they will have;
- ♦ the more joy, confidence, security, faith, and peace they will experience;
- ♦ the more God will work through the pastor's preaching;
- ♦ the more the people will grow spiritually;
- ♦ the more boldness, courage, and passion the people will have for reaching their lost friends, neighbors, and relatives for Christ;
- ♦ the more desire there will be in the hearts of the people to do the work of ministry;
- ♦ the less influence Satan will have on the people of the church and on those they are praying for outside the church;
- ♦ the more opportunities there will be to serve the Lord and be used by Him to advance the Kingdom of God;
- ♦ the stronger the marriages and families in the church become; and
- ♦ the more money people will give.[14]

You should now feel amply motivated to pray! Simply put, prayer is vital for all healthy, growing, Christ followers and for healthy, growing, Christ-following churches. But do we believe this? That is, do we really think that a strong prayer ministry will cause Duke's statements to be true in our church? Bold expectations like these form the foundation of a prayer ministry philosophy that influences a church in a dramatically God-glorifying way.

One Church's Prayer Philosophy, for Example. Every prayer ministry builds from a belief in and commitment to the importance of prayer. How it is valued determines how strong the prayer ministry's wings can become. I am very thankful for my church and its commitment to prayer, so I would like to highlight here some specifics in the development of Central's prayer philosophy as an example to learn from.

Years ago our elders decided to put Central's core values in writing. They worked on them for months, and finally landed on these five:

◆ **All People**

We primarily exist for the sake of those who are not yet part of the Body of Christ, intending to mature all believers into fully transformed, committed, and reproducing followers of Christ.

◆ **The Bible**

We acknowledge the Bible as the revealed truth of God, providing direction for our lives. We desire to communicate its truth in a manner that relates to our culture.

◆ **Authenticity**

We are a community of grace and forgiveness where everyone is allowed, encouraged, and expected to be authentic. This is a safe and practical place to come as you are and grow in your faith; but this is also a place where complacency is challenged.

◆ **Involvement**

Every believer within this community is responsible to use his or her spiritual gifts, time, energy, and finances for honoring God through ministry.

◆ **Future Generations**

We are a community where children and youth are highly valued; we sacrificially share the responsibility of raising godly children and youth.

They were ready to publish these values when one of our elders noticed, "Hey, we don't have anything in here about prayer." To their credit they decided then and there to make prayer one of our core values. They expressed the value this way:

♦ **Prayer**

As a community of believers, we seek God's guidance and direction through prayer in all that we do as a church and in all aspects of our daily lives.

And I'm happy to say our leaders remained sharp even after writing this; they realized that a core value by itself does not necessarily translate into a stronger church of prayer. They were prepared for the work it was going to take. Don't get me wrong, there was already plenty of prayer going on, but they believed there was room for improvement.

Now, before joining the staff at Central I'd had no idea that all of this was going on at the leadership level. I had known Cal, the senior pastor, for years and always liked him. But what was most important to me was that I join a team that would embrace a passion for prayer ministry; I wasn't going to settle for anything less. Most of all, Annie and I wanted to be assured that any ministry we signed on with was of the Lord's leading. As God would have it, Central had the fit we were seeking. We had a leadership that stood solidly behind prayer ministry and were offered an opportunity to develop something new.

So I was able to join the group of leaders who were thinking about prayer. One of the first moves in the development of any ministry philosophy is to decide upon the objectives, the answer to the question, what do we hope to accomplish here? We invested considerable time and energy into determining those goals, but we began by penning our prayer mission statement:

It is our desire to mobilize the congregation to participate in the fulfillment of Central's mission and vision through intentional and specific prayer:

♦ We will encourage prayer in every ministry and aspect of church life.

- We will provide easy entry prayer opportunities for all to participate in.
- We will inspire and motivate our church to love to pray.
- We will provide instruction in prayer and prayer ministry regularly.
- We will recruit volunteers to carry out this ministry.

Accomplishing this will allow Central, as a church, to:

- Ensure that all prayer requests are prayed for.
- Ensure that Central's leaders are supported with specific and consistent prayer.
- Ensure someone is praying for our missions, missionaries, and staff every hour of the day.
- Pray for our local, state, and national leaders.
- Assist other churches wishing to grow in their prayer ministries.

And we chose these two broader churchwide goals regarding prayer.

Goal 1: We Desire to Be What Jesus Called the Church to Be. In Mark 11:17, Jesus speaks of "a house of prayer for all nations." Notice please that Jesus did not say in this passage, "My house will look like a resort for Christian believers," or "My house will be filled with great music." His house was not to be known for its great programs or even for first-rate sermons. Jesus is very clear: "*My house* will be called a house of *prayer* for *all nations*" (emphasis added). God was and is very concerned about lost nations and people. God is pictured throughout Scripture as longing for all people to find salvation. Much of the storyline of the Bible is God making Himself known so that the nations can see His glory and their need for Him. He has charged His church to be doing the same.

But there's that interesting phrase, "a house of prayer." How do you know if you are on the right track to becoming a house of prayer? Cheryl Sacks has written a wonderful book, *The Prayer Saturated Church*, which is helpful in self-evaluation. She differentiates between a "church with prayer ministry" and a house of prayer.[15]

Prayer Ministry	House of Prayer
A limited number of people are involved.	The entire congregation is involved.
Prayer is done by a select few, and the responsibility is always put on them to pray.	The entire congregation takes ownership for doing their "prayer share."
Little or no regular emphasis put on prayer from the pulpit.	There is teaching from the pulpit, and priority is placed on prayer by the pastor.
Very little training is offered in prayer.	Classes and frequent special opportunities are offered on prayer.
Vision for church growth in prayer is limited. The church is content with only a few praying.	The concept of a "prayer band" has grown to the larger vision of a "prayer army."
A few leaders attend prayer meetings with no regular commitment. They carry the burden to pray.	All leaders, staff, and lay-persons have a burden for prayer.
Church groups open meetings with prayer as a main agenda item.	Groups spend time praying together and set times of prayer in addition to regular meetings.

Prayer Ministry (*continued*)	House of Prayer (*continued*)
Something seems lacking in the church atmosphere because prayer is feeble.	There is a fresh-flowing atmosphere of the Holy Spirit due to the whole church praying.
Prayer opportunities are limited for members to have the freedom to pray.	There is a natural flow of prayer going on throughout the church.
Prayer ministry staff is not recognized as a viable part of the church staff.	A paid or volunteer prayer minister and staff are in place.

At Central, we had determined that we would seek the higher, more challenging goal of transforming the church into a true house of prayer like this. We are still in the process, but we know we are on the right track.

Goal 2: We Desire to See Lives Transformed Through Prayer.
We pray because it is the one way to bring about transformation. We are not satisfied with just knowing people are praying; we long to see transformed lives as a result. We desire to see people being renewed by the word, establishing a new or stronger relationship with God, and seeking Him for direction in their lives through prayer.

Matt (not his real name) is a good example of this. When he first showed up at Central he was a painfully shy thirty-something who had never been married and was extremely depressed. He had been on medication for years and felt hopeless. He had been to counselor after counselor with little progress. We started encouraging Matt and teaching him to pray. He joined a weekly intercession time and began to improve. Later we went through our twenty-six-week Life Coaching program for intensive mentoring. Today he is a different guy. He is much more outgoing and even leads our Life Coaching ministry. The goal is transformation by exposure to God's word and much prayer.

Nonnegotiables

There are certain conditions that must be met in order to see our objectives reached. We see these few absolutes as key elements of our prayer philosophy.

Build the Vision Prayerfully. We glean inspiration for new elements of our vision from a variety of excellent sources, including conferences, books, interactions with prayer leaders across the world and, most important, from prayer itself. Of these, prayer is the hardest work and takes the most time, but it is truly a nonnegotiable for us. A man-made vision is eventually going to become difficult to stand behind and nearly impossible to keep propping up. But a vision that has been birthed out of a lot of prayer excites everyone and does not weaken as quickly as a man-made vision. It is essential to take the time to seek out God in prayer for the vision for your prayer ministry.

Maintain Inspiration. A constant state of inspiration is critical to keeping a prayer ministry going. People get all excited about something, but in a month or so they have gone back to their old ways. So our job is to keep prayer in front of them in a gently encouraging way. If we push too hard, we will run people off; but if we don't lovingly encourage them, they will become distracted and lose their way.

Maintain Vision. Perhaps you have heard of the USS *Constitution*, the "world's oldest commissioned warship afloat."[16] This ship is the famous for her actions during the War of 1812 against Great Britain. She earned the nickname "Old Ironsides" for her toughness in the battle against the British warship *Guerriere* in that conflict. She continued to serve in various capacities on through the nineteenth century, and even completed a three-year ninety-port tour of the nation in 1934. *Constitution* has continued to sail occasionally under her own power, as recently as August 2012.[17] This is one tough old ship, with a history of successful service to prove it.

But the truly interesting thing you may not realize about "Old Ironsides" is that she leaks. And she has leaked for years. Two times each day "Old Ironsides" has to be pumped to empty the water that seeps into its hull.[18] Even the tough ones leak!

Humans are very much like that, especially in the area of vision. It's forever leaking out of us. We may become thoroughly excited about prayer ministry or some other ministry in the church, but life steals our excitement and focus. So a part of the job of leading prayer ministry has to be constantly recasting the vision. *Ministry, including prayer ministry, is sustained by the quality of the vision and how often it is reinforced.*

Make It Relevant. One of the reasons people don't return to our prayer meetings is because we have allowed the meetings to get off track. Have you ever been to a prayer meeting where the prayer centered on Aunt Betty's cousin's niece who has a hang nail? I am not saying that we should not pray for these kinds of things but that they should not be prayed for in public settings where people are unfamiliar with the person they are praying for. This kind of praying de-energizes a prayer meeting. We try hard to keep our large-scale prayer meetings focused on major topics that everyone can relate to and away from specific people not known by all.

It is critical that prayer meetings start and stop on time and stay relevant. This approach has proved to be beneficial to the growth and longevity of prayer meetings.

Help your people see the big picture. A statement like this precedes many of our typical prayer meetings: "The meeting tonight is designed to pray for our nation and its leaders. We know that some of you have personal matters that you would like to have prayed over. We will try to get to those at the end of our time. But please understand that personal prayer needs are not the focus tonight. If we don't get to personal prayer, please don't be offended."

Get Senior Leaders Onboard. If you were to do a survey of all the great prayer churches across our country, you would find senior leaders, key people in leadership, who carry the torch of prayer ministry in their congregations. The reason for this is that the people in the congregation take their cues from these individuals who have the true power to actually change things and make bold statements about the church as a whole. In prayerful churches, someone with executive decision-making responsibilities has made the decision to focus on prayer, and Christians watch their key leaders to determine what is ultimately important. In each church, some things rise to the top as level-one priorities while others fit somewhere lower down on the ladder. The rankings are set by the people who have been entrusted with making the big decisions. So if you intend to influence your church toward prayerfulness, you need either to be one of those key leaders or to get them onboard with the vision.

Some executive leaders prefer to delegate prayer and prayer ministry to someone else. It may not be their strongest suit, or they may even be uncomfortable with prayer. This is really not all that surprising. I never took a class on prayer or prayer ministry in college, and I do not know of any pastors who have. Furthermore, the key leaders in many churches do not have formal theological training.

But delegating prayer and the prayer ministry will only have limited success if the key leaders are not also directly involved in casting vision and directing steps. The degree of the success will depend on the leadership skill of the person leading the prayer ministry and the favor he or she enjoys.

Celebrate Victories. I believe great leaders know when to celebrate. Many driven leaders are so focused that they can't enjoy one victory before planning their next attack. You may know people like this. This approach is detrimental to the team and its morale, and ultimately to the success of the ministry in general.

David had to learn this lesson the hard way in 2 Samuel 18 and 19. David and his men went out to fight Israel and David's son Absalom, who had deceptively taken the kingdom of Israel away from his father. At one point in the conflict, Absalom became caught in the fork of a tree and partially hung. David's key military commander Joab took three javelins and plunged them into Absalom's heart. When news reached David of the victory his men had fought for and won, instead of rejoicing at the victory, he was beside himself with grief for his son Absalom.

Joab confronted David with these words from chapter 19:

> "Today you have humiliated all your men, who have just saved your life and the lives of your sons and daughters and the lives of your wives and concubines. You love those who hate you and hate those who love you. You have made it clear today that the commanders and their men mean nothing to you. I see you would be pleased if Absalom were alive today and all of us were dead. Now go out and encourage your men. I swear by the Lord that if you don't go out, not a man will be left with you by nightfall. This will be worse for you than all the calamities that have come upon you from your youth till now" (verses 5-7).

This is an extreme example, but celebrating the victories that God gives you and your associates is a must for the health and well-being of the team. If you don't, people will leave you and join another team that has mastered this principle.

Recruit Men as Leaders. We have made a decision in our ministry to spend our recruiting dollars and energy on men (there's more on this topic in chapter 5). The rationale is that women are naturally more interested in prayer because they are just wired that way. But men are not always ready to pray. We know that if we staff our prayer rooms with women leaders, many men will feel uncomfortable and move on to something else. So for the good of the ministry and for the sake of our families, we try to engage male leaders for our prayer ministry.

Many men would love to pray but don't know how and don't know where to turn for help. We have found that men learn to pray best in community, as a band of brothers. I am talking about being in community with others they can trust deeply who will walk beside them in life and in the spiritual disciplines. For this to happen, a male leader must be willing to love men unconditionally and help them until they get it.

I would love to go deer hunting. I do own a gun, but I have never been in the forest with it. I don't know the first thing about where to start. I'm lacking both the experience to find a spot to hunt and a hunting license. No one has taught me how to make a tree stand, how to keep from giving off my scent, or how to gut an animal, if I were fortunate enough to kill one. Consequently (and that is the key word here), I have never been deer hunting. I have three grown sons who own guns and want to go deer hunting also. I think we would love it and love doing it together. Being in the mountains, smelling the pines, and having time with God in that setting all sound wonderful to me. But I can't be for certain that I would like it because I have never been.

You have by now surmised that I think many men feel the same way about prayer. They have heard about prayer, and it even seems like something they would believe in doing or even enjoy, but they don't know where to start, and they need someone to walk them through it. I have never walked anyone, male or female, through learning to pray who was disappointed or wished they hadn't invested the effort. On each occasion, that person was delighted with his or her newfound ability to talk with God and was thrilled to have some help getting started.

Sam (not his real name) is a good example of a man who needed to learn how to pray. I met him on a mission construction trip to the Dominican Republic. He was a part of a group of guys from our church called "The Sweat Hogs." The Sweat Hogs have gone to the same community in the Dominican Republic for the last ten years, helping the nationals get on their feet. Sam is a building contractor. He is a good man, but prayer was an undeveloped spiritual discipline for him. I watched him during the trip and could see that the other guys looked up to him. He was a leader in more than just the construction arena, but he didn't know it yet. I made it a point to make friends with him, and by the end of the week we were talking about prayer. He was pretty standoffish at first, but I kept after him. Frequently eating lunch together, in time we built a strong friendship. Finally, I invited him to join me in the prayer room for a service. It was rough for him at first, but eventually he got the hang of it. I took him on a prayer journey to Vietnam and continued to help him grow. He joined one of the e-men accountability teams (there's more about these teams later) and even began praying with his wife. Now he leads prayer on one of our campuses, championing it for that campus as well, and he is doing an outstanding job. He has also started a midweek prayer meeting. If you were to ask Sam straight out, he would tell you, "I would have never dreamed I would be in prayer ministry. Using my hands and building something, sure, I am all in, but not prayer." Now he can't imagine life without prayer and is the poster child for the point that *most men would love to pray, but they don't know it because they have never prayed much.* They desperately need someone to lead them along the way.

More Introductory Thoughts on Establishing Prayer Ministry

Don't Give Way to Discouragement! Maybe the toughest thing about initiating and operating a prayer ministry is staying encouraged. Satan does not want your church to have a prayer ministry, and he will do anything to keep it from happening.

I remember some particularly painful discouragement I faced while I was serving as prayer pastor at another church. One of the requirements for the staff of Christ's Church of the Valley was that we stand in the courtyard after each service to recruit people for our ministry. My spot was next to Kevin, the sports pastor. After a single service he would have thirty-five people lined up to register for coed softball, while I would be fortunate to have one person who would even *talk* to me, let alone join in the prayer ministry. Many Sundays I would leave campus discouraged and even upset. *Why are people so shallow? Why would they rather play softball than pray?* But this is cancerous thinking. It is judgmental, and it works like poison in a prayer ministry. It took some time, but eventually the prayer ministry grew, and we had seven hundred to a thousand people involved in it on some level; but it happened one person at a time and out of much prayer. There was no lack of opportunities to get discouraged, but I held on. You will have to also.

Consider This Caution About Negativity. Don't let your prayer ministry (or any other ministry, for that matter) be born out of negativity or be characterized by negativity at any time. Sometimes we may examine our church or church leadership and feel they are not doing enough, not praying enough, not supporting us enough. They may well be missing the high mark we have set for prayer in our church, and we can see that the system is not working as we envisioned it. And that observation—along with the attitude problem behind it, which leaves us thinking we are in charge of other peoples' priorities—can lead to a negative attitude about the church or about ministry or the Christians with whom we fellowship and serve, or even about prayer itself. Birthing a prayer ministry out of negativism will not work; rather, it will be destructive. People can smell a negative attitude like a skunk in the kitchen, and they will just stay away. If you find yourself setting the prayer standards for others, or if you are struggling with negativity for some other reason, then the timing is not yet right for you to launch a prayer ministry in your church. Begin by asking God to change your attitude and your heart.

Matthew 7:1-5 is a wonderful passage to meditate on and use for determining if your heart is right and ready for leadership in a prayer ministry. Jesus says:

> "Do not judge, or you too will be judged. For in the same way you judge others, you will be judged, and with the measure you use, it will be measured to you.
>
> Why do you look at the speck of sawdust in your brother's eye and pay no attention to the plank in your own eye? How can you say to your brother, 'Let me take the speck out of your eye,' when all the time there is a plank in your own eye? You hypocrite, first take the plank out of your own eye, and then you will see clearly to remove the speck from your brother's eye."

At the root of negativity, and plenty of trouble even when negativity isn't obvious, is self-righteousness in the heart of the ministry leader. When a leader of any kind, but particularly a prayer leader, becomes self-righteous about his or her ministry or passion, it can be deadly for more than just the individual in question. I like to refer to key prayer leaders as the "DNA carriers" for the prayer ministry. If this leader is guilty of the very sin of the scribes and the Pharisees that Jesus most vigorously attacked, it may leave the DNA (that is, the core essence) of the entire ministry tainted or even corrupted by that sin. Prayer leaders must never fall into the selfish pit of self-righteousness.

I have had to learn this lesson, and then relearn it, several times. Since I was a senior pastor for many years before coming to work on a large staff, I became accustomed to making things happen on my schedule. So there are times I wish we could move faster or that different staff members would embrace our prayer ministry more passionately. But through the years I have learned to turn all this over to the Lord and let Him build His church in His way, in His timing, and to do what I am called and gifted to do. I have given up setting prayer standards or expectations for anyone but myself, and life is much better now. Don't miss this point; it will save you much grief.

After your heart is right, go to your senior pastor or leadership, and let them know of your burden for prayer and for praying over the life and needs of the church. Go as a servant and an advocate, asking for permission to begin a prayer ministry. Ask about areas that need prayer attention, and listen intently to the responses.

Money Talks! What Is It Saying? At some point you will want to ask for a small budget to get the prayer ministry up and running. In a small church, that number could be $250 a year, or in a larger church it may be several thousand. The amount of money is not as important as what it represents. When pastors commit budget dollars to a ministry, they are giving it real legitimacy. No pastor will ever say a prayer ministry is not necessary, but getting busy, goal-oriented pastors to fully support a prayer ministry can be tough.

Of course, a budget also means the leadership will be expecting results, so be prepared to administrate wisely, investing in purchases that will make an impact and a long-term difference.

Heed This Word About Pastors. Most pastors, especially senior pastors, are overworked and way too busy. They jump from board meetings to weddings and back to funerals all in the same day. Hurting church members may then lay enormous psychological and spiritual needs directly upon their shoulders, expecting God's solution for their pain to come to them through the pastor's next words. Emotionally, all this can be like hiking the Grand Canyon in a single day for the pastor. As a result, there are plenty of senior pastors for whom a new ministry idea from a church member can seem like just another burden to bear when it is first presented.

I know about this, because my wife and I started a church from scratch when I was 26, and I served as the senior pastor for 17 years. People were always coming to me with their pet projects to make the church better. Some ideas had real merit, while some were obviously not in the best interest of the church at all. Many of the ideas were presented by strong, reputable folks who were capable of implementing them, but a few came from people who were not good at follow-through with projects, or who were simply not yet capable of leading a ministry such as the one they were suggesting. Navigating all this was often exhausting for me.

When you go to your pastor, then, be sure not to waste his or her time, and don't go with half-baked ideas. You will not help your cause with the one person who is probably the gatekeeper for the church and the one who can make or break the ministry you want to launch.

THRESHOLD

CHAPTER 4

The Prayer DNA Carrier

"Everything is possible for him who believes."
(Mark 9:23)

One of the men on staff with me at Central was in Africa riding in a minivan across country. Along the way, the Lord told him, "Stop the van and get out and recommit yourself to Christ."

My friend tried at first to reason with God. We have all tried that before, haven't we? "Lord, I will do it when I get back home. I will get on my knees, and I will completely recommit myself to you," he told the Lord silently.

God was not having any of it. "I want you to do it here, and I want you to do it now."

"But God, it will be embarrassing. I will have to ask the driver to stop. The other guys will think I am trying to be super-spiritual or something. Let's just wait till I get home," my friend pleaded. The Lord's reply was a short but strong, "No!"

So my friend gave in, "I'll do it, Lord." He looked out over the horizon and said to himself, "I will do it before we get to the hill up ahead," giving himself enough time to muster up his courage. But he chickened out. The hill in the distance came and went, and he didn't stop the van. So he looked out on the horizon again and made a second promise, "Lord before we get to that hill, I will obey you." But he again failed to pull the trigger. The conviction was growing stronger all the time, so he made another commitment but failed yet again. In the end, it took him seven hills to actually stop the van and recommit himself.

Although it was tough, my friend did it! Give him credit! The truth is I have failed in situations like this more times than I care to remember. How many commitments have I made and not kept? How many times have I backed down, fearing how my obedience might look to others? How about you? How many mountains does it take for you to obey?

Character Is Key. We now need to discuss the *personal* character and the *personal* spiritual work of the prayer ministry's key leader. I call this leader the "prayer DNA carrier" because he or she does even more than pray and administrate a ministry; he or she actually embodies the character of the prayer ministry in his or her own actions and attitudes. Leadership by this one person's example is essential to the success of the prayer ministry, and it can probably be stated categorically that this person will be the one who is most responsible for taking the church across the threshold. Below are a few of the deepest personal character elements of this servant leader. Please understand that these are expressed in complete humility; you need not fear that I have somehow reached a state of perfection in all of these traits, even though I do humbly claim to occupy this role for my church.

Prayer Leadership Demands a High Level of Commitment. The story above about my teammate is an illustration of the kind of obedience that is required of any spiritual leader such as the prayer DNA carrier, who is the primary prayer visionary and leader for a local church. Anything less than utter and complete consecration of this leader's life to prayer leadership will leave his or her prayers weak and leadership anemic. The ability to obey, and to obey even when it is particularly difficult (or awkward or inconvenient), is one of several important prerequisites for excellent prayer leadership.

Prayer Leadership Is a Priestly Role. The Old Testament role of priest is similar to the role of the prayer leader. This applies to all prayer group leaders and especially to the DNA carrier. The priest was responsible to enter the inner court and offer sacrifices to roll back the sins of the Israelites until the time when they could be completely forgiven by Christ's sacrifice on the cross. The priest's work was done on behalf of another and for the other's benefit. Similarly, we prayer leaders bring people and their needs to God and intercede on behalf of others. But we also help them to learn to bring their own prayers to the Father. We teach, we lead, *and* we intercede.

Prayer ministry can sometimes be a tough assignment. During one of the services at Central we hold an intercession time for the health needs of the people in our large congregation. Perhaps doing this would energize you, but I usually find praying for seventy-five people who have terminal and heartbreaking diseases exhausting. Yet at the same time it is deeply fulfilling; what an honor it is to carry these hurting people into the presence of God in their moments of great need. The prayer leader's actions as intercessor are similar to those of the four men who carried their friend on a stretcher to Jesus (in Mark 2:1-12). When they could not gain entrance because of the large crowd, they removed a portion of the roof and lowered him down in front of Jesus; they were essentially "practical priests." If you will serve as prayer DNA carrier and leader, the act of picturing yourself standing before God on behalf of others, much as the priest did for the Israelites, may help you begin to understand your mission as prayer leader and intercessor.

The Prayer Leader Needs Strong Personal Spiritual Disciplines. A prayer DNA carrier needs to have biblical truth always on his or her mind, so he or she needs to spend significant time in Bible reading and study or meditation, and obviously also in personal prayer time. Organization and a workable plan are the keys to success. Here I'd like to share some ways I like to organize my efforts in the spiritual disciplines:

♦ **Stay in the Word.** I have tried many Bible-reading plans through the years, and I like these three the best.

Approach 1. This idea, originally from Dee Duke in Jefferson, Oregon, involves reading thirteen chapters a day. He read two Old Testament chapters (excluding Psalms and Proverbs); five chapters in the Psalms; one chapter in Proverbs; two chapters from the four gospels, Acts, and Revelation; one chapter in the Pastoral Epistles (that is, 1 Timothy, 2 Timothy, Titus, and Philemon); and two chapters in the remaining epistles. This approach gets me through the Old Testament twice a year, Psalms and Proverbs once a month, the gospels four times a year, the Pastoral Epistles twice a month, and the remaining epistles four times a year. I have found reading this amount daily to be very helpful in filling my life with Scripture.

After reading what I have selected for the day, I record the verses that require additional attention. The next step is to pray over the passages that are impacting my life. Praying through the lessons that God is teaching me daily helps me to remember them and build them into my life. I review them each for a couple of days so that they don't get away from me. The goal is to plant them deeply in my heart.

Approach 2. I sometimes read through the Bible in a year using *The Daily Bible* by F. LaGard Smith, a version of the NIV that is organized into 365 readings in chronological order. This is a nice change, because having smaller amounts to read each day allows me to read much more slowly and more deeply.

Approach 3. Sometimes I read focusing on a theme. Recently, I read in search of the declarations in Scripture, of which there are many.

♦ **Organize Your Complex Prayer Life.** It should probably go without saying that the prayer life of the prayer DNA carrier should be well organized. When people find out that you are willing to pray for them, you may begin to receive so many requests that it becomes difficult to handle them all, making organization even more necessary. And there is so much to pray about even without extra requests that any disorganized approach may be disastrous.

Try using a prayer plan to help with this problem. My personal plan is set up in such a way that I pray daily for normal needs like family concerns and major life directional issues. I further break down the rest of my prayers into categories. This is what works best for me:

◊ **Mondays: Partners.** Partners are the twelve people that are praying for our ministry. We don't just ask them to pray for us; we take their concerns seriously as well, and we devote Monday's prayer time to their concerns.

◊ **Tuesdays: UpTeam.** UpTeam is the name of the monthly booklet that we put out with the needs of Central's staff and global workers. The booklet is used by a team organized to conduct uninterrupted prayer throughout the week. The booklet is usually about sixty-five pages long, and I use it for my Tuesday prayer times.

◊ **Wednesdays: Churches and Church Needs.** I pray for the churches I know and love around the United States. These are generally churches in which I have preached or held prayer conferences and made strong connections. I also pray for Central's needs and future on this day.

◊ **Thursdays: People.** On this day I pray for people God puts on my heart. Some are ill; others are planting churches; and still others are people I feel God wants me to pray for, sometimes people I seem to have met by chance. I call them divine appointments.

◊ **Fridays: Nations.** This is a particularly fun day because I pray for the nations. Mostly I lift up the places I have visited on prayer journeys and key areas of the world.

◊ **Saturdays: Central's Prayer Ministry.** I devote time to praying for Central's Prayer Ministry and all its leaders. I pray for their families, jobs, children, and specific circumstances.

◊ **Sundays: Service Intercession.** I am involved for several hours in the during-service intercession at Central; personal prayers round out the day.

By using this system, I am able to cover all the topics and requests I feel led to pray for, but they are spread out throughout the week so that they don't begin to feel overwhelming or burdensome. I usually pray briefly in the morning after my Bible readings, which is usually the first thing I do each day. My favorite spot is on my couch in the family room. Sometimes I am teaching in an early morning Bible study, so my prayer gets pushed to later in the day, but early morning is best for me for personal prayer.

Some people who are otherwise serious about their commitment to prayer make the mistake of only having one potential time for it. So if they miss their regular early morning time, they are sunk for that day. I have several secondary options in a given day: at lunch, after dinner, or before bed. Having multiple slots available throughout the day for a quiet time helps me make sure to honor my commitment to prayer.

Often Annie and I pray together briefly after we finish our morning studies. This lasts from five to ten minutes on average. My longer prayer times for the subjects I described take place at the office, usually in the afternoon before I call it a day.

What I do or what someone else does in personal disciplines is not all that important. Such habits can be a guide or can provide minor direction. Some people are retired and have all the time in the world. Others have huge jobs besides their work at the church, so they have less discretionary time to invest. Do what you can, and give it to the Lord to bless, but *don't compare your disciplines to others'*.

The Prayer Leader Believes God for Good Things—No Matter What. As previously noted, the reason many of us do not pray more is that we are not convinced that prayer will do any good. Obviously, this view of prayer will not lead a church across the threshold into God's transformation; it will not inspire people to pray, nor will it build a prayer ministry. Key to the DNA of the prayer ministry is an unshakable faith in God, and this must be most strongly embodied in the DNA carrier.

So it goes without saying that a prayer leader must have a higher view of prayer than popular culture has embraced. The prayer leader must believe that Mark 9:23 reference presented at the top of this chapter. David Wilkerson once said, "Considering all the power and the resources we have in Christ, most believers have asked almost nothing in His name." The prayer leader must be the person who calls the church back to that foundational belief that "everything is possible for him who believes."

Keeping our trust level high is another tough job in the pursuit of prayer leadership. Each of us will continue to go through peaks and valleys of various kinds, and the flag of faith and hope is more difficult to hoist at some times than at others. I have found some help with this hope problem in an old book written more than three hundred years ago by William Gurnall, entitled *The Christian in Complete Armour*. Gurnall says:

> Hope is a supernatural grace of God, by which the believer through Christ expects and waits for all

those good things promised by God to all believers, things which he has not as of yet received, or has not fully received. True hope is a jewel that none wears but Christ's bride. No soul but the believer's soul is graced with this true, supernatural hope. To be hopeless and Christ-less are the same thing. Hope's subject, then, is the believer.[19]

Gurnall is challenging the prayer leader to say, "I will not, under any circumstance, surrender my necklace of hope or the belief that prayer changes things!"

The Prayer Leader Humbly Depends on God Alone. Great prayer begins with humility and dependence on God. This state of humble dependence is gained through a repeated act of the will, whereby he or she yields to God and puts all personal wishes in neutral.

"Neutral" does not mean *settling* for something less than my heart's desire. Rather, it is *resting* in all of His promises and all that He is. "Neutral" means being content with His will in the situation. Until I am dependent, humble, and in neutral, real prayer cannot begin. Jesus prayed in the garden, "Not my will, but thine, be done" (Luke 22:42b KJV). This one sentence in one prayer of Jesus epitomizes the neutrality that is required.

Unrepented sin blocks effective prayer (see Psalm 66:18). Pharisees in the New Testament prayed, and now sinners of all sorts pray, perhaps especially when their sin and foolishness have landed them in a pot of trouble. They just don't pray effectively. It is of vital importance that the prayer leader's life be free of unrepented, ongoing sin, even though it is likely that he or she will be specifically targeted for temptation. If something affects this humbly dependent relationship with God, which sin certainly does, it must be eliminated.

I personally like to picture prayer as entering the great throne room of God. I see the angels swarming around His throne and the twenty-four elders seated on their thrones. The four living creatures are crying out, "Holy, holy, holy is the Lord God Almighty, who was, and is, and is to come" (Revelation 4:8). Entering the throne room reminds us who is calling the shots. I like to enter the King's throne room and lie down on the altar. I remind myself that I am a servant and that He is in charge. Nothing can be accomplished without Him, and He doesn't need me to set His plans in motion. This mental exercise helps me make sure that I am completely humbled and dependent on God.

The Prayer Leader Spends Extended Time Alone with God. To be completely candid, I need to tell you that prayer is the hardest work I do, and the degree of effort required for that work is compounded when the length of time is extended. For me it is much easier to do something else, pretty much anything else, than it is to pray for long periods, and I can only assume that you will have essentially the same experience. For this reason prayer must be viewed as a discipline; it is a discipline that is *required* of the prayer DNA carrier. (See 1 Peter 4:7.)

Please consider using a wonderful Navigators' program called *Half Day in Prayer.* I have been using this program for thirty years now. On the days I set apart for a half day in prayer, I take my calendar, a Bible, the current book I am reading (usually on prayer), prayer requests, missionary newsletters, and a journal of Bible highlights (that is, the journal entries I have recorded from each day of Bible reading). During these extended times of prayer, I look for themes in my Bible reading. If, for example, on four or five days during the last month, God called me to trust more, then I know that God is working on something in my life that requires more trust. Often, when I pull my calendar out, I can see the hand of God preparing me in my Bible reading (the listening part of prayer) for what is ahead. God's orchestration is hard to perceive as I am living it, but it becomes clear as I look back and see the patterns.

Why insist on *extended* times in prayer? Why do I need to pray in long stretches? Isn't it best to "pray continually," as 1 Thessalonians

5:17 says, meaning "as I'm driving, eating, showering, or resting in the evening"? To be clear, praying continually and while doing regular daily activities is both a scriptural and very practical solution to many prayer-problems. But there are benefits to extended times in prayer that cannot be achieved by a busy person who never completely pauses from his or her busy-ness to get alone with God. Consider these reasons to pray in long stretches:

- ◆ Significant time spent in prayer helps us to gain and clarify perspective, to see ministry, relationships, and spiritual matters more clearly.
- ◆ Jesus gave us the example. He was often alone for extended periods in prayer. And He should, of course, be serving as our prayer DNA carrier and primary example.
- ◆ Much of the direction God gave to His leaders came out of times when they were alone with God. Think about some key Bible characters and especially the leaders: Moses and the Ten Commandments, Abraham, Nehemiah; all of them gained vision and direction from time alone with God.
- ◆ Extended times alone with God allow me to more thoroughly and unflinchingly examine my motives and my heart in general.
- ◆ Alone time gives God an opportunity to communicate with me while He has my undivided attention. We live such hurried lives that there is often no time for God to speak an undistorted message. We have the phone, TV, Internet, and every other kind of media, and each can effectively crowd out God's instructions to us.

Quality prayer is not likely to occur while we are driving or working, generally, nor when we're praying in bursts of short, sentence prayers. The most transformational and complete prayer occurs when I set aside periods of time to be with the Lord and tell Him my requests, and then listen for His responses.

We have noticed this principle in action in our service intercession times. The good stuff in prayer usually does not come at the beginning. The best praying comes after we have prayed everything we can think of and we have grown silent. Sometimes, in that stillness, God leads us to something that is so rich that we all know it is from Him and not something we have concocted. All this is not to say that the other prayers are not important; they are. But frequently the best prayer comes as we grow still.

The Prayer Leader Seeks Hard After God. Evidence of the DNA carrier's intense relationship with God should permeate his or her life. This should be seen as an act of service to the church, because it will have a positive effect on everyone in the prayer ministry and beyond.

I recently attended the wedding of a couple working in the Muslim world. As a part of the reception, several video clips were shown that had been sent in by people they serve with who were unable to attend the wedding. All the clips had one theme. They described the groom as someone who is seeking hard after God. The bride, who came from the church Annie and I started years ago, has the same kind of heart for God. How many people do you know whom you would describe as seeking God *hard*? People can tell, one way or the other, what a leader's heart is really seeking after, so the prayer DNA carrier needs to be seeking hard after God.

The Prayer Leader Learns to Stoke the Fire in His or Her Heart. A prayer leader must be passionate about growing his or her prayer life. He needs to be constantly training that passion by reading on prayer, listening to others speak on prayer, trying new personal approaches in prayer, and experimenting with corporate prayer services.

I buy almost every CD at every prayer conference I attend and listen to them repeatedly. I have a mentor in prayer who has proved to be invaluable to my growth. I love biographies of great men and women of prayer. *Rees Howells: Intercessor* by Norman Grubb and *George Müller: Delighted in God!* by Roger Steer are so good for my soul and faith that I go back and read them again every couple of years. If you are going to keep the fires of your faith and your commitment to prayer burning, you must keep training those passions.

The Prayer Leader is Growing in Communion with the Father. This communion derives from maintaining attitudes of servanthood and brokenness and is accomplished largely in the extended prayer times previously discussed. But the prayer leader is not in the leadership position so that others will be impressed by his or her spirituality. He or she serves as a prayer leader for the joy of serving others, passing on the benefits of that communion to them.

The Prayer Leader Must Deal Properly with Failure. The prayer leader will fail in various ways from time to time. While it is completely normal to fail, it is not to be considered normal to be content with failure. Prayer leaders who have failed or fallen in some way must do whatever it takes to get back on track. No level of radical obedience should be too much to pay.

When a man or woman of God chooses to take on this role, harassment from Satan is to be expected. Attacks may come in all forms. One method he seems to use to attack me is to cause expensive items around the house to break! He may also attempt through various means to disrupt relationships. Another weapon is to bring about disheartening circumstances or, even more common, to attempt to cause us to feel more miserable during normal, difficult circumstances. His great hope is that you will become discouraged and leave your post as prayer leader, to determine that the role is just too emotionally costly to maintain. The good news is that God is in charge and will not allow us to be tempted beyond what we can endure. (See 1 Corinthians 10:13.)

In closing, please do not be afraid that the standards expressed in this chapter are absolutes. But I do see them as useful guardrails. These thoughts about the proper character and identity of *the leader I need to be* help keep me on track, much like the guardrails the Arizona Department of Transportation sets out along the tricky mountain roads north of where I live. The road is treacherous, and I need to stay on the paved surface. So much of importance is at stake.

THRESHOLD

Building a People of Prayer

I would rather teach one man to pray than ten men to preach.
—Charles Spurgeon

I remember quite well my first prayer ministry recruit at Central. His name was Rick, and he owned his own alternator and generator rebuild shop. We seemed to hit it off. I got to know him around campus and eventually invited him to join me in the prayer room to pray during one of our services. I was careful to ask him if he would come once and try it. He accepted my invitation and was with me in the prayer room the next weekend. I explained to him what we do and how we do it, and told him that he didn't have to say a word, just watch and listen as others prayed. He made it through the first week and came back the next. Eventually he began to pray during those times and started to really grow. If you were to ask Rick today, he would say, "I didn't realize it, but I really wanted and needed to learn to pray. But I didn't know how, and I needed a safe place to get my feet wet."

Rick is like most American Christians. They need to pray, they genuinely want to pray, but they need someone to model prayer for them. Potential pray-ers need a person who is brave enough to invite them to a prayer meeting and who is willing to walk with them along the way. Now Rick leads our Half Day in Prayer ministry and has become a campus prayer coordinator for one of our five campuses. He and many others who have come from prayerlessness to become prayer heroes all prove the point that *the only reason some people do not pray is that nobody has asked them to.*

Build Relationships First. If you want to start a prayer ministry, you need to understand that all ministry of all types is all about relationship. It is very rare for us to win people to the prayer ministry team without an investment in the relationship. The time taken to build the friendship helps protect us from selecting someone too quickly, and it allows the process to happen naturally instead of in a manner that feels forced.

After you have recruited *your friends*, look next to *form friendships*. Nearly anyone can join you in prayer ministry, but allow me to suggest that you first emphasize forming new friendships with people who are leaders and influencers, for the purpose of winning them to the prayer ministry. (We will look more closely at the topic of adding gifted leaders in a moment.) People with these characteristics are always going to be leaders and influencers, so they will lead and influence others for prayer if they become engaged. They will help get the movement in your church started more quickly. But the key for all recruitment efforts is to begin with a relationship, a friendship, not with an offer of a key position in an exciting new ministry.

Cultivate the Prayer Leadership Wisely. As I have just indicated, the first step in the challenging process of prayer leadership cultivation is, perhaps not surprisingly, to look for the best leaders you can find. Some of these will be leading in other ministries, not prayer, but you will be able to tell they are great leaders. For me, selecting leaders is often based on gut feelings, not on characteristics I can put on paper. Maybe my selection comes from the thought, *Would I want to follow that person?* If the answer is yes, I will pursue that person further. Remember, prayer leadership not just prayer, so the leadership qualities of the leaders you recruit need to be strong.

After a potential prayer leader has been identified, try to get him or her involved in the prayer ministry at an introductory level. You may give the person a job to see how he or she responds to the challenge. Are these people procrastinators, or can they get the job done in a timely fashion? Do they respond to e-mail messages or blow them off for a week or two? Do others seem to follow their lead? Do they seem to be energized by the work, or is it drudgery to them? If they do well in their first task, try giving them a second, slightly more difficult, one for further evaluation.

Another challenging aspect of leadership selection concerns correctly identifying the right season for a potential new recruit's leadership. Effective leadership does not consist of skill alone, but also availability. We all go through periods when life seems like a wild river and we do well simply to navigate the rapids. Inviting someone to join your team who is experiencing major turmoil may be a mistake, even though he or she may show genuine desire to enlist in prayer ministry leadership and may have the skill set to do the job. Bringing someone on at the wrong time can sour him or her for later, more fruitful ministry.

At Central, we watch people for several months and listen to our hearts, praying about their involvement. If the vision begins to grow in them for prayer ministry, we poll the rest of our leadership team to get their feedback. If the response is positive and the life season question is right, we then invite them to join the team.

The next step in recruiting a good leader comes when you place the vision and challenge of threshold-crossing prayer ministry in front of him or her. Pose the questions, "What could our church look like if we had more prayer going on?" and "What kind of value would it add to our work if we could do this?" Most have never given these questions any thought.

As we already discussed, many of the leaders you will attempt to recruit are very gifted, so they could make significant contributions to any number of the ministries in a local church. Our job is to invite them to use their gifts for the Lord in the prayer ministry, so make them want it: "Instead of selling sugar-water like some Coca Cola marketer, why not *really* invest in the Kingdom of God and help the church learn to *pray*?" We are obviously not saying that other ministries and teams in the church are like Coca Cola, but you get the idea. Prayer ministry has a seriousness about it that is appealing to people of substance. And once people of character and quality have come to comprehend the vision, they too will understand that serving in prayer ministry is supportive of and fundamental to all parts and teams of the church.

Invest Deeply in the People You Lead. This eight-part leadership task looks something like this:

- Pray for them. Ask for their prayer needs, and follow up on them.
- Love them. Again, ministry leadership is primarily about relationship.
- Challenge them. I asked one of our prayer leaders to lead the devotional thoughts for one of the days of a prayer journey we were on together. When we got done, he asked me, "What did you think?" I said, "You did a good job with the material, but I was not convinced you believed what you were telling me." That really stopped him in his tracks, and he admitted I was right. Frank discussions and this kind of give-and-take help people grow. (See Ephesians 4:15.)
- Spend time with them. Eat lunch with the leaders as often as you can. Invest your precious time in the relationships, and press them for more growth.
- Invest in them in other ways (training, materials, and meaningful meetings, for instance) and make sure that they know you believe in them.
- Take them with you on trips. I don't like to travel alone, so I often bring one of our prayer leaders along. Some of the best times of mutual encouragement have come on these trips as

we talk and ponder how we can help our church grow in the area of prayer.

♦ Talk with them about your struggles. They need to understand what you are dealing with so that they can watch you in the real action, see how you turn to prayer in the struggles, and take notice as God answers and strengthens you even in the hardest spots. Some leaders reveal little of their personal lives to their teams, but that makes them appear plastic. But this is an area in which balance is required; if you reveal too much, you can appear self-focused and selfish. So go slow, and don't overdo it.

♦ Be approachable. Encourage both dissent and creative input for the sake of the ministry, soliciting the thoughts and ideas of your team so that when they have a fresh idea or notice a potential problem, the first thing they want to do is to share it with you. Also encourage them to speak openly about their own lives and struggles with you (as described earlier in this list).

Again, Recruit the Guys. Allow me a bit of repetition: as I already discussed at some length in chapter three, at Central we have chosen to be very intentional about recruiting men to pray. (The reason for this, in case you're skipping around the chapters of this book, is that women are often much more sensitive to spiritual things than men are, and women are therefore more likely to be drawn to prayer and prayer ministry. Women, of course, do a wonderful job in prayer ministry and often outperform men in terms of service and leadership. But when men see a ministry run by women, they may simply move on to something else. We don't want to let men off the hook that easily!) We actively recruit men for all our prayer ministry areas. We have found that if we get the men to pray, other men will join in. We have also found that the women will pray no matter what.

The American church's primary active demographic for prayer is women. It is not uncommon to have 75 percent women in a prayer ministry, but because of our intentional focus on recruiting men at Central, we are much closer to 50 percent. Some of our service intercession times are all men (more on service intercession in a later chapter). We certainly want women praying as well, but we focus more attention on getting the men to pray.

To be most effective, intentionally use only masculine colors for your prayer ministry advertising, and gear all your decorations at events toward men. At Central, for example, it is very common for us to ask the question, "What would a potential new male pray-er think about this promotion piece, article, or event?" If it is not masculine, we pitch it or change it.

This topic affords me the opportunity to share one of my most embarrassing blunders in prayer ministry, although I am sure there will be many more to come. Recently, I was speaking at a workshop for a national conference. Annie, my wife, had come along with me this time, as had several of our prayer team members. The subject was "How to Start a Prayer Ministry from Scratch," and things were going pretty well. When I got to the point in my talk where we began to discuss recruiting, I said, "We only go after men for our prayer ministry. I can have all the women I want." At this, our prayer team members hooted and hollered, which left me a bright shade of mortified pink. At least everyone had a good laugh at my expense.

But the point is solid, and it is critical for the success of prayer ministry at your church: recruit men, and you will have men in your ministry. Just don't forget that recruiting efforts with men must be intentional and deliberate.

Provide Easy Access Points. Chapter 7 will cover prayer access levels and the kinds of prayer ministries that fit them, but we need to address this topic here in the context of building a team of committed pray-ers in your church. Work diligently at providing ground floor prayer opportunities that will expose people to prayer and yet not demand too much commitment from them at first. These entry-level events should not be intimidating, such as praying for an hour during a service, but rather fun and stimulating. Such events are important to expose people to prayer and prayer ministry without overwhelming them.

An example at the entry level prayer might be a local event associated with the National Day of Prayer. At Central we plan an all-church gathering and invite everyone to attend. It is one hour long and includes a variety of prayer elements. We are especially careful to make the night relevant, appealing, and low-pressure. We do not want to cause anyone to feel uncomfortable by asking them to come to the stage and pray from the platform, for example. People leave that service having enjoyed it and, I hope, desiring more prayer.

Thinking about these easy-access events reminds me of window-shopping in a fancy mall. Merchandisers know that the window space at the front of their store is prime real estate, and they treat that space with great care, spending real money on the way these displays look and the way they make the shoppers *feel*. These special prayer events and opportunities for prayer beginners must be just as carefully and artfully crafted so that attendees are prompted from within to give serious thought to trying out a prayer ministry.

Inspire Your Pray-ers with Answered Prayers. Some churches encourage prayer or even publish a list of prayer needs, but you seldom hear about any answers to those prayers, if there are any. Telling stories of God's movement and His faithfulness is incredibly motivating and inspiring.

We have a couple in our church who had been homeless; they had lived for a while in a fifty-two-inch drainage ditch pipe. But they found their way to our ministry for the homeless called Acts Ministry. Acts meets two Saturdays a month, inviting the homeless to our campus for showers, clean clothes, haircuts, prayer, counseling, and a host of other services. This is easily one of the best, most exciting ministries of our church. We prayed our couple through getting jobs, finding a place to live, and several other practical needs. Then one evening, we gathered for an all-church prayer and worship time and told their story to the church. We highlighted how God had moved in their lives. The church erupted with praise and gratefulness to God. This is the kind of inspiring occasion that helps large groups of people in a church become motivated to pray, because everyone can relate to a story of struggle and God's faithfulness. And a report like this is even more motivating for those who have already invested their time in prayer.

Inspiration is extremely valuable, and then, just one step beyond that, there's encouragement. It might be impossible to over-emphasize the importance of encouragement to us human beings. I recently bought a used exercise machine that came with a feature called the "personal performance monitor." I discovered my first morning, as I was working out, that if I'm going 3.5 miles an hour or slower, there is a little note that appears on the screen that says, "Get going." However, if my speed is more than 3.5 miles an hour, the same monitor reads, "Way to go." It is truly amazing the extra effort I will exert to see those three little encouraging words.

We are all built that way; we love to be inspired and encouraged. In fact, we are starved for these feelings that remind us that we are alive and part of something. So remember to include inspiration and encouragement as you make plans for your prayer teams.

Infiltrate Every Area of the Church. You want to build a prayer team for the Student Ministry, Small Group ministry, and every other ministry at your church, putting prayer exactly where it belongs: everywhere.

At Central, we look for a leader who is already on that ministry team, a champion of prayer to direct the prayer efforts for that ministry. Often ministry teams are so overworked and understaffed that they don't feel as if they can spare a key leader to become the prayer champion in their ministry, but this is flawed thinking. Church leaders often get caught in the "tyranny of the urgent" frame of mind, which says, "I have to get this job done, and I need to be the one to do it," instead of bringing all needs to God in faith and asking Him to fill the needs. If we have prayer in its proper place, we will have much less struggle keeping a given ministry effort going. By making the decision to appeal to God first in prayer, we activate His power to help with the needs we face. Gently paint the vision of *prayer first* for each ministry in your church, one by one, and watch God work.

Get the Kids Involved. Kids bring passion and excitement, so involve them in everything you have going. When we have major prayer events, we have learned to invite the youth to lead in key areas so that they will grow and develop a heart for prayer. Including students builds leadership among the youth and opens the door for a move of God among them.

We were thrilled at the development we saw among the youth during one service intercession time at our Gilbert campus. We made a tough leadership decision to turn that intercession time over to the students, and it paid off. And they don't pray like the adults, who sit on the couches and remain completely composed. Students pace back and forth, move the furniture, prostrate themselves before the Lord, and call out in loud voices. The student-led intercession time has provided some of the most powerful prayer times I have ever been a part of. None of it would have happened if we had tried to get them to fit into the existing pattern or to maintain control of the session. We had to relinquish the leadership to them and get out of the way.

Involving the youth has also come with some somewhat predictable difficulties: we have had seasons when we had many kids involved and other times when we did not have any. Success depends on several leadership elements, including the effectiveness of your prayer leadership in casting the vision to the youth ministry staff and leaders, and the ability to raise up key youth who will model prayer and lead their peers.

Get Them Reading. As I've already mentioned in other contexts, books are a great way to teach your people about prayer.

Consider recommending and lending or giving great books and articles as a way to inspire others to pray. Get familiar with the excellent works that are available, and then handpick the best ones and get them into the hands of the people you want to motivate. Don't forget to do this specifically with men.

You and I can only be talking with one or two people at a time, and then usually only for brief moments. Books and articles will do some of your leadership work for you during those hours when you have no access to the people. And if a potential new pray-er reads a powerful book on prayer and becomes enthusiastic about it, it's likely he or she will soon look for an opportunity to take on some new challenge. A list of some favorite books on prayer is provided in the Appendix at the back of this book.

Put Ministry in Their Hands. I find small portions of baseball watching to be relaxing and enjoyable. The key phrase here is "small portions," because my attention span limitations cause me to become bored very quickly. It is much more fun to be on the diamond making the plays and swinging the bat than it is to watch. There is a lesson in this for ministry: ministry was not designed to be watched. We were designed to have a part in it. When all we do with ministry is talk about it or watch someone else doing it, we quickly lose interest.

If you want a vibrant prayer ministry and people who are engaged in that ministry, then *give it away*. Don't make the mistake of doing it all yourself; give major portions of prayer leadership to others. Make their contributions so significant that if they fail to follow through, the work will suffer. This will ensure they have "skin in the game" and will feel the importance of their service.

At Central, we have servant leaders who spearhead each area of our prayer ministry. These individuals are carefully selected and trained, and they carry the weight of the program. Then I get to be the one who looks on as they excel, and as ministry happens. That is the one sort of ministry watching that will always be one of the genuine joys of my life as a leader.

It is clear that the apostle Paul gave ministry away and allowed others to lead. Take a moment to review Romans 16:3-15, looking for those who carried the ministry in their hands under Paul's supervision. It is an impressive list:

> Greet Priscilla and Aquila, my co-workers in Christ Jesus. They risked their lives for me. Not only I but all the churches of the Gentiles are grateful to them.
>
> Greet also the church that meets at their house.
>
> Greet my dear friend Epenetus, who was the first convert to Christ in the province of Asia.
>
> Greet Mary, who worked very hard for you.
>
> Greet Andronicus and Junia, my fellow Jews who have been in prison with me. They are outstanding among the apostles, and they were in Christ before I was.
>
> Greet Ampliatus, my dear friend in the Lord.
>
> Greet Urbanus, our co-worker in Christ, and my dear friend Stachys.
>
> Greet Apelles, whose fidelity to Christ has stood the test.
>
> Greet those who belong to the household of Aristobulus.
>
> Greet Herodion, my fellow Jew.
>
> Greet those in the household of Narcissus who are in the Lord.
>
> Greet Tryphena and Tryphosa, those women who work hard in the Lord.
>
> Greet my dear friend Persis, another woman who has worked very hard in the Lord.
>
> Greet Rufus, chosen in the Lord, and his mother, who has been a mother to me, too.

> Greet Asyncritus, Phlegon, Hermes, Patrobas,
> Hermas and the other brothers and sisters
> with them.
> Greet Philologus, Julia, Nereus and his sister,
> and Olympas and all the Lord's people who are with
> them. (New American Standard Bible)

You Know You're Getting There When . . . A couple years ago we had a tragic death in our congregation. A father accidentally backed over his young child with the family car. The church staff and body were devastated, and everyone wanted to do something, but no one knew what to do.

Unbeknownst to me, a group of people from the church organized a prayer time. Someone asked the family for permission to pray for them on their property at an arranged time. Our pray-ers met at the house on that evening, circled the property silently and prayed. They didn't go in or try to speak to the family, since this was just a day or two after the accident. But they did stand with the family on their property in heartfelt and urgent prayer. These volunteer pray-ers knew something needed to be done, and they didn't need me to make it happen. When well-organized prayer gatherings and potent prayer ministry of this magnitude happen spontaneously, without the leader being the spontaneous one, you know your church is heading across the threshold to being a house of prayer.

CHAPTER 6

Constructing a Transformational Prayer Ministry

After they prayed, the place where they were meeting was shaken.
(Acts 4:31)

Get started! If you have some names in mind for the leadership roles discussed in the last couple chapters, then you're probably ready to take some more concrete steps to begin the prayer ministry that God may use to take your church across the threshold. For the purpose of this book, I have broken the process down into seven steps. Some of them can be very exciting to walk through, while others may feel more like hard work. In fact, it will start with some of that work. There is little that can be done until you know what challenges you face and what resources are already in place. So the first step in the ministry-development process is to take inventory of everything that is currently happening and to get familiar with the needs in the church.

Step 1: Get Informed. You will need to assess your whole church to gather general information and discover what is being prayed for and what is not. At this point, here at the beginning, also be sure to invite the Lord into the process by seeking His will about it. See if He reveals to you the area or areas that are on His heart for the prayer ministry at your church. To begin the assessment step, here are a few questions to get solid human answers to help you think and pray clearly. If your church is like most churches just starting out in prayer ministry, you will probably find the answers to be revealing.

- Who, if anyone, is praying for those in the body who are in need?
- Is anyone in your church really praying for your global workers? Who?
- What about pray-ers and prayer for the senior pastor and family?
- Is anyone praying for your other pastoral staff and church leadership?
- Is anyone praying that the services will be impactful? (Don't underestimate the power of during-service intercession. At times, total strangers who have visited Central have made comments such as these:
  "We felt the power of God on us during the service."
  "It was exceptional. Were there people praying for us during this service?"
  "We felt something we have not felt other places?")
- Who, if anyone, is praying for the children of the church? The youth?
- Are the elders and other leaders gathering for prayer, not just business? For example, when I was a senior pastor, our elders met every other week. One week we worked on the business and spiritual needs of the church, and the other time we gathered solely for prayer.

That short list of questions should have you thinking! Answer them unflinchingly and as thoroughly as possible, in writing. Do the same with the list that follows, which is much more in-depth, keeping in mind that it may be more difficult to come up with some of the answers. Make notes about what you already have in place, what you don't have, and what strikes you as a perfect fit for your church. Just remember that each answer will tell you something about what you have to work with and how you need to begin to move toward the vision of a transformational prayer ministry.

Useful Questions for Evaluating Your Church's Prayer Life

General Data: the Church and the Prayer Ministry as They Are Today

- What is the size of your church? (Average attendance? Membership?)
- How many adults do you have in the congregation?
- How many prayer groups are gathering for prayer weekly in your church?
- What percentage of your congregation is involved in official (recognized by the leadership) prayer ministry?
- What percentage of your prayer ministry team is male?
- What percent of your prayer ministry leadership is male?
- Do you have leaders for each part of the prayer ministry?
- Are your prayer leaders running the ministry, or do they merely have the title?
- Does your church have multiple sites or campuses? If so, what provisions have been made for unity in prayer across multiple sites? Do you have prayer ministries at each location? If so, what types?
- What are the five most important prayer needs for your congregation at this time?
- Gather a list of the major ministries of the church (that is, organized ministries with at least a team leader in place). Which of these ministries have someone praying for them?

Pastor's Questions. These questions are intended for the use of the pastor in evaluating his ministry only. They are not designed to give the prayer ministry members ammunition to shoot at the pastor for his lack of prayer emphasis!

- Am I, as senior pastor, committed to prayer, and does it show? How?
- Do I talk about my prayer life with the congregation during the weekend service(s)?
- Is prayer mentioned and modeled in the pulpit in the weekend service(s)?
- Do I attend the prayer ministry's events or gatherings?
- Do I believe prayerlessness is a weakness or a sin? How should my answer influence how I teach and lead with regard to prayer?

Questions About the Church's Prayer Life. Please see these questions as a means to stimulate reflection and evaluation. They are not intended to be used as ammunition against the bride of Christ.

- Does the church have prayer teams for each special event?
- Is the evangelism effort covered in prayer, and does it have its own prayer team?
- Is there a way for church members to submit prayer requests easily, and is there a prayer team in place to pray over the requests?
- Are there opportunities for continuing education on the subject of prayer and prayer ministry?
- Does the church have service intercession teams for each service and campus?
- Does the church have a staff member championing the prayer effort?

- Do members and guests have the opportunity during worship services to pray for each other?
- Are there prayer partners available at the end of the service prepared to pray with those who have pressing prayer needs?
- Does the church have a prayer room, and is it used?
- Is the prayer room nicely furnished? Is it the nicest room in the church?
- Are answered prayers announced and celebrated?
- Are prayer testimonies celebrated?
- Does the growth of the prayer life of each member have a high value?
- Is prayer part of the DNA of the church, or just another ministry?
- Is prayer a part of each ministry of the church?
- Is the prayer ministry welcomed and encouraged or merely tolerated?
- Does the church have a weekly corporate prayer meeting and, if so, is it attended by senior leadership?
- Is there a sense of God's presence in the church overall and during the weekend service(s)?
- Has the church mobilized and organized itself to be effective in prayer and prayer ministry?
- Does your church have a prayer strategy and plan?
- Does your church have a budget for prayer ministry? Is it generous?
- Is prayer being taught and modeled in the children's ministry?
- Is prayer being taught and modeled in the youth ministry?
- Do you have any teen prayer warriors?
- Does your church use prayer as a way to transition from one element to another in a service? Or is it strictly used for honest communication with God?

Ministry Staff's Questions. It serves no value to set expectations for how the staff is to pray. These questions may be used as items for the staff to discuss and pray about during a regular staff meeting, or for a period of time.

- Does the staff gather regularly for prayer?
- Are we as staff members sharing our prayer needs with each other and praying for each other?
- What percent of our staff is comfortable with praying for others in times of need?
- Would other church members describe our staff as prayerful?
- How unified is our staff? Is our unity made evident by agreeing in prayer?
- Which staff members are especially committed to prayer ministry?

Leadership's Questions. These questions may be used by the church's elders and lay leadership for evaluating their participation in and commitment to prayer and prayer ministry.

- Do the elders or leaders gather strictly for prayer at any other time than their regular meeting times?
- Are major decisions of the leadership prayed over extensively?
- Is there a prayer history of the church? In other words, when the church history is told, does it include dates and specific requests that were given to God in prayer? Are there inspiring stories of His answers to those prayers?
- Is that prayer journey shared with the people?

Now summarize your findings, analyze and pray. Take some time to make generalizations from the information you've gathered, and to identify particular strengths and weaknesses. Discuss among your prayer leadership what you may have discovered that is surprising, or particularly encouraging for the future, or particularly difficult to face. Maybe your church is not all you would like it to be with regard to prayer; still, you are much better off knowing exactly what the situation is. In the real world of leadership, ignorance is not bliss. Finally, and most important, look again through the list and pick out some areas that need prayer and *begin praying specifically* for those needs.

Step 2: The First Big Meeting. Once you have evaluated the church and have some solid items to talk about, call a meeting of all the people in your church who are interested in prayer and potentially interested in prayer ministry. Encourage, beg, and if necessary, bribe the senior pastor and other senior leaders to come and participate if at all possible. You want to hear from all of these parties about what prayer is going on that you may not be aware of, and you want to get their assessment and input. You also want to begin to lead, or to provide an opportunity for the leadership to crystalize out of the group.

Consider our first meeting at Central. We started by saying thanks to those who were interested in the work, and then I shared some of my prayer testimony. Then we showed one of the *Transformation* DVDs by George Otis Jr. (We used the one featuring Hemet, California; there are three different vignettes on this DVD. The purpose is to paint the vision of what can happen if a church gets serious about prayer.) Then we discussed what was going on in prayer and prayer ministry at Central at that time.

The next segment of the meeting was spent identifying all the prayer ministries we had decided to add immediately. These included School of Prayer, Service Intercession, and prayer partners.

After we described those new ministries and their value, we moved into a discussion of some ministries we could add. These were ministry ideas I had read or heard about that were working in other churches. I explained each ministry and wrote its title on a large flip chart page. Then I stuck each flip chart page on the wall somewhere in the large room. I asked each person in attendance to pick out three favorites among the suggested ministries. Then I gave them three colored dots: one red one, which was their first choice and worth three points; one blue one, which was their second choice and worth two points; and one green one, which was their third choice and worth one point. Then I asked them to place their colored dots on the flip chart page that was their favorite, then the second favorite, and then the third favorite. This way I had quantifiable evidence of what they were interested in, and everyone had a chance to weigh in.

After I got a feel for what they valued, I asked them who they looked to for leadership, both male and female, when it comes to prayer. I gave them an index card and had them write three male names on one side and three female names on the other. This step was designed to give me a better sense of who in the congregation was being looked to for leadership so that I could consider approaching them as potential leaders for the ministry.

Step 3: Strategize. Now that you have input from the people in the prayer ministry in your church (by the way, I should mention that the most important person you need to get input from is the senior pastor), you can make some preliminary determinations about which of the unprayed-for areas are most important. Don't try to fix all the areas of your church that need prayer all at once. Tackle them one at a time and with great care. If you start too soon or with a weak plan, your attempts will fail, and it will become harder to get people on board next time. So go slowly, and deliberately make a list of priorities. Develop a plan, and begin to carry it out.

Step 4: Solve Some Problems, Creatively. Begin looking for a creative strategy to rectify a few of the deficiencies you have discovered. The key word here is *creative*. Let's say the prayer covering for your kids is lacking. Now the task is to come up with an appealing, interesting, and engaging way to pray for the kids that will also be sustainable and helpful. I know of a church in Saint

Louis that makes baseball cards of all their junior high and high school kids. Then they have a special Sunday and recruit adults to take the card of a specific kid and pray for him or her during the year—a great idea. Implement a creative solution like this one for a couple of the deficiencies in your current prayer ministry, and people will begin to take notice.

Step 5: Get Key Leadership Buy-In. Once you have done an assessment and have a creative plan to begin the prayer ministry, make another appointment with your senior pastor to get his or her active support for the plan. In larger churches, the decision maker may not be the senior pastor, but rather an executive leader or leaders; if so, then this leader or team is more important. Do not attempt to move forward until you have secured their approval. As you present your plan, be careful to listen for their input as well. Sometimes your senior leaders see or know things that you don't know. Their guidance can be critical to the success of prayer ministry.

Step 6: Recruit. Once you have the approval of senior leadership, get started with building your team. You are looking for prayer team members and for prayer leaders for the various ministries. Begin by inviting your friends to take part. When your friends are all participating, or have at least all been invited to participate, then begin to speak to leadership-gifted individuals about joining in. (See Chapters 3 and 5 for more about building your leadership team and prayer teams. Again, many people would love to pray, but they don't know it yet. They are either uncomfortable with prayer or have had a bad experience somewhere along the way. Maybe they attended a prayer meeting that went on for way too long and only a few droned on in prayer; there was no team approach. Sometimes prayer meetings are not very relevant, and this discourages people. Maybe they were called on to pray out loud at a large function and were unprepared for the task. Unpleasant experiences like this can cause people to avoid prayer. So start with people who trust you, remember the importance of relationship, and ask them directly and nicely. Make sure nothing is uncomfortable for them, and proceed slowly.)

Step 7: Carefully Craft Your Access Levels. It is probably best to divide your ministry into various levels of access, or degrees of difficulty: entry level, which is appropriate for anyone; intermediate level for those who are willing to grow and ready for more challenge; and advanced level for those who have progressed to a high degree of commitment to prayer. The next chapter will present a wide variety of prayer ministries that may be specifically targeted for each of these levels. The idea is to help people connect well to prayer and to challenge them without overwhelming anyone.

CHAPTER 7

Prayer Ministries
and Access Levels

"See to it that you complete the ministry
you have received in the Lord.
(Colossians 4:17b)

Even a prayer ministry that is carefully set up to help people make a healthy beginning in prayer doesn't always work the way it's designed. Sometimes people dive into prayer ministry too quickly, despite your efforts to help them ease in slowly, at a level that is appropriate for them. These people believe they can join right in at the highest level, and they struggle and suffer for it. Especially in prayer ministry, the experience of people like this is much like that of a person who hasn't yet learned to swim, but who jumps into the deep end of the swimming pool anyway. Thankfully, others follow the suggested, slower approach, starting with entry-level prayer ministry opportunities, and they find it much easier to grow. Perhaps the key for prayer leadership to remember is that people who are interested in prayer are not all alike and need careful shepherding as they progress through the learning curve.

What follows is a breakdown of ministries into access levels as we use them at Central. You will come up with even more creative ideas for your church.

Entry-Level Opportunities

School of Prayer

A number of different approaches can be taken to the School of Prayer idea, as long as the primary focus is teaching and coaching. At Central, the School of Prayer is a four-hour session held once a quarter. Each SOP offers topics designed to teach people to pray and time to practice what they have learned. The SOP is designed to teach three topics: one basic topic, such as "How to Pray Out Loud"; one intermediate topic, such as "Praying as a Couple"; and one advanced topic, such as "Praying for the Nations." Each session is forty-five minutes long and is followed by fifteen minutes for practicing what we have learned. We have a refreshment time that is catered, and we provide handouts so that participants can begin to build a prayer notebook. We rotate about fifty topics, so you could attend every SOP for several years and not hear the same material. Sometimes we have in-house teaching, and other times we bring in a guest speaker. For more information, see Chapter 12, which goes into more detail about schools of prayer.

Prayer Garden

Central has its own Prayer Garden on one of its campuses. The garden offers a quiet place on campus for members, staff, and friends to pray. There are six stations in the garden with inspirational thoughts for prayer at each station. The meditations are scheduled in such a way that they are changed out monthly, so the material presented in the garden is always fresh. We use themes that reflect the current time of year. For example in September we pray for the kids and teachers starting a new school year. In

November we feature areas to be thankful for, and in February we pray for families and marriages.

Prayer Conference

Our prayer conference features some of the finest speakers, authors, and teachers available, who share their expertise on the topic of prayer. The speakers lead stimulating Friday night and Saturday morning sessions to motivate and challenge participants in all phases of their prayer lives. If it works out, we also try to get the speaker to share in our weekend services. God has used this event to focus the attention of the whole church on prayer. The conference has inspired people to pray more and stimulated many to join the prayer ministry.

Andy is a good example of someone who got connected to the prayer ministry at a prayer conference. He approached me a week or two after one conference and told me how inspired he had been by it. I made an appointment with him to get to know him better. It turned out he was a former Campus Crusade staffer and knew his Bible well. I invited him to join me in the prayer room to pray at one of the services, and the relationship was off and running. Andy loves to teach, so we asked him to help us develop a curriculum for small groups, which he did. Andy's teaching in this setting is helping many people become excited and passionate about prayer. He also assists in our Vision Team, which strategizes the next steps for the prayer ministry. (There's more on the vision team later in this chapter.)

24-7 Prayer Time

Each year in November, Central's prayer team hosts a 24-7 prayer room featuring ten interactive, creative prayer stations for members and friends. The 24-7 is open all week long, offering an uninterrupted, quiet time of prayer for participants. Many people point to this event as the time they learned to pray. We invite members and guests to sign up for one-hour slots during the 24-7 week and enjoy powerful times of directed prayer.

The 24-7 had a huge impact on a man I'll call Ronny. I bugged him to take a prayer slot in our 24-7, so he did. He decided to take a 2 a.m. slot. Without my knowledge, he devised quite an elaborate plan. He thought to himself, *I can't pray for an hour, so I will show up twenty minutes late. When I arrive, I will visit with the host for ten minutes so there will be only thirty minutes left.* (There are hosts in the prayer room at all times to keep the stations stocked with consumables, give people an initial tour so that they understand what to do at each station, and make sure that people are quiet and do not disturb others praying.) *If I follow my plan I will only need to spend three minutes at each station to fill up my time.* Ronny worked his plan flawlessly. He was late, visited with the host, and had only thirty minutes to pray. But his plan fell apart. After praying at each station he returned to his car, where he noticed the clock: he had spent more than two hours in prayer and loved every minute of it.

The key to the success of our 24-7 events is the interactive character of the stations. One year we did a station that featured praying for the homeless people in our homeless ministry. We obtained prayer requests from some of our homeless friends and put them on sticky notes inside a large cardboard box that had been constructed like a crude house. We had a fake fire, a shopping cart with plastic bags in it, and an old rotten tire for a seat. People crawled in the house and felt what it was like to be homeless for a short time. Soon they were writing prayers on sticky notes for the homeless, and it was clear to everyone that God was moving. This station was one of the most powerful stations we have ever used.

At another station we prayed for the lost. Someone from our team made hundreds of paper fish with hooks and attached them to a fish net, which was strung over the top of the booth. People secured their fish to a net with names of the lost they wanted to pray for. Eventually the net was stretched out of shape with the weight of the paper fish. It was stunning to see the names of all those who needed salvation.

By the way, we kept the fish with all the names on them and used them in our service intercession time that focuses on evangelism. This allowed us to continue to pray through the following year for the salvation of those mentioned in the 24-7.

This is a sample of what was used in publicity.

Virtual 24-7

In 2012 we made our first attempt at a *virtual* 24-7. This included the same topics as our live 24-7, but it was developed for and prayed through on the computer. We felt that it was important for us to attempt a virtual 24-7 because now, with five campuses, it will not be possible to set up a 24-7 on each campus. The virtual 24-7 gives people all across Arizona and even around the world a chance to participate in the 24-7, no matter where they live. We plan to continue developing this venue for encouraging people to pray.

What follows are some examples of prayer stations we have used in the past years for Central's 24-7s.

Make sure your stations are attractive.

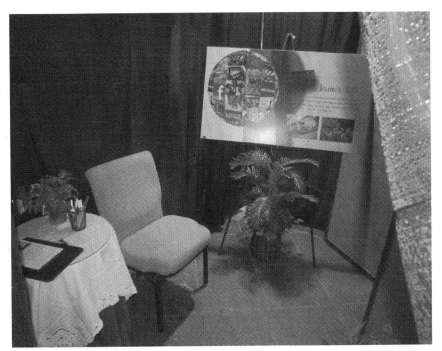

This station was for prayer for the unborn.

Our struggles were handwritten on a stained-glass vinyl material and attached to a light box.

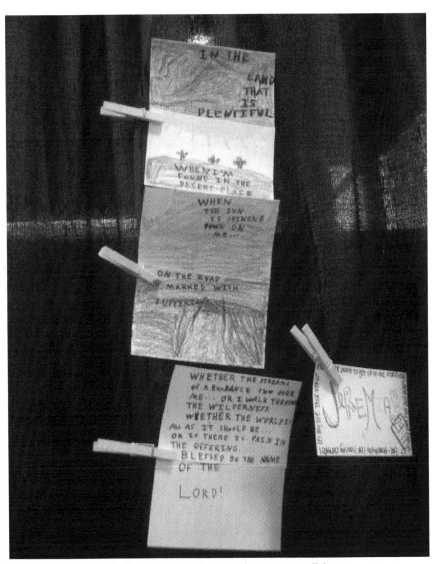

Make sure your stations are as interactive as possible.

This station reminded us of the danger of the tongue.

This station called us to worship God.

This station depicted sins that needed to be nailed to the cross.

Global Workers' Needs Groups

Many churches invest significant resources into the sending and support of global ministry workers from among their own ranks, yet few take this opportunity to consistently saturate that sending and that support with prayer. But there is intense interest among the church family in what these courageous workers are doing, and that interest provides an impetus for their families and friends to organize behind them in prayer.

Central has adopted a church-based team approach to global ministry, and we have identified North Africa as the place we want to do overseas work. Most of our global workers are in that region, and we are hoping to make significant impact in this area in the years to come. One of our church-based teams is already at work in one of these African countries, and several more of our families are now raising support to join them. If you have ever had to raise money, you know that it can be tough, so we decided to start a prayer group that focuses on just their country and their needs. The global workers who were on the way to the field and needed support were glad to join. One family wanted to host the prayer group in their home, so we were able to get started right away. Groups like this one provide several benefits:

- These groups give people who are trying to get to the field the prayer support they desperately need.
- These groups create among their members who are not going a stronger sense of affinity for, and identity with, the global workers in the group who are preparing to go.
- These groups give their members a chance to include friends and family members who want to be supportive of the future work of their friends. These friends or family members may also, at the same time, learn much more about prayer.
- These groups are a good training ground for running similar prayer groups on the field. (Most churches in unreached countries are small house churches, which are similar to the

small prayer group we created here for support. Being a part of a vibrant prayer group here can be very helpful for those considering starting a prayer group in the field or even here at home.)

♦ Finally, these groups give leadership a glimpse of the leadership abilities of the group members. If a mission candidate can run an effective prayer meeting here in the States, he or she will likely also do well abroad; if he or she struggles with such a role in the States, chances are the struggle will be even greater in a global work context.

Prayer e-Newsletter

One way we get the message out about prayer needs and opportunities is through a prayer newsletter. Central's monthly e-newsletter is created by Jayne, who is a great servant minister. Cathy, my associate in prayer ministry at Central, assigns several of us topics to write about, and Jayne compiles all the information to make an impressive e-newsletter. The newsletter helps pray-ers know what is coming and what to sign up for next. If you create a newsletter, make sure that it is well done, and don't forget to use masculine colors and themes. Again, all our publicity is designed with a male audience in mind.

Staff Prayer Lunches

This idea features a three-dollar lunch on staff meeting days, with an opportunity for staff members to pray for each other after eating. The entire lunch was exactly one hour, so we could eat during the first half hour and pray during second. We made a card that each staff member filled out with space for a couple of personal prayer requests on it. (See the Appendix for the card we used for this.) After eating, we split up into pairs, men with men and women with women, and exchanged our cards. I would pray for someone on the staff for that next month, and he would pray for me. It worked well, and people enjoyed becoming better acquainted and praying for one another.

Prayer Rooms

We have a prayer room or two on each campus. Prayer rooms need to be the nicest rooms in the church, so we have them decorated by someone with a flair for interior design. Prayer rooms have pictures of some of our global workers and their families on the wall as well as a beautiful framed map of the world. Each room seats ten to twelve people. We use our prayer rooms for life coaching, for midweek prayer, for spontaneous prayer when someone stops by, and for service intercession during the services. To be honest, we don't have all our problems solved: in three of our newer campuses we do not yet have dedicated prayer rooms. One campus uses the campus pastor's office, another uses a hallway not far from the worship center, and a third uses a changing area for stage productions. These rooms are not ideal, but they are better than nothing until we can get a permanent place of our own.

Make sure that you insulate these rooms for sound, and do not position them under or near the air handlers for the worship center; the noise can be distracting and detrimental to concentration and prayer.

Daily Devotional on Prayer and Podcasts

We found a source for a daily devotional on prayer and put it on our webpage. It is from Harvest Prayer Ministries and my good friend David Butts. This devotional is powerful, and we encourage our people to use it. The devotional keeps prayer in front of them with excellent daily thoughts.

Several years ago we hosted the National Prayer Leaders annual meeting on our campus. Originally we planned a gathering each night to expose our people to these amazing prayer leaders. But as we thought about it more, we realized that this was just too much, so we looked for another approach. It was then suggested that we record fifteen minutes of their best material on prayer and put it on our website as a monthly podcast, so we did. The podcasts have been a wonderful entry-level option for our people.

Intermediate-Level Opportunities

LIFT

LIFT is our weekly prayer meeting. But this is not your grandma's prayer meeting! We approach it as a battleground with territory to be taken for the Kingdom. It is one hour long, and we do not let it become focused on our personal needs but keep it focused on kingdom issues. Typically we pray over a worldwide issue such as a famine in Africa or a military conflict. Then we pray for national concerns; for example, in the fall of 2012 we were praying about the presidential elections and in the spring of 2013 about the bombings at the Boston Marathon. Next there is a state topic such as immigration, which has again recently been a major focus in Arizona. After state matters, we then pray for the churches in the Phoenix area as specifically as we can and cover our own church in prayer. We like to teach people to pray for other churches as much as or more than we pray for our own church. It would be very arrogant to think God is doing something only within the walls of our church. We use multiple types of prayer at these gatherings, such as popcorn style, everyone praying out loud at the same time, individual prayer, and praying in groups of two and three. The goal is never to use the same kind of prayer two weeks in a row so that LIFT stays alive and fresh. Honestly, corporate weekly prayer has been the hardest for us to build. Our people seem to respond better to prayer-focused special events than they do to weekly ones.

Web Prayer Team

The Web Prayer Team prays for the requests turned in during weekend services and on Central's website. All requests are available online for an interactive prayer session. All that a participant needs to get started is the use of a computer with Internet access, a short training session, and a password.

The web team is how we pray for the needs of our body. Prayers can be entered under any one of these categories:

- health issues
- finances/job
- marriage/relationship problems
- comfort and grief
- current events
- depression/anxiety
- family issues
- spiritual warfare
- the nation
- global outreach
- God's will
- the persecuted church
- praise report
- prayers for Central
- salvation/rededication
- suicidal tendencies
- the homeless
- the incarcerated
- travel
- youth
- hospitalization
- life transitions

After logging into the website, the pray-er selects the areas he or she wants to pray for and then begins the prayer session. The system is set up with an option for writing a note of encouragement to the one who is asking for prayer. All requests and responses are screened to make sure that all communication is appropriate. We have limited all requests to two hundred and fifty characters.

Sometimes our screeners have to sterilize a request because it has too many unnecessary details. Although Central's system was created several years ago, we have continued to use it ever since, and it is still serving the church's needs well. (If you are interested in using this system, which relies on Arena, web-based software designed for churches, please contact us, and we can help you get started.)

Prayer Partners

Prayer partners are members of the prayer ministry who pray following a worship service with those who come with specific needs. Prayer partners serve following the service they attend, so it is very convenient for them. Prayer partners are not to provide counseling, but rather prayer support. God has done some incredible things during these prayer times, not only in the lives of those we are praying for but in our lives as well. Having prayer partners weekly has created a climate of prayer. It is not uncommon to see a small group gather at the front of the worship center to pray with one of their members. Sometimes you may see a husband and wife joining hands to pray with a Prayer Partner or an entire family praying with a prayer partner.

We do a background check on each prayer partner to ensure everyone's safety. Prayer partners are also provided about an hour's training. Our experience has shown that this is sufficient to allow them to do a wonderful job of serving those who need prayer.

Service Intercession

Service intercession is a prayer group session that takes place during every worship service. At present we have ten services, so we have ten intercessory prayer teams. Each service intercession time is identical in method, but each service's prayer focuses on a different theme.

We begin with *confession* (out loud). This may seem intimidating, but good prayer comes out of a clean heart. This pattern is in our

DNA, and our people have embraced it. They would not describe it as weird or uncomfortable in any way. Next we praise God. Then we pray for the *people in the service* and *those leading the service*. We pray for their faith, their marriages, their children, and anything else the Lord puts on our minds. We often ask the Lord to direct our prayer time and He does so in astounding ways. Often we find ourselves praying about something that surfaced during the service intercession that we had not thought of before we asked God to lead us in our praying. It is not uncommon to share a sense that these are indeed the things on God's mind. They have a different depth and intensity to them. Finally we pray for the *theme* of that service intercession time. At the first Sunday morning service in Mesa, the prayer theme is our global workers. Deciding on a theme and praying for it weekly is a key to successful service intercession. Some service intercessor participants come to pray for a particular service because they have a heart for the people attending that service. Others come because they have a heart for the theme, such as our global workers.

These are the themes we use most often: the nation; global workers; marriage and family; health; and the lost.

We use this time as a training ground for people who want to learn to pray. Jo wrote to us about her service intercession experiences:

> Since I joined the prayer team, I've gone from treating God like a vending machine to realizing there is a battleground that I am in the middle of. I now believe there really are forces of evil wanting a piece of me, and I am learning to pray more strategically and aggressively.

Barry also joined me in the prayer room to pray during one of our services. The theme for that service intercession times was major health issues. It is not uncommon for us to face the challenge of organizing and praying for seventy-five major health-related requests, some of which are nothing short of desperate. After about three weeks, Barry announced that he did not want to do service intercession anymore. "This is work, and it is too hard. I want to be in a ministry that is more fun," he said. We talked for a long time about his perspective, and he began to realize that although praying is work, it is vital and a privilege, not an obligation. He still serves as one of our service intercessors.

Prayer Small Groups

This is an eight-week course for existing small groups, strictly on prayer. The idea is to offer this course to small groups who are looking for something on prayer, or to those groups whose leaders need a break. We have found that the groups and the leaders are delighted for the eight-week break, and we have a great chance to teach on prayer.

At Central, two of us on staff team-taught the course the first time, and then another member of our team took our material and added his perspective as well as additional insights and created a small group curriculum for Central. This approach is still new for us, but it has worked well. The topics are preset; we made a determination about what we thought were the most important topics to teach on prayer. We teach them and take the time to practice them in the small group setting. The participating groups have all grown exponentially, and most have joined the ministry in one form or another.

Prayer Shield

The purpose of the Prayer Shield ministry is to cover with prayer the key leaders (senior pastor and executive leaders), who are at the forefront of the church's efforts. At Central, we have several prayer teams that pray specifically for Cal (our senior pastor) or for the chairman of the elders or one of the campus pastors. The goal is for these teams to meet once a quarter with their key leader, who openly shares his needs and struggles; then the team covers those needs for the quarter in prayer. It takes some time for the prayer shield team to build the trust of their senior leader, because the leaders need to feel completely sure it is safe to share their concerns with confidentiality. Once the trust is established, it is an enormous blessing to the leaders.

A prayer shield does require some work, but it is worth the time and investment. I used to believe that it was my job to pray for others, so I almost never shared with anyone *my needs* for prayer. Several years ago I went on a prayer journey to British Columbia, with one of my favorite people, Dean Trune. Dean leads Impact Ministries, is a trained life coach, and has been leading in prayer ministry for years. I was sharing with him some of the bizarre things that Annie and I were going through. He interrupted me midsentence, and asked, "Do you have anyone praying for you?" I said, "No, I feel like it is my job to pray for others." He went on to tell me that he has one hundred and forty-four people who pray for his work and ministry. He challenged me to recruit a team to pray for us. So we did. We have twelve people, but the difference they have made is massive. Once we experienced the power of a prayer shield, we were sold, and have enjoyed the benefit of their prayers and of praying for them for years now. Prayer shields can be powerful, and each senior pastor should have a team praying for him in your church.

Advanced-Level Opportunities

Half Day in Prayer

Half Day in Prayer is a Navigators program in which an advanced-level prayer-ministry member retreats to a remote place to spend three and a half hours alone with God. Loren Sanny wrote the Navigators material in the '80s, and it is still available online. His article helps pray-ers catch the significance of investing long periods of time alone with the Lord, instead of the more common brief sporadic moments. He explains what to bring on the half day and how to make the most of the time. Many people have never prayed for any extended period of time, so this can be a genuine turning point in their growth. In the more than 30 years I have been working with the Half Day, I can't recall anyone having a negative experience with it. My wife treasures the special notebook she has used over the course of those years to record all the things she has learned on half days in prayer.

What I like best about a half day in prayer is that it gives me time to look back over the last month or two for things in my journal that God has been teaching me. We believers often miss the orchestration of God in our lives because we don't take this kind of time to reflect. I find the process incredibly comforting. I never really have the time to sacrifice for a half day; whenever they come along on the calendar I can always think of a thousand pressing things I need to be doing instead of spending that time in prayer. But each time I make room for it, God more than makes up the time, and I am better off for having been in His presence.

Sometimes, when you go on a half day in prayer, things may not go smoothly. I remember one occasion when the gnats were so bad that I couldn't concentrate. Another time Annie and I were chased by biting horseflies. At another one I almost stepped on a rattlesnake. I was praying at my cabana when I needed to stretch my legs. I stood up, started to walk, and noticed a rattlesnake coiled up and ready to strike. I was so scared that I let out a girlish scream (this style of scream is famous at our house; we call it the "Covert Scream") and jumped completely over the snake in one hop. Neither the snake nor I was hurt, but it did compromise my concentration for the rest of our half day.

UpTeam (Uninterrupted Prayer)

The goal of the UpTeam ministry is to maintain twenty-four-hour-a-day, seven-day-a-week prayer covering for the church, its staff, its new church plants, and its global outreach workers. UpTeam members pray one prearranged hour each week.

At Central, we create an online book each month, full of fresh prayer requests, which we make available to team members who have login credentials. The book is controlled so that each respondent sends one praise, three ministry requests; and two personal requests. Each entry must be less than two hundred and fifty-five characters so that the book remains manageable and the team does not get overwhelmed. This project is very labor-intensive, but it bears fruit. One volunteer proofs the entries, and another gathers the needs from our global workers; I work on getting the prayer requests from the staff. An administrative assistant then compiles the book from the submissions we receive from our staff and global workers. We are convinced there is power in this ministry because someone is praying for these needs every hour of the day, seven days a week.

E-men's Groups and E-women's Groups

E-groups are rigorous prayer accountability groups that report to each other via the Internet. Participants work at the disciplines of daily prayer, Bible study, praying for their spouse, exercising, reading, and praying for their neighborhoods. E-groups have proved to be life-changing. The groups also meet quarterly in person for fellowship and encouragement.

Tony, an E-group member, writes:

> By being held accountable, I have seen my marriage
> strengthened and have learned to pray with my wife
> regularly. Also my time in the Bible and in prayer
> has moved from sporadic to a daily habit. I know
> beyond a doubt that I would not have been as
> consistent in these areas if I were not being held
> accountable by a group of such caring
> Christian men.

A couple of years ago we noticed some very significant patterns. Usually when people come to us, they are broken. They may have lost a home or be out of work or be facing some other significant crisis. Originally, I thought if we could teach them to pray and get them praying consistently, they would recover nicely. So we started the E-groups to help fill this need. What we discovered was that getting people praying regularly does stabilize them, but it does not resolve the problems that got them into trouble to begin with. These issues require discipling, and relational or emotional healing. Out of our new understanding of these dynamics, Life Coaching was implemented.

Life Coaching

Life Coaching is a twenty-six-week one-on-one discipling study with a huge emphasis on cleaning up the relational debris each of us carries. Life Coaching provides clear Bible teaching to help us begin to view things from God's perspective and not ours. It is intense and painful at times but has proved to be powerful in the lives of those who have chosen to take the challenge. We use the *Called to Obedience* material by Howie and Denny Dowell. This material is not available for purchase; you must be discipled to obtain it. This website provides more information: http://www.ctoministries.org/.

Prayer Journeys

Prayer journeys take participants to different countries around the world to pray for the outreach and effectiveness of global field workers. These trips are not designed as sightseeing adventures, but rather act as heavy intercession campaigns, and they can be extremely rewarding.

Central's prayer ministry does at least one of these each year. Our most recent trip as of this writing was to the Far East. We had a seven-member team, and not all were seasoned pray-ers. But by the end of the ten days, all had made drastic steps forward in their prayer lives and developed a stronger heart for the lost and the nations. We prayed several hours each day and met with local workers to understand their needs and struggles. Some of our time was spent visiting with nationals who were not yet believers, and we even spent a couple days staying in their homes. This was the highlight for most of the team. Prayer journeys are a wonderful laboratory for learning to pray at an advanced level and developing a passion for the world.

Vision Team

You can't make anything better if you don't know where you are going, and it is vital to have people thinking about where *this* ministry is going at all times. We have a Vision Team for the prayer ministry that meets one or two times each year. They are all servant ministers, and they give up their day to help us think about prayer ministry, strategizing for the future. These leaders are usually people who run organizations and see the big picture well. We ask our most strategic thinkers to join this team so that they can help Cathy and me to stay on track and chart the course for the future. Our Vision Team meetings don't happen very often, but when they do, they last the entire day. We look at last year's objectives to see how we have done at attaining them and seek God for the next year's objectives. Usually these are minor corrections to help keep us on course.

Threshold Intensive

The Threshold Intensive is a four-day interactive immersion in prayer ministry for church teams, college students, and prayer leaders. The hands-on sessions provide foundational information about prayer as well as practical suggestions for growth and development in prayer ministries of all types. Built into the experience is time to learn as well as to pray into practice what has been taught. Intentional leaders who want to grow prayer in their churches or ministries find this time invaluable, even transformational, as it has been for the Catalyst Church (described in the Introduction of this book).

You Can Do This!

Prayer ministry is one of the hardest ministries in the church (because of the prayerlessness of so many), but it is also one of the easiest (because God is in it and blesses it). *God wants your church to grow in prayer*, and *He will show up* in noticeable ways if you plan times and places for Him to do so. Simply get a structure in place and rely upon His promise: "For where two or three come together in my name, there I am with them" (Matthew 18:20). I tell you emphatically, you can do this because *He* can and *He* wants to.

As you are dreaming and planning, don't be afraid to call in an expert to help motivate, inspire, and evaluate your prayer ministry. Budget dollars spent on events and training that focus on prayer are well spent. And sometimes input from outside helps a church to envision what is possible more clearly than another idea from someone who is well-known within the church.

Ministries like the ones described in this chapter can help your church step across the threshold into God's glory, but of course every church is different. We have been at it ten years now, and we do have some successes, but also several failures, to show for it. What works for us may not work for you and in some cases might not even be appropriate. So this list of the prayer ministries we use at Central is provided only as a way to get you thinking about access levels and about what you and your church could be doing. Undoubtedly, some of the best prayer ministry ideas have not yet been imagined. Ask God what He has for you, and He will lead you on the adventure He wants you to experience.

CHAPTER 8

Leveraging Special Events for Momentum

God does nothing except in response to believing prayer.
—John Wesley

Almost everyone loves special events, whether they are at church, at work, at our kids' schools, or anywhere else. Many people even love big political events. Large special events act as anchors in a church's annual calendar. For the sake of the Kingdom of God, the key is learning to bathe the church's special events in prayer. Doing so invites God to take His proper place in the church calendar and opens the door for His power to be displayed and for lives to be changed. But these events also allow the prayer ministry to pick up new pray-ers and to gain valuable momentum for engaging the entire church in prayer.

Here are a few categories of special events, any and all of which may be leveraged to gain momentum in the prayer ministry:

- Holidays and seasonal events
- City or community events
- Church outreach events
- Youth events and camps

- Sports events
- Elections and political events
- Special prayer events

Some Observations About Large Events and Prayer Ministry

- Churches regularly forget to include prayer in special events planning and implementation, and the events suffer for it.
- Leading other leaders to include prayer in their events is a responsibility the prayer DNA carrier must bear.
- People are willing to work harder and to pray for something big. It is therefore possible to capitalize on that openness to teach them how to pray for special events, and more important, how to pray in general.

Teaching our teams to pray over special events helps build their faith, it allows them to be dependent on God for outcomes (a very positive kind of dependency), and it helps them learn firsthand the value of making prayer a part of all that happens at church.

So Don't Forget. At one of the churches where I served, the senior leaders decided to purchase ten thousand tickets to an Arizona Diamondbacks baseball game as a means of attracting new unchurched friends. I was on the implementation team for this event and had the chance to build prayer into the planning. So we designed two smaller events to pave the way for the game. Each small group member was encouraged to select a couple individuals they wanted to invite to this all-church outing. In preparation for the game, we encouraged our small group members to pray for those individuals for thirty days and then to invite them to an ice cream social at their small group meeting location in early June. In July we again asked each small group member to pray for the same people for thirty more days and then to invite them to a barbeque again with their small group.

Our hope was that the friends would feel more comfortable with the people in the small group after these two preparatory events were completed. All the prayer, combined with the positive, low-stress interaction, set the stage for the invitation to the Diamond-backs game. We anticipated that this would spark interest in the church and the small group in the future.

That August we were able to sell and use all ten thousand tickets, and many of those we prayed for attended. Not only that, but *our church's attendance jumped by five hundred the Sunday after the game, and did not go back down.* Lesson learned: praying over a special event makes a dramatic difference in the lasting effects of the effort.

Sadly, the lesson didn't stay learned. For the preparations for the next major event of this kind, the church went back to the old habits: lots of excellent organization without the foundation in prayer. You guessed it; the event did not bring the powerful results the prayer-covered event had brought. Now, these comments are intended merely to point out what we see over and over again in churches across America: we regularly neglect to take advantage of strategic prayer for events that are otherwise carefully strategized, and God's blessing is sadly missing.

It has also taken time for strategic prayer to move into all major events in the life of Central, but we have seen good progress.

Get the Word Out Clearly. As the information about an upcoming major event begins to flow, it's important to use electronic means to put out plenty of clear information and encouragement about praying for them. The prayer ministries that flourish that take full advantage of the web, e-mail, and social media.

At Central we use a *combination of website and e-mail* communication to connect our E-men and E-women accountability groups. The technology allows us to stay in touch with seventy-five to one hundred people without meeting with them weekly in small groups. Although e-media-based accountability ministry is not as effective as face-to-face meetings, it is working and helping people stay in touch and stay in prayer for each other.

Facebook works very well for letting people know about our upcoming Schools of Prayer and other major events. Many experts believe that it has become impossible these days to be truly successful in creating a movement or coalescing a major event without using Facebook. That may be an overstatement, but Facebook and *Twitter* and other social media can be great tools to create a buzz about an event.

E-mail has proven sufficient for the distribution of monthly prayer newsletters and the receiving of prayer requests. Especially as your people become aware that they will regularly receive the prayer news and can readily get their requests into the hands of people who pray, information can move much more quickly than in the days of the old telephone prayer chain and paper bulletins. More rapid communication means prayers are more timely, and emergencies can frequently be prayed about by large numbers of people in real time.

We use our *website* for a few important purposes. First, it is used to register those who are interested in our events. Then, this past year we conducted a virtual 24-7 on the website as an experiment, and it went very well for the first time. The possibilities the website offers have become increasingly necessary because we now have five campuses, with more to come, spread across the Phoenix metropolitan area.

Each week in our weekend services we have a preservice slide that provides a number for people to *text prayer requests* during the service. Since we have a team in the prayer rooms during the service, we can pray for the need in real time. We are finding, however, that people are saving the number and texting us not just during the services but any time they have a need.

We have worked hard to get some of our teachings on the website in the form of *podcasts*. Doing so allows our people to watch and learn from the comfort of their homes or offices.

Here are a couple examples of how we have mobilized prayer coverage for major events:

- ◆ **Camp E-mail Blasts.** These are sent out each day while the kids are at summer camps with items for parents and prayer teams to pray about. These e-mails are carefully worded and specific in asking God to enrich our students' camp experience. We do this kind of e-mail blast for many major events. Be sure to check the Appendix for examples of these e-mails.
- ◆ **2012 Election Prayer Campaign.** Before the last major election we organized a forty-day prayer and fasting event. The communications are provided below in some detail because you may be interested to see the scope of the event and the specific way the publicity and flow of information were organized. Below are the contents of the e-mail messages we sent out to everyone for whom we had an e-mail address. We sent out each of these the day before the date listed.

* * *

Forty Days of Prayer and Fasting for the Nation
Beginning September 30

Cathy *(this is the other prayer minister on staff with me)* and I have not seen a time when we believe there has been a greater need for prayer for our nation than right now! So, for the next forty days Cathy and I will be praying and fasting for our nation. We would like to ask you to join us.

Here is the way it will work:

Each Monday you will get an e-mail message from us with some things to pray for during the week. We would like to ask you to include those in the things you are praying.

How you choose to pray and/or fast is up to you. You can set a time each morning to pray over our nation or find a time each evening that works well for you.

Fasts look different from person to person. Some people will not eat anything for a day. Others will give up a meal once a week. I have known of people giving up chocolate or TV for the period of the fast. If you decide to fast, choose something that will be a stretch and will prompt you to pray often.

* * *

Forty Days of Prayer and Fasting for the Nation
October 1

It is very obvious in Scripture that God is the one who places people in office.

Romans 13:1: "Let everyone be subject to the governing authorities, for there is no authority except that which God has established. The authorities that exist have been established by God."

Invite God into the process of our elections.

Ask God to glorify Himself with the outcome of our elections.

Pray, "Lord, we want Your will to be done for our nation, state, and local governments."

Pray, "Lord, we pray for divine protection over the integrity of the election process."

* * *

Forty Days of Prayer and Fasting for the Nation
October 8

Here are some prayer thoughts for the week. Please include them in your times of prayer.

Ask God to raise up governing officials who will honor life, marriage and family, and religious liberties. Pray for leaders who are faithful to the nation and to their spouses and children (Malachi 2:15-16).

Pray that each American voter will serve this country by placing his or her vote.

Ask God to help America with our foreign affairs and for leaders who will be effective in this arena.

Pray for a Congress that is not deadlocked, but can accomplish the needs at hand.

* * *

Forty Days of Prayer and Fasting for the Nation
October 15

Here are some prayer thoughts for the week. Please include them in your times of prayer.

Pray for a government that can find solutions to our debt crisis.

Ask God for leaders who will lead with integrity. Pray that our leaders would be granted wisdom, knowledge, and understanding, and have the courage to do the right things (James 1:5).

Pray for leaders who can create jobs and help turn our economy around.

Ask the Lord to have mercy on our nation.

* * *

Forty Days of Prayer and Fasting for the Nation
October 22

Here are some prayer thoughts for the week. Please include them in your times of prayer.

Ask the Lord to stop the sex trade industry and porn industry in our nation and around the world. Forgive us as a nation for not standing up against evils of our day. Forgive us, Lord, for immorality, abortion, filth, greed, and selfishness.

Pray for our military men and women who serve this nation so faithfully. Pray that the leaders will direct our military wisely.

Thank the Lord for the abundance of His blessings we have received to this date.

Pray for those who will go to bed hungry or homeless today. Pray for leaders who will have a heart for the hurting.

* * *

Forty Days of Prayer and Fasting for the Nation
October 29

Here are some prayer thoughts for the week. Please include them in your times of prayer.

Pray for leaders who care deeply about our education system and lead very positively for our children.

Pray, "Lord, we pray for the pastors who lead your churches. Give them a boldness that will steer us on the right path again as they teach and preach. We have tolerated compromise long enough. Call us afresh to righteousness."

Pray, "Lord, call the churches to be prayerful for this election and for churches to make their views known to their leaders."

Pray for leaders who will find solutions to our immigration issues. This issue has been unresolved for way too long.

Lord, give us leaders like Abraham Lincoln, who put the good of the country over his own popularity or re-election hopes. Pray that our leaders would be God-fearing and recognize that they are accountable to Him for each decision they make (Proverbs 9:10).

* * *

Forty Days of Prayer and Fasting for the Nation
November 5

Here are some prayer thoughts for the week. Please include them in your times of prayer.

Pray for revival in the nation and a return to godly principles. "We ask You to awaken our nation to its need for godly leaders. Make us a country of people hungry and thirsty for righteous leaders" (Proverbs 25:5, Proverbs 29:2).

Pray that true positions and views are revealed to voters instead of spin.

Ask the Lord to help our politicians to recognize their inadequacy and to seek God's will. (Proverbs 3:5-6).

Ask the Lord for protection for our nation from those who would like to hurt us.

Pray for others who are taking this forty-day adventure with you.

Pray that it has been a blessing for them as it has been for you.

Thanks for taking this ride with us! We trust that it has been a blessing for you. May God honor our prayers.

Some Other Major Events We Cover in Prayer. At Central, we do a summer event on the Fourth of July called Fire in the Sky (FITS) with fireworks, food, and inflatable bouncers for the children. The leader who runs this outreach is very cognizant of the need for prayer coverage. He makes a point of calling for and building strategic prayer into the FITS schedule. This past year we prayed over many aspects of this gathering, including the weather. Weather is a concern in Phoenix, since it can be 117 degrees in July.

Interestingly enough, this year it was only 94 degrees on July 4. We had a small storm that passed through early in the day, and the temperatures dropped to the lowest numbers Phoenix had seen on that date for more than one hundred years.

Central also hosts a satellite location for the Willow Creek Global Leadership Summit each year, and our prayer leadership organizes prayer covering for the event. We ask God to raise up leaders in our church and the other churches represented by all who attend the Summit. This year, for the first time, we offered service intercession throughout the entire conference. Each year we also offer prayer partners and a private prayer room for all who attend.

We also have Summer Camp ministries and Vacation Bible Schools for students and youth. These special events are obviously important to the parents, so they are motivated to pray.

The Prayer DNA Carrier Leads the Event Leaders. Major events are a great way to help other ministries develop a prayer team for their ministry and for their major events, but experience shows that the church's prayer DNA carrier will need to step in to help make things happen, and even then the results may be mixed. Some ministries' leaders are shortsighted and content to have the prayer ministry pray over their events. But other ministries' leaders will instantly catch on and want a prayer team of their own to support their ministry.

When I hear about a major event coming to our church that will be led by one of our staff members, Cathy or I stop by the office of the person organizing the event to ask how we can pray for him or her. Usually that leader is experiencing stress in one area or another. After that, we ask about including prayer more broadly in the event organization, and the leader almost always jumps at the chance to have the event covered in prayer. We then suggest some things we could do to get people praying. We allow the event leader to pick the items that will work for him or her and their event. Usually I also take them an article that I wrote, one containing some of the ideas that eventually made it into this chapter, and I leave it with the leader to read. The article speaks especially about the benefits of including prayer in major events and why it is so important.

For some team leaders, this is their third or fourth year at leading a major event. Each year we find that most of them become progressively more open to prayer coverage for their event than in the previous year. This is because God *shows up*, that is, there are noticeable positive differences and a sense of God's presence, when we pray. It is critical to work patiently and gently with all event leaders. A prayer leader must never come across in a condescending or self-righteous manner.

Remember to Capitalize on Holidays. Each year at Easter we send out e-mail messages to recruit large numbers of people to pray in the prayer rooms for the Easter services and the people who will be attending. We have seven prayer rooms on our five campuses and several Easter services at each campus. Our goal is to have teams of people praying in the prayer rooms during each service. We invite entire small groups, couples, and even the youth to take a service for prayer. This year we had 182 who participated on all our campuses.

For many, this special event provides the opportunity for their first exposure to corporate prayer. Some are afraid at first, but before long they are into it. Most will say as we conclude, "Has it been an hour already?" Once they see firsthand that service intercession is not nearly as difficult as they thought, some begin to join in regularly. We have small groups that participate year after year, and a portion of our new people in the prayer ministry come from seasonal prayer efforts.

For the next year I made plans to reserve one of the two prayer rooms (on the campuses that have two prayer rooms) strictly for small groups. Then I began recruiting small groups to fill up these times. People seem more willing to give service intercession a try in a group they feel comfortable with, so I recommend that you capitalize on this tendency.

I challenged one of the men I am life-coaching to bring some of the boys he mentors. I asked him something like, "You know the most important thing you can teach those boys, don't you?" He answered no and asked what it was. "Teach them to pray," I said, "and you have given them a tool they can use all their lives. Why don't you see how many you can get to pray with you at Easter for one of our service intercession times? I will make sure you have one of the prayer rooms all to yourselves." He loved the idea and had ten young men praying with him that night.

Prayer Conferences Work. In an effort to get more people exposed to prayer, consider a prayer conference, which is a perfect example of a prayer special event. Select and invite a national speaker, and begin publicity far in advance. The publicity works best if you can arrange for the conference speaker to speak at the weekend services sometime earlier in the year so that the people will be acquainted with him or her before the conference. If that is not possible, an excellent video may also be used.

We have used radio, print, preservice worship slides, mass e-mail, service videos, service announcements, Facebook, bulk mail, and our website all to get the word out about the prayer conference. Our conferences are usually Friday night and Saturday morning. Our time is slightly restricted because we have to turn the campus around for weekend services beginning at 4 p.m. on Saturday, so it makes for a tight day for us. But your situation will offer different challenges and opportunities.

We sometimes have people say, "We did not know we even had a prayer ministry." In a large church it can be very difficult to get stage time, so you have to be creative to make your people aware of an upstart prayer ministry! Those of you who work in smaller venues have the advantage over those in larger ones in this area of stage time. Use it wisely!

So the prayer conference provides a wonderful introduction to the prayer ministry for many. We have spent years collecting the e-mail addresses of the people in our church and around the state who are interested in prayer. Now, when we have an event, we use that list to get the word out. Some ministries are not diligent about collecting e-mail addresses, so they have trouble communicating their message. Make data collection a priority.

Schools of Prayer Work. Another common prayer special event through which people can connect with the prayer ministry is a School of Prayer (see chapter 7, Entry-Level Opportunities). At Central we do one of these each quarter. At the end of the teaching time, the leader of each Prayer Ministry team explains that ministry and invites people to join in. Sometimes five to ten new attendees want to try one of these ministries. The School of Prayer has been a consistently excellent way to recruit new people and inspire the people we have to continue to grow in prayer.

Building Campaigns Need Prayer, Too. Undergird your building campaigns with prayer and with God's blessing. In 2008, Central held its "And One Campaign" to raise money for our second campus. There were several prayer components that made the campaign different from most and helped to leverage it for prayer.

First, we organized a bus tour down to the new property so that people could see the land firsthand. The leadership team had an artist's conception drawn up for people to view, along with a narrated video presentation to explain the entire project. We hired four charter buses for several nights, and hundreds rode down to the property on the buses. The video was played, and many questions were answered en route to the new property.

Once we arrived at the new campus, we introduced the people to prayer walls we had constructed. These walls were designed so that people could post a prayer for the use of the land and ask God to do something special with it. When the tours ended, we had hundreds of heartfelt, meaningful prayers recorded from our people.

With God's help we were able to build as we felt led to build. And by the way, the new place was packed within three months of its opening. The Gilbert campus is now our largest. What role did all that prayer play? We will never know this side of heaven, but make sure you plan into your building campaigns a strong prayer emphasis.

We have found using prayer walls to be effective.

Prayer is not the idea of men, but of God. If you include lots of prayer in your special events, you'll be glad you did, for various reasons. Obviously, your event will gain the benefit of prayer coverage. But I am also convinced that the process actually teaches your people much about prayer that they can use in their own lives; at the same time it teaches the church as a whole about the importance of prayer.

CHAPTER 9

Types and Fresh Methods of Prayer

The prayer power has never been tried to its full capacity.
If we want to see mighty wonders
of divine power and grace wrought in the place
of weakness, failure, and disappointment,
let us answer God's standing challenge,
"Call unto me, and I will answer thee, and show thee
great and mighty things which thou knowest not!"
—J. Hudson Taylor

Not long ago, I was asked to speak to a group of men on the subject of prayer. I struggled with how to make the talk so straightforward and to the point that they would be sure to grasp it.

Eventually the Lord led me to Revelation 3:20, which says, "Here I am! I stand at the door and knock. If anyone hears my voice and opens the door, I will come in and eat with him, and he with me." I used this verse to explain that God is standing at the door, waiting to listen and help us with life; all He asks is that we open the door and invite Him into our lives and struggles by taking the time to talk with Him. Prayer is no different from simply talking to a friend who cares about our lives, and we do that all the time. Right?

If only it *felt* that simple. In fact, many Christians struggle with how to fill, or use, their prayer time. "What do I talk about?" or "What should I say, exactly?" are common questions. And the prospect of filling an extended period of time with one-sided conversation can be very intimidating.

Once we have decided to make the effort to talk with God, we will benefit greatly if we give some genuine thought to figuring out what that conversation needs to look like. The material that follows is designed to provide some help with typical prayer problems and questions. I have specifically included types of prayer and exercises that are applicable for individual use as well as for prayer ministry or group settings, even in large prayer ministries. By the way, these methods and patterns are good examples of the kinds of material we present at Schools of Prayer.

Types of Prayer

To begin, it makes sense to categorize the prayers we pray in order to help us think clearly about this all-important activity of talking with God. I am convinced that it is most healthy to pray different types of prayers, depending upon the situation. This kind of flexibility helps us learn and increases our interest, and both of those benefits will serve to increase our commitment level. This list is not intended to be exhaustive, but rather to start this topic by getting us thinking a bit more critically.

Rote Prayers. These are prayers we pray from memory. An example of rote prayer would be, "Now I lay me down to sleep, I pray the Lord my soul to keep. If I should die before I wake, I pray the Lord my soul to take." Another rote prayer that is not as elegant would be, "Good bread, good meat, good gosh, let's eat!" Many have prayed rote prayers at one time or another, and there is nothing necessarily wrong with praying this way. But rote prayer should not be our primary method. One of the dangers of rote prayers is that they can be prayed without even engaging our minds because they are memorized. Praying with an unengaged mind is not beneficial.

Jesus encouraged us in His Sermon on the Mount not to pray with meaningless repetition. See Matthew 6:7.

Crisis Prayers. These arise out of feelings of desperation in difficult times. An occasion for crisis prayer might be a doctor's report, which might motivate us to pray this way: "Oh Lord, I simply cannot believe I have cancer . . . God, you've got to get me out of this somehow! Let me go on living! Help me know what to do!" We pray like this when we have no place to turn but to God. These, too, are very much normal prayers to bring to God in the times that call for them, and there is certainly nothing wrong with praying this way. But again, if the only time we pray is when we find ourselves in some sort of crisis, we may take that as a sign we have some growing to do in the area of prayer.

Casual Prayers. These are prayers that we see have little lasting significance. A casual prayer could be, "God, you know I am late for this doctor's appointment. So please make every traffic light between here and there green, and let the elevator be on the bottom floor when I get there." Casual prayers are not full of desperate feelings like crisis prayers, but are prayed much more frequently. Do pray casual prayers, but again, these should not represent the majority of prayers we pray.

Prayer List Praying. This is a favorite of many believers. Praying a list of petitions to God is a good way to pray, because the creation of the list over time essentially keeps you from sacrificing valuable prayer time in casting around in your memory for things you wanted to pray about. You will not forget anything that God has placed on your heart if you've written it down in advance. Some people don't like the lack of spontaneity in praying a list, and choose another form, but I love it. I find that it helps me stay on track and keeps my mind from wandering.

Kingdom Prayers. These are petitions focused on matters of the kingdom of God. These are not just impersonal prayers like, "Thy Kingdom come, Thy will be done on earth," but rather much more personal expressions of that same thought. I have a friend, Dean, who moved his family to Seattle, Washington, to start a church. The people of our church have invested much time in prayer for Dean and for his family, and also specifically for the church they started. These requests on behalf of them are kingdom prayers, because I am asking God to extend His Kingdom here on earth through Dean's life as a church planter and through his work. I am not praying for myself, nor for any of my interests. The emphasis is solely on extending the work of God on earth.

Intercession. In this context, the act of interceding, or going between, is praying for someone who is in need. This morning I was praying for Jon, one of the guys I took on my last prayer journey. His father had a heart attack in an airplane while flying home from England on a business trip and has struggled ever since to regain his health. To date he has been in the ICU for one hundred and twenty-five days and is still very critical. As I pray for Jon and his dad, I am interceding for them, representing their case before the Father. I am bringing them before God and asking Him to help them in this season of trouble. Intercession is something Jesus expected us to do for each other. You can read more on this subject a bit later in Chapter 10.

Listening Prayer. This is a kind of prayer that requires almost no words from me. One of my pastor friends called me up and wanted to meet at Starbucks. We have spoken on several occasions about our struggles with prayer, but this time he told me about a breakthrough he was having in his prayer life. He said, "I go out on my patio, and I tell God, 'Here I am, Lord, I give you this 30 minutes I have. Please speak to me. I am listening,'" then he simply waits for what he will hear from God. He freely admits that sometimes he doesn't hear much, but says that other times it is as though God is speaking right to him on that patio. He told me that this kind of listening prayer has revolutionized his prayer times.

Spiritual Warfare Praying. This is doing battle in prayer with the evil one and his associates. This topic will be addressed in detail in Chapter 12.

Learning to Pray, Patterns of Prayer

For the important purpose of helping yourself or your church's people become more comfortable with prayer, a prayer model or prayer pattern may be very useful. Even advanced pray-ers may find these patterns helpful at times, and the application for new believers or inexperienced pray-ers should be obvious.

PRAY. Use the word "pray" to remember these four actions when you pray:

- Praise God for His glorious work, His character, and His grace.
- Request God's providence for Kingdom concerns and for the needs of others.
- Ask God for the things you need.
- Yield to his Lordship in your life, and rest in it.

The Five P's of Prayer. Use these words that start with "P" to remember five actions when you pray:

- **Praise.** Offer praise and honor to the Lord.
- **Provision.** Ask God for His daily provision for all your needs.
- **Pardon.** Request forgiveness, and commit to forgive others.
- **Protection.** Plead for the Lord's protection for all who are dear to you.
- **Purpose.** Seek His kingdom, and make it the first priority in your life.

BLESS. Use this acronym to remember five topics for prayer:

- **Body.** Pray for health, strength, and safety.
- **Labor.** Pray for favor and excellence at work and for employment needs.
- **Emotions.** Pray for encouragement, joy, and peace for facing life's challenges.

♦ **Spirit.** Pray about your personal walk with God and position in the home.
♦ **Social.** Pray for godly and strong friendships.

Use the Lord's (Model) Prayer as a Pattern. When a disciple of Jesus came and asked Him how to pray, He responded with the Lord's Prayer (or model prayer) we have come to know and love. This instruction of our Lord should not be taken lightly or left out of our practice of prayer, but I do not believe it was intended to be quoted, but rather to be used as a pattern or model for right praying.

Below is the Lord's Prayer, outlined for in-depth prayer. The words of Jesus (from Matthew 6:9-13) are in bold as section headings.

Our Father in heaven, hallowed be your name. . . . Think of the qualities and names of God that may be especially meaningful to you, such as these:

♦ Father
♦ Peace
♦ Always present
♦ Protector
♦ Righteousness
♦ Answers prayer
♦ Provider
♦ Shepherd
♦ Faithfulness

Your kingdom come, your will be done on earth as it is in heaven. Pray that God will accomplish His will through these parties.

♦ Our church and its staff in these different ministry areas:

◊ Preschool

◊ Children's
◊ Youth
◊ Single
◊ Adult
◊ Recovery
◊ Small Groups
◊ Prayer and Missions
◊ Worship
◊ Preaching
◊ Sports Ministry

- Our elders
- Our national leaders
- Our state leaders
- Our city officials and local leaders

Give us today our daily bread. . . . Recognize and affirm that God is the source of all good things.

- Confess your faith in God's ability to provide.
- Humbly petition God for your needs.

Forgive us our debts, as we also have forgiven our debtors.

- Ask God to forgive you.
- Confess your sins to Him.
- Extend forgiveness to others.

And lead us not into temptation, but deliver us from the evil one.
Put on the full armor of God (see Ephesians 6:10-18).

(Note: The armor of God is not to be seen as a sort of rabbit's foot or lucky medallion that we call upon for extra protection from bad things that might happen. In the Ephesians passage, Paul uses the "once for all time" verb tense to command his readers to put on the armor, indicating that it is not to be viewed as an action to be duplicated daily. In this prayer, we appropriately acknowledge the armor that we have put on as Christians, humbly affirming that its power to defend and fight comes from God Himself.)

- ◆ Belt of truth
- ◆ Breastplate of righteousness
- ◆ Feet fitted with readiness from the gospel of peace
- ◆ Shield of faith
- ◆ Helmet of salvation
- ◆ Sword of the Spirit, which is the word of God
- ◆ Pray with all kinds of prayers
- ◆ Pray for God's protection from temptation over family, friends and leaders
- ◆ Claim your victory over the devil

For yours is the kingdom and the power and the glory forever.

- ◆ Give God all the glory.
- ◆ Recommit yourself to His purposes and kingdom.
- ◆ Ask God for revival in our nation.
- ◆ Ask God to draw seekers to Himself.
- ◆ Ask God to bless the work of the global workers who are laboring in a foreign field.

Biblical Prayers for Other Believers as Models for Our Intercession

Intercession for the needs, interests, and spiritual well-being of others—or praying for each other, is a tremendous honor and privilege each believer enjoys. In order to help us think more clearly about how to pray for each other, it may help to examine how the Christian leaders in the Bible went about it. If you have never undertaken a study of this subject, the following passages may surprise you as you look at them in this light. Take special note of the contents of the prayers the Apostles Paul and John make a point of mentioning, and consider praying in these ways for some other believers in your life or your church.

Ephesians 3:14-21. This is the second prayer of Paul for the Ephesians:

> For this reason I kneel before the Father, from whom his whole family in heaven and on earth derives its name. I pray that out of his glorious riches he may strengthen you with power through his Spirit in your inner being, so that Christ may dwell in your hearts through faith. And I pray that you, being rooted and established in love, may have power, together with all the saints, to grasp how wide and long and high and deep is the love of Christ, and to know this love that surpasses knowledge—that you may be filled to the measure of all the fullness of God.
>
> Now to him who is able to do immeasurably more than all we ask or imagine, according to his power that is at work within us, to him be glory in the church and in Christ Jesus throughout all generations, for ever and ever! Amen.

Philippians 1:9

> And this is my prayer: that your love may abound more and more in knowledge and depth of insight, so that you may be able to discern what is best and may be pure and blameless until the day of Christ, filled with the fruit of righteousness that comes through Jesus Christ—to the glory and praise of God.

Colossians 1: 9-14

For this reason, since the day we heard about you, we have not stopped praying for you and asking God to fill you with the knowledge of his will through all spiritual wisdom and understanding. And we pray this in order that you may live a life worthy of the Lord and may please him in every way: bearing fruit in every good work, growing in the knowledge of God, being strengthened with all power according to his glorious might so that you may have great endurance and patience, and joyfully giving thanks to the Father, who has qualified you to share in the inheritance of the saints in the kingdom of light. For he has rescued us from the dominion of darkness and brought us into the kingdom of the Son he loves, in whom we have redemption, the forgiveness of sins.

Colossians 4:12

Epaphras, who is one of you and a servant of Christ Jesus, sends greetings. He is always wrestling in prayer for you, that you may stand firm in all the will of God, mature and fully assured.

1 Thessalonians 1:2

We always thank God for all of you, mentioning you in our prayers. We continually remember before our God and Father your work produced by faith, your labor prompted by love, and your endurance inspired by hope in our Lord Jesus Christ.

1 Thessalonians 3:10

Night and day we pray most earnestly that we may
see you again and supply what is lacking in
your faith.

Philemon 6-7

I pray that you may be active in sharing your faith, so
that you will have a full understanding of every good
thing we have in Christ. Your love has given me
great joy and encouragement, because you, brother,
have refreshed the hearts of the saints.

3 John 2

Dear friend, I pray that you may enjoy good health
and that all may go well with you, even as your soul
is getting along well.

Ephesians 1:16-23. This is the first prayer of Paul for the
Ephesians, saved for last here because it is so rich.

I have not stopped giving thanks for you,
remembering you in my prayers. I keep asking that
the God of our Lord Jesus Christ, the glorious
Father, may give you the Spirit of wisdom and
revelation, so that you may know him better. I pray
also that the eyes of your heart may be enlightened
in order that you may know the hope to which he
has called you, the riches of his glorious inheritance
in the saints, and his incomparably great power for
us who believe. That power is like the working of his
mighty strength, which he exerted in Christ when he

raised him from the dead and seated him at his right
hand in the heavenly realms, far above all rule and
authority, power and dominion, and every title that
can be given, not only in the present age but also in
the one to come. And God placed all things under
his feet and appointed him to be head over
everything for the church, which is his body, the
fullness of him who fills everything in every way.

Pray the Pictures of Jesus

Many find it very satisfying and even exciting to pray about a
particular snapshot of Jesus we see somewhere in Scripture. For
example, take the picture of Jesus holding the little children on His
lap in Mark 10 and apply that scene to your church's Vacation Bible
School program and weekly kids' gatherings and to your own
children. Here is a sample of how that prayer might sound: "Father,
as I think of Jesus holding and loving the little children, I ask You
to hold and love our kids in the children's programs this morning.
May each child feel as though You are personally holding them and
caring for them. May our children be conscious of Your wonderful
love. I ask You to release Your power into their lives and their
families; give them a hunger to know You, and to grow to love You
in return. Build them into the young people and adults You want
them to be."

If you selected the picture of Jesus calming the storm on the Sea
of Galilee for His disciples, the prayer could be prayed like this:
"Jesus, just as You calmed the storm on the sea, will You please calm
the turmoil in my life today. I am afraid, just as the disciples were,
and I am asking You to interrupt my troubled situation and bring
Your peace, as You did for the disciples."

You could pray the picture of Jesus returning on a white stallion
in Revelation 19:11-16 like this: "Thank you for bringing victory
with you, a complete vanquishing and demolition of all foes and
enemies. Jesus, Your victories leave no enemy with any claim on

You or Your Kingdom. Please bring this kind of victory into my life, my circumstances, and this church. Allow no enemy to have any claim on me, my life, or the ones I love. Lord, I ask You for this form of victory in Jesus' powerful name."

Praying the pictures of the Scriptures can be practiced personally as we spend time in prayer privately, or it can be done in a corporate prayer setting, which is where I have found it to be most exciting. Either way, praying the pictures of our Lord in action will certainly spice up a tired prayer life.

Pray Scripture Declaratively

One woman I have known for years has become a truly powerful prayer warrior. Her husband is also. They have spent years praying for the nations around the world. Much of their prayer has been on location in one of those countries. They recently taught our church to pray "declarative prayers" from Scripture. Here is a list of some passages I have found that can be prayed this way.

1 Chronicles 16:24

Declare his glory among the nations, his marvelous deeds among all peoples.

Psalm 5:3

Morning by morning, O LORD, you hear my voice; morning by morning I lay my requests before you and wait in expectation.

Psalm 9:10

Those who know your name will trust in you, for you, LORD have never forsaken those who seek you.

Psalm 9:14

That I may declare your praises in the gates of the
Daughter of Zion and there rejoice in your salvation.

Psalm 19:1

The heavens declare the glory of God; the skies
proclaim the work of his hands.

Psalm 31:19

How great is your goodness, which you have stored
up for those who fear you, which you bestow in the
sight of men on those who take refuge in you.

Psalm 33:4

For the word of the LORD is right and true; he is
faithful in all he does.

Psalm 33:5

The LORD loves righteousness and justice; the earth
is full of his unfailing love.

Psalm 34:5

Those who look to him are radiant; their faces are
never covered with shame.

Psalm 71:17

Since my youth, O God, you have taught me, and to this day I declare your marvelous deeds.

Psalm 89:2

I will declare that your love stands firm forever, that you established your faithfulness in heaven itself.

Psalm 125:1

Those who trust in the LORD are like Mount Zion, which cannot be shaken but endures forever.

Psalm 138:7

Though I walk in the midst of trouble, you preserve my life; you stretch out your hand against the anger of my foes, with your right hand you save me.

Psalm 138:8a

The LORD will fulfill his purpose for me.

Proverbs 21:30

There is no wisdom, no insight, no plan that can succeed against the LORD.

John 9:39

". . . I have come into this world, so that the blind will see and those who see will become blind."

1 Corinthians 2:14

But thanks be to God, who always leads us in triumphal procession in Christ and through us spreads everywhere the fragrance of the knowledge of him.

Ephesians 5:3-5

But among you there must not be even a hint of sexual immorality, or of any kind of impurity, or of greed, because these are improper for God's holy people. Nor should there be obscenity, foolish talk or coarse joking, which are out of place, but rather thanksgiving. For of this you can be sure: No immoral, impure or greedy person—such a man is an idolater—has any inheritance in the kingdom of Christ and of God.

1 John 1:5

This is the message we have heard from him and declare to you: God is light; in him there is no darkness at all.

The idea of this style of praying is to pray in a declarative fashion the truths that are expressed and the promises that are made in a given passage of Scripture. As you noticed in these passages, sometimes a verse does not contain the word "declare" or is not even phrased as a declaration, but there is a truth or promise within it, which may be expressed declaratively.

For example, if we were praying Psalm 34:5 as a group, someone might pray it this way: "Lord we declare that those who look to you are radiant and their faces are never covered with shame." If we were praying Psalm 138:8 we might say, "The LORD will fulfill his purpose in me, and I declare it to be so." At the end of each declaration the entire group says in unison, "We agree!"

Many of us have found this to be a thrilling way to pray and one that helps us stand on the truths given to us in God's word.

Pray Favorite Scriptures

Especially in groups that are new to corporate prayer, it is often helpful to teach them to pray their own favorite scriptures. Most everyone who has been a believer for a while has a favorite scripture, but not many people have thought of reformatting that scripture that so forcefully speaks to them into a prayer.

For example, if your favorite scripture is Lamentations 3:22-23, your prayer could go like this: "God I thank you that your steadfast love never ceases and that your mercies are new every morning. Lord, this is so incredible! Thank you!"

This approach helps groups get a feel for praying Scripture and removes fear because they are simply using the words of their favorite verses as a guide.

Prayer Exercises for Groups

Learn to Listen to God. Praying in a group can lead to some exciting experiences of God's leading as the group focuses on hearing what He is saying. A friend who has spent his life praying for missions and missionaries taught me a couple of ways to listen to God that are the best I have seen.

Two Men in the Middle. This is a somewhat complex method or exercise, but an intensely interesting one that depends upon the Spirit's leading to function. The group begins by taking a few minutes to prepare hearts, and then waits and listens to receive a direction from the Lord as to what to pray regarding the topic at hand. In this exercise, if at any time a pray-er gets no specific sense of direction from the Lord, then he is free to choose a topic based on his own thoughts.

1. Start with two people facing each other in the middle, about six feet apart—persons A and B.
2. Person A begins by praying about the concern God gave him.
3. Once person A is finished, person B then prays about his own subject, while person A quietly chooses someone else in the group to take his place in the middle. So there are always two people facing each other in the middle praying or preparing to pray.
4. The interrupt line: At any point while one of the two people in the middle is praying, someone else in the room (person C) may either find that pray-ers A or B are interceding about the same things person C felt God directing him or her to pray about; or person C may feel something stirring inside related to what person A or B is praying about. At this point, person C may step up to the middle, between the two people (A and B) praying, and wait for A or B to finish praying. Others who want to pray over the same matter can join the interrupt line by lining up behind person C. Once C is done praying, instead of the prayer shifting back to person B, those who have made a line behind person C take their turns praying. When that line is finished, the prayer resumes with person B, who now begins praying over a new subject. Then, as before, if anyone in the room is burdened to pray over that topic, he or she prays as well.

The interrupt line is designed to help cover one topic completely until it is finished before moving on to the next. This approach is both interesting and spontaneous, and it makes ample room for the Spirit's leading.

Distilling God's Direction. This is also somewhat complex, but consider what may be gained by intentionally allowing the Spirit to direct the prayers of an entire group as you work out this method.

1. Form groups of four.
2. Choose a theme for prayer, such as the nations or your church, and then ask God, "What is on Your heart today for us to pray about?"
3. Take three minutes (or more if you want) to prepare hearts, and then wait and listen to receive a direction from the Lord as to what to pray regarding the topic at hand. As in the two-men-in-the-middle exercise, if someone doesn't get any bearing from the Lord, then he or she is free to choose another topic based on his own ideas. This encourages listening to God, something most Americans don't do often or well.
4. Then, each person in the group of four shares with the others in that group what he or she sensed they should be praying about it.
5. Now pray what you identified you were to be praying about around the circle for five minutes. Short, focused prayers usually work better than long prayers by any one person.
6. Next, repeat the prayer circle, but each person adopts the prayer topic of the person on his or her left in the group of four, taking that prayer need on as if he or she had been the one who had originally heard it from the Lord. (This can be humorous as many people realize they don't know what the person next to them was praying and need to ask.) This approach encourages deep listening to and empathy for other pray-ers. Next, have each group of four choose one person to send to the group on their left and another person to send to the group on their right so that the groups are nicely shuffled. Now each person in the new group of four shares what he or she sensed they should be praying about.

7. Then pray for five minutes. Again, short focused prayers usually work better than long prayers by any one person. When the five minutes are up, repeat the prayer time, but each person adopts the prayer topic of the person on his or her left in the group of four, taking that prayer need on as if he or she had been the one who had originally heard it from the Lord. As previously stated, have each group of four choose one person to send to the group on their left and another person to send to the group on their right so that the groups are nicely shuffled. This process is repeated several times until you run out of time or until most of the participants have prayed with most of the pray-ers partaking in the exercise.

8. The final groups of four decide which of the four prayer items they felt God was giving special emphasis to as they were praying. (We say, "This prayer had the breath of God under it," or it "had that little bit of extra Holy Spirit oomph to it.") At times, groups resist this, but encourage them by saying, "If you had to choose one, which would it be? Was there a topic we prayed over together that seems to be rising to the surface to make an impression?" They have to choose—and it can be fun to force them. This encourages weighing the things God gives us to pray.

9. Each group chooses one person from their group of four to pray out loud in the larger group focusing on the topic they have chosen in the previous step. It is often amazing to see how the Holy Spirit has either given a high level of similar attention to all the groups on a given subject, or made sure that the whole range of topics that needed to be covered was exposed, by giving a different emphasis to each group.

Turn Church Business Meetings into Prayer Events. If you are familiar with typical church leadership meetings, then this idea and set of recommendations may be remarkably refreshing to you.

Charles M. Olsen has written very wisely about different methods of prayer for a church board meeting. He disdains the common "bookend prayers" employed to open and close a meeting, and the equally common problem of leaving prayerfulness out of all that occurs between those prayers. This method, he says, "traditionally separates out the spiritual aspects of the meeting from the 'business at hand.'" It's as if the spiritual is simply forgotten, and the meeting proceeds according to the pattern of non-church meetings, with "an emphasis on efficiency, a reliance on 'reasoned' judgments, and a structure based on parliamentary rules," culminating with a vote "by majority rule."

To combat this troubling practice and the even more troubling worldliness it reveals, Olsen suggests several different prayer activities for the meeting, including these:

- **Gleaning for Prayer.** Olsen means we should use the meeting as a research exercise for topics to pray about, which are then prayed about in the meeting.
- **Offering Prayers of Confession.** The gathered leaders take time out to confess to God their failings and sins.
- **Taking Prayer "Time-Outs" Throughout the Meeting.** Pause after each twenty minutes of discussion or debate to pray about what is being discussed.
- **Praying Scriptures as a Group of Leaders.** The Lord's Prayer and Jesus' prayer in John 17 are two suggestions.
- **Acknowledging Subliminal Prayer.** This involves intentionally seeing to it that one or more attendees are praying quietly about what is being discussed, or for the others in the meeting.
- **Framing the Meeting as Worship.** Any meeting of church leaders can be viewed as an act of worship, so intentionally think of it that way and watch what happens. Make the meeting an opportunity to worship together with deliberate pauses for worshipful prayer.[20]

Olsen's ideas offer a higher vision of church leadership meetings, a vision that is more akin to what we see in Scripture. Pass on these ideas to the board or leadership of your church, and encourage them to consider rethinking their meeting style with an emphasis on prayer and the leading of God's Spirit. If an entire church is to cross the threshold into an explosion of God's glory, the leadership will need to participate fully, and there is no better place to start than in their regular meetings.

CHAPTER 10

Toward Deeper, Fresher Prayer

Who you become will be determined by how you pray.
—Mark Batterson, *The Circle Maker*

If your church is to be one that crosses the threshold into the richest blessings of God, there will need to be an increasing number of people with a deep and abiding commitment to prayer. Experienced prayer warriors know that it pays to maintain an arsenal of prayer ideas to keep their communication with God fresh and interesting. In the previous chapter we looked at some tried-and-true patterns and prayer methods, and in this one we will examine some more intense ones. These ideas should be considered appropriate for the intermediate- to advanced-level pray-er and may be integrated into your church's instruction on prayer.

More About Praying the Scriptures

Pray the scriptures frequently because they are so rich in meaning and so helpful in guiding our prayer. Scripture is about God, whose depths are unfathomable, and Scripture also addresses nearly every imaginable aspect of human existence, which is also a sufficiently complex topic. So, for example, the Bible provides not only the deep theological truths and beautiful imagery to increase our love of God, but also wonderful patterns for praying for the people on earth we love and care for. Look at these two examples and consider pausing to pray them now for someone you love.

Ephesians 1:16-23

> I have not stopped giving thanks for you, remembering you in my prayers. I keep asking that the God of our Lord Jesus Christ, the glorious Father, may give you the Spirit of wisdom and revelation, so that you may know him better. I pray also that the eyes of your heart may be enlightened in order that you may know the hope to which he has called you, the riches of his glorious inheritance in the saints, and his incomparably great power for us who believe. That power is like the working of his mighty strength, which he exerted in Christ when he raised him from the dead and seated him at his right hand in the heavenly realms, far above all rule and authority, power and dominion, and every title that can be given, not only in the present age but also in the one to come. And God placed all things under his feet and appointed him to be head over everything for the church, which is his body, the fullness of him who fills everything in every way.

Matthew 17:15. This is a verse I have prayed many times over my sons: "Lord, have mercy on my son." This very brief passage inspires me to ask God to look upon them, to see their needs and to meet them.

Hebrews 4:12. Praying Scripture frequently along with our other prayers and petitions to God helps us to keep our prayer lives fresh and exciting, as this well-loved verse teaches us:

For the word of God is living and active. Sharper than any double-edged sword, it penetrates even to dividing soul and spirit, joints and marrow; it judges the thoughts and attitudes of the heart.

Here, then, are a number of other benefits we gain when we pray the word of God, along with some passages to pray that make the point. Internalize these concepts and consider teaching them to believers you have the privilege to train in prayer.

Praying the Scriptures Teaches Us to Pray According to God's Will

It is easy to see how Jesus wrestled in prayer with regard to accepting and obeying God's will. Some are troubled by the thought that Jesus needed to wrestle with this, but His wrestling and His victory in this area should, in fact, be a tremendous encouragement to us. The wrestling process of lining up our prayers with the will of God is aided by the praying of passages of Scripture, which teach and explain His revealed will to us.

Notice Jesus' prayer in Matthew 26:36-42:

> Then Jesus went with his disciples to a place called Gethsemane, and he said to them, "Sit here while I go over there and pray." He took Peter and the two sons of Zebedee along with him, and he began to be sorrowful and troubled. Then he said to them, "My soul is overwhelmed with sorrow to the point of death. Stay here and keep watch with me."
>
> Going a little farther, he fell with his face to the ground and prayed, "My Father, if it is possible, may this cup be taken from me. Yet not as I will, but as you will."
>
> Then he returned to his disciples and found them sleeping. "Could you men not keep watch with

me for one hour?" he asked Peter. "Watch and pray so that you will not fall into temptation. The spirit is willing, but the body is weak."

He went away a second time and prayed, "My Father, if it is not possible for this cup to be taken away unless I drink it, may your will be done."

Luke 22:43-44 adds another dimension:

An angel from heaven appeared to him and strengthened him. And being in anguish, he prayed more earnestly, and his sweat was like drops of blood falling to the ground.

I can't tell you the number of times I have begun to pray about something, and as I pray and pour out my heart to God, a verse comes to mind to confirm that I am on the right track. At other times, a passage surfaces in my thoughts to alert me that what I am praying about is not God's will at all. It had felt perfectly normal to pray about that subject when I began, but as I prayed, the topic was weighed and discovered to be wanting in light of God's revealed truth and will. Intentionally praying a scripture helps to streamline this process, putting me immediately on track with God's will. Then I am able to move on to other topics in prayer, in confidence that I'm off to a solid start.

Praying the Scriptures Helps Us to Become Grounded in God's Word

As we pray Scripture, we also learn it and actively build it into the fabric of our lives. Unlike simply memorizing the words of the Bible, praying them causes you to deeply consider the content, all while intentionally under the influence of the Spirit.

Luke 21:33

Heaven and earth will pass away, but my words will
never pass away.

John 15:7

"If you remain in me and my words remain in you,
ask whatever you wish, and it will be given you."

Praying Scripture Gives Us a Vocabulary for Prayer

The complaint, "I don't know what to say when I'm praying!" is
a common one, and it's no wonder. For a new believer or pray-er,
praying can make him feel as if he's talking to himself. But Scripture
is full of examples of prayers, and of the language of Jesus and the
apostles, the prophets, and the psalmists about all sorts of spiritual
themes. Scripture helps us to pray in a very practical way by actually
providing for us many of the very topics and words we want to pray.
Consider how you could pray these two passages, for example:

Colossians 1:10-13

And we pray this in order that you may live a life
worthy of the Lord and may please him in every way:
bearing fruit in every good work, growing in the
knowledge of God, being strengthened with all
power according to his glorious might so that you
may have great endurance and patience, and joyfully
giving thanks to the Father, who has qualified you to
share in the inheritance of the saints in the kingdom
of light. For he has rescued us from the dominion of
darkness and brought us into the kingdom of the
Son he loves.

1 Timothy 4:12

Don't let anyone look down on you because you are young, but set an example for the believers in speech, in life, in love, in faith and in purity.

Praying Scripture Helps Us Develop an Intimate Relationship with God

Consider the deep intimacy and the passion for God and His purposes that is evident in the words of so many of the biblical writers. Allowing the Scriptures to guide our prayers allows us to feel right along with the likes of King David, who was a man after God's own heart. Pray with David when he says, for example:

Psalm 63:1-8

O God, you are my God, earnestly I seek you; my soul thirsts for you, my body longs for you, in a dry and weary land where there is no water.

I have seen you in the sanctuary and beheld your power and your glory.

Because your love is better than life, my lips will glorify you.

I will praise you as long as I live, and in your name I will lift up my hands.

My soul will be satisfied as with the richest of foods; with singing lips my mouth will praise you.

On my bed I remember you; I think of you through the watches of the night.

Because you are my help, I sing in the shadow of your wings.

I stay close to you; your right hand upholds me.

Praying Scripture Keeps Us Focused

I love any form of prayer that guides me along the way, and praying the Scriptures does just that. Read through 2 Thessalonians 1:3-4 and 11-12:

> We ought always to thank God for you, brothers, and rightly so, because your faith is growing more and more, and the love every one of you has for each other is increasing. Therefore, among God's churches we boast about your perseverance and faith in all the persecutions and trials you are enduring.
>
> . . .
>
> With this in mind, we constantly pray for you, that our God may count you worthy of his calling, and that by his power he may fulfill every good purpose of yours and every act prompted by your faith. We pray this so that the name of our Lord Jesus may be glorified in you, and you in him, according to the grace of our God and the Lord Jesus Christ.

Read it again slowly, noticing how Paul's thoughts, through the Spirit's guidance, can guide you to pray for those who are in your church or small group. Using this passage and others like it as a prayer guide is a perfect way to stay on track as you intercede for others.

Praying Scripture Gives Us Authority to Stand Against the Enemy

As we confidently pray the ideas and words of Scripture that address the spiritual battles we face, our negligible personal authority with respect to Satan is strengthened by the absolute authority of Scripture. Ponder the significant *extra armor plating* we can add to our prayers by expressing in them the truths in these passages:

1 John 2:14

I write to you, fathers, because you have known him who is from the beginning.

I write to you, young men, because you are strong, and the word of God lives in you, and you have overcome the evil one.

Ephesians 6:10-18

Finally, be strong in the Lord and in his mighty power. Put on the full armor of God so that you can take your stand against the devil's schemes. For our struggle is not against flesh and blood, but against the rulers, against the authorities, against the powers of this dark world and against the spiritual forces of evil in the heavenly realms. Therefore, put on the full armor of God, so that when the day of evil comes, you may be able to stand your ground, and after you have done everything, to stand. Stand firm then, with the belt of truth buckled around your waist, with the breastplate of righteousness in place, and with your feet fitted with the readiness that comes from the gospel of peace. In addition to all this, take up the shield of faith, with which you can extinguish all the flaming arrows of the evil one. Take the helmet of salvation and the sword of the Spirit, which is the word of God. And pray in the Spirit on all occasions with all kinds of prayers and requests. With this in mind, be alert and always keep on praying for all the saints.

2 Corinthians 4:16-18

Therefore we do not lose heart. Though outwardly we are wasting away, yet inwardly we are being renewed day by day. For our light and momentary troubles are achieving for us an eternal glory that far outweighs them all. So we fix our eyes not on what is seen, but on what is unseen. For what is seen is temporary, but what is unseen is eternal.

2 Corinthians 10:3-6

For though we live in the world, we do not wage war as the world does. The weapons we fight with are not the weapons of the world. On the contrary, they have divine power to demolish strongholds. We demolish arguments and every pretension that sets itself up against the knowledge of God, and we take captive every thought to make it obedient to Christ.

Praying Scripture Helps Us to Know and Fulfill God's Will and Purposes for Our Lives

Admittedly, some passages of Scripture can be quite difficult to interpret and apply to our lives. Others, meanwhile, speak to us with piercing clarity, as if we have been given a bank of floodlights to shine on our path through the night. The passages that clearly teach us what we are called by God to do should be celebrated, because that clarity creates peace and direction in our lives. When we pray such verses, our hearts and minds are centered on clear teaching, and our wills are effectively brought into submission to His. Celebrate the clarity in these verses and many others like them, and pray them for clarity in your life.

1 Thessalonians 5:16-18

Be joyful always; pray continually; give thanks in all circumstances, for this is God's will for you in Christ Jesus.

Philippians 2:13

. . . for it is God who works in you to will and to act according to his good purpose.

Psalm 32:8

I will instruct you and teach you in the way you should go; I will counsel you and watch over you.

Psalm 86:11

Teach me your way, O LORD, and I will walk in your truth; give me an undivided heart, that I may fear your name.

Isaiah 30:21

Whether you turn to the right or to the left, your ears will hear a voice behind you, saying, 'This is the way; walk in it.'

Isaiah 48:17

This is what the LORD says—your Redeemer, the Holy One of Israel: "I am the LORD your God, who teaches you what is best for you, who directs you in the way you should go."

Praying Scripture Builds Our Faith and Gives Us Confidence in God's Provision

James teaches in two places in his short book the importance of praying in faith (James 1:6 and 5:15). When we pray the Scriptures, we can be sure about the truths we are praying, and that increases our faith for prayer and for all of life.

1 Peter 1:25

". . . but the word of the Lord stands forever."
And this is the word that was preached to you.

James 5:15

And the prayer offered in faith will make the sick person well; the Lord will raise him up. If he has sinned, he will be forgiven.

1 John 5:14-15

This is the assurance we have in approaching God: that if we ask anything according to his will, he hears us. And if we know that he hears us—whatever we ask—we know that we have what we asked of him.

Praying Scripture Gives Us Joy for Each Day

Prayer does not always need to be an exercise in melancholy. Obviously, we come to God with a serious demeanor when we are in great need or when the circumstances of life have us cornered in a dark place. But what about the rest of the time, when we can pray with a light, joy-filled heart? Scriptures that fill us with joy are a wonderful tool for steering our thoughts toward God and the joy of His salvation. There are hundreds of verses like this to help experience all the joy God has for us. Pray them to positively affect your days and your prayer life.

1 Thessalonians 5:16-18

> Be joyful always; pray continually; give thanks in all circumstances, for this is God's will for you in Christ Jesus.

Praying Scripture Allows the Holy Spirit to Work in and Through Us

Most believers are familiar with Ephesians 6:17:

> Take the helmet of salvation and the sword of the Spirit, which is the word of God.

If we take "the sword of the Spirit," in other words, intentionally focus on the word of God, *during prayer*, then we actively invite the Spirit of the sword to cut and remake us as He also defends us against the enemy's attacks. Consider again these other verses about the role of the Spirit, and pray them to allow Him to work in you.

John 14:26

> "But the Counselor, the Holy Spirit, whom the Father will send in my name, will teach you all things and remind you of everything I have said to you."

Romans 8 5-9a

> Those who live according to the sinful nature have their minds set on what that nature desires; but those who live in accordance with the Spirit have their minds set on what the Spirit desires. The mind

of sinful man is death, but the mind controlled by the Spirit is life and peace; the sinful mind is hostile to God. It does not submit to God's law, nor can it do so. Those controlled by the sinful nature cannot please God.

You, however, are controlled not by the sinful nature but by the Spirit, if the Spirit of God lives in you.

Praying Scripture Helps Us Develop the Fruit of the Spirit in Our Lives

This is another way in which the Spirit uses the sword to change us and grow us. These passages are full of direct descriptions of the character He is building in us. Praying them and others like them speeds and directs the process.

Galatians 5:22-23

But the fruit of the Spirit is love, joy, peace, patience, kindness, goodness, faithfulness, gentleness and self-control. Against such things there is no law.

Matthew 7:16

"By their fruit you will recognize them. Do people pick grapes from thornbushes, or figs from thistles?"

John 15:4

"Remain in me, and I will remain in you. No branch can bear fruit by itself; it must remain in the vine. Neither can you bear fruit unless you remain in me."

Colossians 1:10

And we pray this in order that you may live a life worthy of the Lord and may please him in every way: bearing fruit in every good work, growing in the knowledge of God.

Praying Scripture Daily Provides Us Daily Guidance and Instruction

Imagine the vast difference between two people who are praying every day, one of whom is unfamiliar with the truth God's word sheds on human life, and the other person, who meditates on His law day and night (Psalm 1:2) and brings what he learns into his prayers. While both prayers are perfectly audible to God, the prayer of the man or woman who knows little Scripture is likely to be full of confusion and lies. When we pray passages like these below, God's answers will be useful for us in seeing and living out the truth.

Psalm 119:33-38, 59, 105

Teach me, O LORD, to follow your decrees; then I will keep them to the end.

Give me understanding, and I will keep your law and obey it with all my heart.

Direct me in the paths of your commands, for there I find delight.

Turn my heart toward your statutes and not toward selfish gain.

Turn my eyes away from worthless things; renew my life according to your word.

Fulfill your promise to your servant, so that you may be feared.

. . .

I have considered my ways and have turned my
steps to your statutes.

. . .

Your word is a lamp to my feet and a light for
my path."

Luke 6:47-48

"I will show you what he is like who comes to me
and hears my words and puts them into practice. He
is like a man building a house, who dug down deep
and laid the foundation on rock. When a flood
came, the torrent struck that house but could not
shake it, because it was well built."

James 1:22

Do not merely listen to the word, and so deceive
yourselves. Do what it says.

Praying Scripture Helps Us Pray for the Things on the Heart of God

Scripture is a clear window into the thoughts and heart of the
Creator of the universe, who also made our souls and hearts. *What
is God thinking about?* may seem like a strange, even presumptuous
question, but we do, in fact, know much of what He considers
important with regard to life on earth and His purposes with us.

Jeremiah 31:3 and 9

The LORD appeared to us in the past, saying:
"I have loved you with an everlasting love; I have
drawn you with loving-kindness."

. . .

"They will come with weeping; they will pray as I bring them back. I will lead them beside streams of water on a level path where they will not stumble, because I am Israel's father, and Ephraim is my firstborn son."

Matthew 9:37-38

Then he said to his disciples, "The harvest is plentiful but the workers are few. Ask the Lord of the harvest, therefore, to send out workers into his harvest field."

John 17:20-23 and 26

"My prayer is not for them alone. I pray also for those who will believe in me through their message, that all of them may be one, Father, just as you are in me and I am in you. May they also be in us so that the world may believe that you have sent me. I have given them the glory that you gave me, that they may be one as we are one: I in them and you in me. May they be brought to complete unity to let the world know that you sent me and have loved them even as you have loved me."

. . .

"I have made you known to them, and will continue to make you known in order that the love you have for me may be in them and that I myself may be in them."

Praying Scripture Encourages and Uplifts Us as We Stand on His Promises

Nothing is more encouraging or stabilizing for our thoughts and our hearts than establishing them on solid scriptural truth. The activity of praying the promises of Scripture is like a triple shot of encouragement. God's promises are not only *true*, they are also *positive*, and they are positive truth about *benefits for us*, all at the same time. Pray and meditate on these and the other many passages that contain His promises.

Joshua 1:5

No one will be able to stand up against you all the days of your life. As I was with Moses, so I will be with you; I will never leave you nor forsake you.

Jeremiah 20:11-13

But the LORD is with me like a mighty warrior; so my persecutors will stumble and not prevail.

They will fail and be thoroughly disgraced; their dishonor will never be forgotten.

O LORD Almighty, you who examine the righteous and probe the heart and mind, let me see your vengeance upon them, for to you I have committed my cause.

Sing to the LORD! Give praise to the LORD! He rescues the life of the needy from the hands of the wicked.

Praying Scripture Honors and Glorifies God

In summary, when we focus on God's revealed will in His word and pray it back to Him, we give Him the honor He is due. Praise God for His word; praise Him with His word.

John 11:4

When he heard this, Jesus said, "This sickness will not end in death. No, it is for God's glory so that God's Son may be glorified through it."

John 14:13

"And I will do whatever you ask in my name, so that the Son may bring glory to the Father."

1 Thessalonians 5:18

Give thanks in all circumstances, for this is God's will for you in Christ Jesus.

Isaiah 42:12

Let them give glory to the LORD and proclaim his praise in the islands.

1 Chronicles 16:29

Ascribe to the LORD the glory due his name.
Bring an offering and come before him; worship the LORD in the splendor of his holiness.

Intercession

Intercession, as we discussed briefly in an earlier chapter, is praying to God on behalf of another. It is difficult to imagine a committed pray-er who is not committed to intercession. It is even more difficult to imagine a church crossing the threshold into God's richest blessing without many in that congregation exhibiting excellence in intercession.

I sometimes share a sermon on intercessory prayer called the "Man in the Middle," taken from Luke 11:5-13.

> Then he said to them, "Suppose one of you has a friend, and he goes him at midnight and says, 'Friend, lend me three loaves of bread, because a friend of mine on a journey has come to me, and I have nothing to set before him.'
>
> Then the one inside answers, 'Don't bother me. The door is already locked, and my children are with me in bed. I can't get up and give you anything.' I tell you, though he will not get up and give him the bread because he is his friend, yet because of the man's persistence he will get up and give him as much as he needs.
>
> "So I say to you: Ask and it will be given to you; seek and you will find; knock and the door will be opened to you. For everyone who asks receives; he who seeks finds; and to him who knocks, the door will be opened.
>
> "Which of you fathers, if your son asks for a fish, will give him a snake instead? Or if he asks for an egg, will give him a scorpion? If you then, though you are evil, know how to give good gifts to your children, how much more will your Father in heaven give the Holy Spirit to those who ask him!"

This passage teaches a number of principles, at least one of which applies directly to the topic of intercession. A guest shows up late at night, and proper hospitality is so important in the culture of this land that it demands the "man in the middle" go to a friend (possibly a wealthier friend) to ask for food *for the guest*. Now, we may be too far removed from that culture to completely understand what kinds of social implications this act may have had. But the man in the middle clearly went because his guest had need.

This is a simple but striking picture of the act of prayer intercession. In prayer, the same motivation that drove this man in the middle to his friend expresses itself through one man taking another man's needs to God. When I preach this sermon, I often pick out three people from the audience to represent the characters, and it is fascinating to watch people grasp the joy of intercession as they come to understand it.

When we read Scripture, we find ample evidence that God values intercession and expects us to be interceding for others. Here, for example, are a few biblical characters we see doing the work of intercession.

♦ **Abraham.** Genesis 18 shows Abraham interceding on behalf of Sodom, pleading and wrestling with God on behalf of an evil city.

♦ **Moses.** Moses intercedes for the Nation of Israel with regard to their sin, as recorded in Exodus 32:30:

> The next day Moses said to the people, "You have committed a great sin. But now I will go up to the LORD; perhaps I can make atonement for your sin."
>
> So Moses went back to the LORD and said, 'Oh, what a great sin these people have committed! They have made themselves gods of gold. But now, please forgive their sin—but if not, then blot me out of the book you have written."

♦ **Anna.** In Luke 2:36-38 we read:

> There was also a prophetess, Anna, the daughter of Phanuel, of the tribe of Asher. She was very old; she had lived with her husband seven years after her marriage, and then was a

widow until she was eighty-four. She never left the temple but worshiped night and day, fasting and praying. Coming up to them at that very moment, she gave thanks to God and spoke about the child to all who were looking forward to the redemption of Jerusalem.

♦ **Stephen.** Stephen intercedes for his murderers with his dying breath:

Lord, do not hold this sin against them" (Acts 7:60).

♦ **Jesus.** Our Lord's present ministry is one of intercession. Hebrews 7:25 says:

Therefore he is able to save completely those who come to God through him, because he always lives to intercede for them.

The following passages may be used to form a solid biblical basis for holding up intercession as an essential element of the doctrine of prayer. It is one of the topics that must be taught and modeled in a complete church prayer ministry.

Ezekiel 22:30

"I looked for a man among them who would build up the wall and stand before me in the gap on behalf of the land so I would not have to destroy it, but I found none."

Ephesians 6:18

And pray in the Spirit on all occasions with all kinds of prayers and requests. With this in mind, be alert and always keep on praying for all the saints.

Colossians 1:9-11

For this reason, since the day we heard about you, we have not stopped praying for you and asking God to fill you with the knowledge of his will through all spiritual wisdom and understanding. And we pray this in order that you may live a life worthy of the Lord and may please him in every way: bearing fruit in every good work, growing in the knowledge of God, being strengthened with all power according to his glorious might so that you may have great endurance and patience.

Colossians 4:2-3

Devote yourselves to prayer, being watchful and thankful. And pray for us, too, that God may open a door for our message, so that we may proclaim the mystery of Christ, for which I am in chains.

Colossians 4:12-13

Epaphras, who is one of you and a servant of Christ Jesus, sends greetings. He is always wrestling in prayer for you, that you may stand firm in all the will of God, mature and fully assured. I vouch for him that he is working hard for you and for those at Laodicea and Hierapolis.

1 Timothy 2:1

I urge, then, first of all, that requests, prayers, intercession and thanksgiving be made for everyone.

James 5:16b-18

The prayer of a righteous man is powerful
and effective.
Elijah was a man just like us. He prayed earnestly
that it would not rain, and it did not rain on the
land for three and a half years. Again he prayed, and
the heavens gave rain, and the earth produced
its crops.

The Importance of the Ministry of Intercession

The last half of Numbers 16 describes a struggle over the spiritual leadership of the nation of Israel. Men such as Korah, Dathan, and Abiram felt as if they could run things as well as or better than Moses. But God judged them by causing the ground to open up, swallowing them and their families. A second group took up the attack, and this time a plague broke out. Eventually things had become so out of hand that God was ready to deal with the entire nation, but Moses intervened with some fast action.

Moses sent Aaron to stand among the people with a censer burning incense to intercede for the people. (Incense should be viewed as a picture of prayers ascending to heaven.) Notice the wording of Numbers 16:47-48:

So Aaron did as Moses said, and ran into the midst
of the assembly. The plague had already started
among the people, but Aaron offered the incense
and made atonement for them. He *stood between the*

living and the dead, and the plague stopped
[emphasis added].

We stand between the living and the dead when we parent
teenagers and guide them away from evil. We stand between the
living and the dead when we muster the courage to speak saving
spiritual truth to a waiter at a restaurant or to a misguided neighbor.
We stand between the living and the dead when we pray for our
nation and for the soldiers fighting our nation's wars. What a
privilege and what a responsibility.

Then consider these thoughts about a man who is known as a
powerful pioneer of world missions:

> Two hundred years ago, a shoe repairman in
> England began to be concerned about the world's
> heathen peoples. As he pounded away on shoes, he
> would look at a map above his workbench on which
> he had written the few facts he had been able to
> garner from *Captain Cook's Travels* and other books.
> He prayed for the salvation of people in
> distant lands.
>
> William Carey—who described himself as a self-
> educated, ungifted plodder—went on to become one
> of the fathers of modern missions. Through his
> influence, Britain's first missionary society was
> formed, but only after Carey overcame great
> reluctance among his Baptist brethren. Carey, feeling
> led of God, made the decision to go to India even
> though his wife at first refused to go with him and
> refused to allow their children to go. She eventually
> was persuaded differently and joined her husband in
> the work.
>
> Once in India, where he spent forty-two years,
> Carey and his coworkers translated the entire Bible

into twenty-five Indian languages and the New Testament or parts of it into fifteen more.

Many books have been written about William Carey, but to my knowledge not one has been written about his little-known sister, a bedridden invalid. She and Carey were very close, and from India he wrote to her about all the details and problems of his work. Hour after hour, week after week, she would lift these concerns to the Lord in prayer. So . . . who was responsible for the success of William Carey's ministry? How does God apportion credit?[21]

Powerful Service Intercession

Praying during for the worship services while they are under way, or Service Intercession, is an extremely important part of a threshold-crossing prayer ministry. Bathing the primary gathering of the church body in prayer brings the power of God to the service and engages church members in meaningful ministry to the body. Some principles of service intercession have become clear to me over time and have made our service intercession at Central easier and more fulfilling.

Always Have at Least Two Hooks in the Water. First of all, let me discuss a basic element of prayer ministry, which is recruiting people to participate in service intercession. Many members may be willing to engage in this important prayer opportunity if they are properly led to do so.

As a kid, I went trotline fishing in Missouri with my dad and grandpa. In case you're unfamiliar with it, I'll explain that trotline fishing involves tying a long rope to a large tree on each bank of a river or creek. Once the line is secure, fishhooks are attached to the rope about every eighteen inches apart; then these are baited with worms or crawdads. Next, the line is weighted and buoyed so that it rests about two feet from the bottom of the creek. Because you have fifteen or twenty hooks in the water at the same time, you increase your chances of catching more fish. At Central, we use this principle (multiple hooks in the water) in our prayer rooms to engage more people in this key prayer ministry.

The first "hook" is to assign *themes* for each service intercession session, and the second one is to pray for the *church service* that is going on as you are praying. People are drawn to participate who have a heart for the chosen topic (missions or our nation, for example), as are those who are passionate simply for intercession and who feel called to pray for those in the service or leading the service.

Themes for service intercession could include these topics:

◆ the nation
◆ lost friends and family members of those who attend the church
◆ health issues
◆ missions and missionaries
◆ marriages and family issues
◆ the prayer ministry of the church

We have chosen these themes at Central because they represent areas of spiritual need we always want to keep in front of our service intercession teams. We draw our themed prayers from those submitted to our Web Prayer website, and we pray for only one or two themes in each hour of intercession, along with prayer for the worship, the message, and the youth and children's programs. We usually run out of time before we run out of things to pray for. We also take personal prayer requests for team building at each session, but we don't always get to those before the time runs out. If we run out of time, I encourage our pray-ers to pray for others on the team during the week as God brings them to mind. This helps our team members learn to put others' needs before their own and keeps the time focused on intercession for others.

Give God Control. Another key to powerful service intercession is to ask the Lord to direct your time of prayer. Even though we always have a theme and a pattern, there are times when God causes us to hit upon something, and we can tell we are somehow touching heaven. We can feel a difference in the anointing on those prayers. It's not that our normal times are not good, but every now and then something truly special happens. The prayers are fuller and richer, and we sense a different level of fervor. Often, the prayers are accompanied by tears of joy and repentance and by other strong emotions, even fear. These prayers may or may not be related to the predetermined theme for the session, but if it is of the Lord, we stop everything else and go with what the Lord is doing. It is not uncommon for us to spend an entire hour praying for something that none of us envisioned when we started our service intercession time, but God's involvement guides us, and that makes intercession exciting.

Use the Same Pattern for All the Services. This is our pattern:

1. **Purification.** Begin your time of prayer with a period of personal repentance and confession. This time is designed to remove anything that might encumber our prayers for that hour. Good prayer cannot flow from a heart in which evil has not been properly addressed. When we enter this time of repentance in the service intercession session, we choose not to share our deepest, darkest burdens. Those sins absolutely need to be dealt with and can hinder prayer, but they require more extended times of confession, seeking the Lord, and a level of privacy not afforded by our somewhat brief confession time in the prayer room.

   Some leaders might shy away from including a time of confession and repentance because they fear it would put people off. But we have done it for so long, openly and relationally, that this time is now part of our DNA. We don't demand that the pray-ers share openly, but we make the invitation. Usually, it is not long before even a new intercessor understands the value of this time and joins in confession.

2. **Praise.** This seems to be the doorway into the throne room of God and the factory that manufactures faith and boldness. Psalm 100:4-5 reminds us to, "Enter his gates with thanksgiving and his courts with praise; give thanks to him and praise his name. For the Lord is good and his love endures forever; his faithfulness continues through all generations." We noticed major improvements in the prayer sessions when repentance and praise took their rightful place and priority.

3. **The Body.** The people in the pews, all the facets of the service, and the children's activities and any other church-related needs, such as upcoming special events.

4. **The Theme for the Hour.** When it is time for this portion of the hour, be sure to make every effort to stay on that theme unless the Lord is clearly leading away from it.

5. **Personal Requests of the Service Intercession Team Members.** These come last. These are not prayed about unless we have time at the end. We always state that we may not get to these so that those making the request will not be offended. This seems to prevent the time from becoming a personal prayer session instead of a strategic time of intercession.

Practice Healthy Corporate Prayer. Probably the hardest part of leading a church to excellence in service intercession is teaching people to pray corporately. Many have no background in corporate prayer, or they did it poorly twenty years ago and never want to do it again. Therefore, continually teach principles of corporate prayer at each service intercession time. Regularly remind pray-ers of these pointers:

- Pray loud enough to be heard.
- Pray short.
- Pray on subject. Complete the subject before you move on.
- Don't preach.
- Don't develop another dialect for prayer; use your normal speech. King James has been dead for four centuries now, so use English that others on the team can understand and agree with you in.
- Pray to God, not to the others in the room.
- Don't pray in order around the circle of pray-ers. Doing so puts new intercessors on the spot as their time approaches. Pray as the Spirit leads, and respond to what others are praying. At Central, our prayer times seem a lot like popcorn kernels popping, as we bounce around the circle, with no clear order.
- Listen while others are praying, and pray in agreement with them.
- Don't be afraid of silence.

Invite Special Guests. If one of our missionaries is in town, we invite him or her to join in our Sunday morning service intercession for our missionaries. It helps the people pray more passionately for our missionaries and helps the missionaries feel connected to the church.

Make the Room Nice. Your prayer rooms should be (if possible) some of the nicest rooms in the church. The room's decor would ideally give the impression that corporate prayer has been planned for by providing pray-ers a space that promotes sacred communication.

Service intercession is not rocket science. All you need are some sincere hearts and some time. People may take a while to catch on, but once they do, look out! You can expect service intercession to become a birthing place for God to express His power, a catalyst for growth, and a comfortable and natural place for amazing ministry.

Some Specifics to Pray About for Those in the Service

Praise and Worship of God. Pray that praise and worship would be sincerely offered up by worship leaders and by the congregation, with no elements of entertainment or show. Pray for full and heartfelt worship from all in the worship center, asking God to glorify Himself through the music, words, emotions, and songs (see Psalm 147:1).

Prepared and Teachable Hearts. Pray that hearts would be open to receive whatever God wants to teach them. Pray for freedom from distractions and the ability to listen to and focus on the Lord throughout the service (see Ecclesiastes 5:1-2).

Conviction of Sin. Pray that the Holy Spirit would do His work to convict the worshipers of sin, righteousness and judgment (see John 16:8).

Decisions of Faith. Pray for people to trust God to act on the things he prompts them to do (see Hebrews 11:6).

Response to God's Word. Ask the Lord to bring about His work in each life through the reading of His living and active word (see Hebrews 4:12).

Humility to Receive Help. Pray against all pride and self-sufficiency so that the needy would seek out prayer and assistance (see 1 Peter 5:6).

Decisions for Salvation. Remind the Lord of His desire that none should perish (see 2 Peter 3:9), and ask Him to do His work of salvation and regeneration in the lives of those in attendance who do not yet know Him (see Acts 2:37-41).

Generous Giving. Request the Lord to free up the hearts of those who can and should be giving so that all is done with a cheerful heart and not grudgingly and under compulsion. Ask God to abundantly provide for the needs of the church through the offering (see 2 Corinthians 9:6-7).

Protection for Pastors and Leaders. Pray for a hedge of protection around the teaching pastor, the worship leaders and all who are a part of the service. Pray for physical safety, emotional strength, and a commitment to living out the truth to combat Satan and his lies (see Ephesians 6:12). Pray for the elders and decision makers of the church.

Pray for All to Be Doers of the Word and Not Just Hearers. Pray that the lessons and convictions from the worship service are not forgotten as soon as people drive away from the campus but that all would honor the applications and commitments they were prompted to make (see James 1:23-25).

Pray for the Ministries at This Hour. Consider praying for these ministries and any others that exist at your church (1 Corinthians 12:12):

- Advisors for New Attenders
- Worship Music Team
- Baptism Hosts
- Greeters
- Junior High and High School
- Parking Lot Attendants
- Prayer Partners
- Stage Staff
- Ushers
- Children's Ministries
- Tech Team
- Security Officers

Perseverance in Prayer

Annie and I raised three boys, and they are all wonderful young men. However, I can remember back to when they were little, when I was always worn out by their incessant asking for all kinds of things. They requested big and little things: "Dad, can we have an airplane ride?" "Can we have a pool?" "Can we spend the night?" "Can we have friends over?" We tend to see God as we are with our children—weary from all our asking.

You may wonder if He gets tired or annoyed with all your requests. The answer is *no!* He invites and encourages persistent prayer. We have the freedom to march boldly and confidently into the throne room of God to ask Him to respond to our prayers. We *must* therefore stop being apologetic! We must conquer our feelings that try to tell us we are bothering God and take on our God-given role as partners with God in His kingdom. It is not, of course, that we deserve to have our prayers heard or answered. Rather, He loves us so much that He gave His Son to open the door to this blessing.

In general, I cannot advocate the "name it and claim it" theology that is prevalent in some churches today. I am convinced that this is not what Jesus had in mind when He taught us about prayer. But on the other hand, I know people who never pray for their own needs because they lack confidence in prayer, or who worry about asking God for more than one or two things per day. These feelings, and the practice of holding back in prayer because of them, are simply unfounded.

God's word describes the situation for us in Hebrews 4:14-16:

> Therefore, since we have a great high priest who has gone through the heavens, Jesus the Son of God, let us hold firmly to the faith we profess. For we do not have a high priest who is unable to sympathize with our weakness, but we have one who has been tempted in every way, just as we are—yet without sin. Let us then approach the throne of grace with confidence, so that we may receive mercy and find grace to help us in our time of need.

God intended for us to ask Him and to invite Him into every area of our lives. It is *impossible* to wear Him out with our asking. In fact, it would seem He is particularly drawn to persistent prayers.

Perseverance Is Important Because Jesus Taught It. Luke 18:1 says, "Then Jesus told his disciples a parable to show them that they should always pray and not give up." I am convinced that this teaching means exactly what it says, namely, that we are never to give up on prayers that we are praying.

Similarly, the verbs in Luke 11:9 are "ask," "seek," and "knock." The form of these verbs in Greek indicates that the action is ongoing or repeated: *continue* asking, *continue* seeking, and *continue* knocking; or keep on asking, never stop seeking, never lose hope, keep on knocking. Don't give up.

In the book of Hebrews we read about people who were praying for things they never saw realized in this life. One of the reasons they are mentioned in chapter 11 is that they were undaunted, even though they did not see the answers to what they were praying for. It appears that persistence is a highly valued character trait.

Perseverance Is a Gauge of Our Faith. Luke 18:8a is worth pondering. It says, "I tell you, he [God] will see that they [the oppressed] get justice and quickly." The context of this verse is the parable of the persistent widow who kept pleading with an unjust judge for justice. The idea, at least in part, is that God is unlike an unjust judge that has to be begged or cajoled into taking action on behalf of those in need. We can make the connection pretty easily from this parable that we should continue to pray.

But what does the second part of the same verse, Luke 18:8b, mean when it asks, "However, when the Son of Man comes, will he find faith on the earth?" What is Jesus referring to here? The best answer seems to be that it is also about persistence in prayer. When Christ returns, will believers still be faithfully praying and asking for the needs of the kingdom, or will they have given up and moved on to something else? Jesus' question in that verse is a forceful call for perseverance in prayer, and a clear indication of what He will be looking for when He comes.

Perseverance Is Important So That We Don't Miss the Blessings God Has for Us. Dee Duke, in his public speaking on prayer, uses an illustration of a huge teeter-totter one hundred feet long. On one side there are three heavyweight men on the teeter-totter, and on the other, a huge box about six feet square. Obviously, the teeter-totter is down on the side of the large men and up on the side of the box. Now suppose that each time you pray, you drop a large rock in the box. After you pray one time what happens? Nothing. After you pray two times what happens? Nothing. After you pray, let's say, 165 times, and the next rock/prayer is added to the box, what happens? That time, the box is slowly lowered to the ground, and the big guys are raised to the sky. What happened? Was the last prayer better than the ones that preceded it? No. But perseverance is required for most prayers to be answered, and that perseverance takes the form of many individual prayers. Sometimes we pray, and the answer comes almost immediately, but most of the time we must continue to pray and wait faithfully on God to work His will.

So what would have happened if we had stopped praying at 164 rocks? The answer is that we don't know, but it seems quite possible that the prayer would have gone unanswered because we quit praying one prayer too soon. There may be flaws in this illustration, but the concept is an important one. We need to keep praying and not give up. I sometimes wonder how many blessings we have missed because we stopped praying too soon.

Persistence in Prayer Is One of the Truest Forms of Worship We Can Offer God. Let's be honest: when we pray a long time for something and don't see any tangible results, we have a tendency to put God and His goodness on trial. But the truth is, if we feel we have to understand everything God is doing, we are attempting to micromanage God. Moreover, we should be *happy* we *can't* comprehend all that He is working on. He should be doing things that are too complicated for us to understand.

When we continue to pray even when we can't see any movement in the earthly realm, that it is one of the truest forms of worship, because it is an expression of our genuine trust and confidence in Him. The Old Testament character of Job comes to mind and those who persevered in Hebrews chapter 11.

I remember teaching about this topic to a small group in our church. In the group were a husband and wife who had a child who was born with a heart defect. They had nearly lost the child over and over again, but all along the way they had prayed for him to be healed. As I was talking to the group about persistence in prayer, I could see them visibly responding. They understood for the first time that their prayers were indeed an offering of faith and worship. Just as the woman broke open the box of nard and anointed Jesus with it in worship (see Mark 14:3), they were worshiping Him as they prayed and waited on Him to heal their son. Their perseverance in prayer was an act of pure and simple worship and faith not based on their feelings or even on the health of their son.

Persistence Helps Purify Our Desires. We sometimes ask God to bless our work, and that is a good prayer to pray. But the motive behind that otherwise healthy request may be a selfish desire to reap the lucrative benefits of success in the vocation. Or maybe we pray for our children to behave well, but we desire this so that our reputations will remain unsullied. These prayers are not very godly.

As we mature in the faith, however, our desires begin to change, and this maturation is directly reflected in the things we pray for. We may begin to pray for wisdom to use our finances wisely instead of praying for the Powerball ticket we bought to have the winning jackpot numbers. We might ask that our children walk in faith instead of praying that they stay out of trouble to protect our reputations.

Perseverance in prayer does not only purify our desires but also helps prepare us for His answer. A premature answer might cause us to glory more in the gift than in the Giver. As we persevere in prayer, our hearts are being prepared to enjoy the gift in a way that will enhance our fellowship with God.

Persistence in prayer helps to develop our life and character, and Scripture makes it clear that one of God's priorities is to help us develop Christian character. He calls us to persistent prayer to bring us under His loving authority and to allow us to understand our dependence on Him.

Perseverance Allows Us to Grow into a More Intimate Relationship with Him. In any relationship, the time the parties spend together adds depth. It is difficult to imagine that a believer has a close relationship with God if he has spent little time and effort consistently seeking God's answers to his prayers. A deeper and more satisfying relationship with God is to be expected when we repeatedly ask Him for the desires of our hearts. Psalm 37:4-6 talks about this:

> Delight yourself in the Lord and he will give you the desires of your heart.
>
> Commit your way to the Lord; trust in him and he will do this:
>
> He will make your righteousness shine like the dawn, the justice of your cause like the noonday sun.

Is Perseverance a Condition for Answered Prayer? We have already begun to look at Luke 18, a passage that clearly teaches the value of determination in prayer. Look again at Jesus' entire parable in the first eight verses.

> Then Jesus told his disciples a parable to show them that they should always pray and not give up. He said: "In a certain town there was a judge who neither feared God nor cared about men. And there was a widow in that town who kept coming to him with the plea, 'Grant me justice against my adversary.'
>
> "For some time he refused. But finally he said to himself, 'Even though I don't fear God or care about men, yet because this widow keeps bothering me,

I will see that she gets justice, so that she won't
eventually wear me out with her coming!'"

And the Lord said, "Listen to what the unjust
judge says. And will not God bring about justice for
his chosen ones, who cry out to him day and night?
Will he keep putting them off? I tell you, he will see
that they get justice, and quickly. However, when the
Son of Man comes, will he find faith on the earth?"

I see these prayers of perseverance as the deep waters of prayer.
If you are discouraged by an unanswered prayer you have been
praying for some time, please do not give up. Instead, learn to enjoy
the spiritual battle. Perseverance in prayer is a wonderful offering to
the Lord. In fact, it seems to me that prayers of persistence are likely
the sweetest prayers of all to God because they come from faith in
Him. There is no outward sign that anything is changing, yet the
believer, the faithful one, prays on, believing and trusting God for
what is not yet seen. The Lord must be pleased with that kind of
faith and obedience.

Now seems a good time to invite you to read Daniel chapter 10.
Daniel has a vision for his people, but he does not know what the
vision means. So he begins to fast and pray for twenty-one days.
After the twenty-first day, an angel appears to him and explains the
vision. The angel reveals that from the first day Daniel began to
pray, his prayer was heard, but that the angel was prevented from
coming to Daniel "by the prince of the Persian kingdom." I don't
claim to understand all of what is going on here, but I am confident
this is a reference to spiritual warfare. There was a great cosmic
battle going on over the answer to this prayer. Amazing as it may
sound, the same kinds of battles are being waged in heavenly places
over *your* prayers. What if Daniel had stopped praying after twenty
days and given up? The Bible does not give us the answer, but my
hunch is that the prayer would not have been answered. How many
times have we quit praying too soon? We sometimes stop praying

when we are just a few days from the breakthrough. Reading Daniel chapter 10 motivates me to keep praying until the answer comes.

After I learned that it took twenty-one days for Daniel's prayer to be answered, I decided to go back and look through my prayer journal that I kept for five years. I wanted to see how long it took to see the answers to my prayers. You would be astounded how many times it was eighteen days, twenty days, or maybe twenty-two days. We stop praying far too quickly.

George Mueller speaks to the need for perseverance when he says:

> The great point is to never give up until the answer comes . . . . The great fault of the children of God is: They do not continue in prayer; they do not go on praying; they do not persevere. If they desire anything for God's glory, they should pray until they get it.[22]

Pray Big

I am convinced that one reason our prayer ministries are weak is because we ask for little things. When I go fishing I am not fishing for guppies but for bass. I want a monster. No one goes fishing for guppies. But when it comes to prayer we often ask for small, insignificant items. God's love and promises invite us to pray bigger and with greater faith. Pray big, and ask for big things that only God can do.

February 8, 2004, was one of the most frightening days of my life. It was the day God called me to pray big. I had begun to work as prayer pastor at Central in August of 2003. Central is a megachurch in the Phoenix area that had, and still has, a desire to pray. We began praying during each of our services on January 1, 2004.

I was praying during the Sunday 9:30 a.m. service, and the theme we had set for our intercession was our global field workers.

We began with confession and then praise, as we continue to do now. Next, we prayed for the band and for Cal, who was bringing the message that day. We were just about ready to move on to begin praying for the global workers when I felt God prompting me to pray that the offering would double. This was completely unexpected, out of the blue. Our leadership team had scheduled four weeks to teach on giving. They had purchased a book for everyone in the church to read by Barry Cameron called *The ABC's of Financial Freedom*.

God's words were in my head so clearly: "Pray that the offering doubles." Being the spiritual giant I am, I said, "No!" "Lord," I prayed silently in a frantic internal voice, "I have just been working at Central for five months, and if I pray something this big—that the offering doubles—and it doesn't, then I will look like a fool. Besides, the treasurer's wife is in here, as well as *my* wife, so it is not like I can pray this and it will just go unnoticed if You don't answer." And I prayed, "They are not expecting a prayer like this, and You can bet they will take note. Besides, everyone knows that when megachurches do stewardship campaigns, if the offering increases by 10 percent or maybe 20 percent, it is considered a real success. No one does a stewardship campaign where the offering doubles!" Maybe you can see where my fear was coming from. I can remember my terrified heart was beating much faster than normal. God was speaking, and I did not like what He was calling me to do. God impressed these words on me quickly and with force. "We are not negotiating here. Now start praying." Reluctantly, I relented.

I stepped out in faith and began to pray out loud in frightened obedience for the offering to be doubled. Later that night, I ran into our business administrator and told him what God had led me to pray. The next morning he informed me that our offerings were up significantly (25 percent) over the previous year's offering on the same day. I was pleased, but still concerned. I remember thinking, "That is good, Lord, but we are a long way from double." The next week, I continued to pray, and the administrator informed me we were up again, this time closer to 35 percent.

By the following week it was obvious to all that God was doing something big. The giving that week was up by 75 percent year to date. By the time the campaign was over, the offerings had increased by 101 percent over the previous year. Please don't misunderstand me here; there were clearly a variety of factors involved in the dramatic increase: great teaching, much spade work done by our diligent leadership, and so on. But prayer had a part as well, and I believe a significant part.

To be balanced, please don't think that you can go into the prayer room any time you want and pray that your offerings will double in one month and it will happen. Praying this way was far from my mind. I was prompted to pray this way so that God would get the glory, and He did. The prayer came from His direction, not from my will. My job was to be obedient (and I was certainly less than stellar in the obedience category). But praise God for His mercy and grace.

So listen carefully for the promptings of God and pray into those. Pray big into those.

CHAPTER 11

Stumbling Blocks

Satan dreads nothing but prayer. His one concern
is to keep the saints from praying. He fears nothing
from prayerless studies, prayerless work, prayerless religion.
He laughs at our toil, he mocks our wisdom,
but he trembles when we pray.
—Samuel Chadwick

In his teaching ministry on prayer, Dee Duke presents some reasons for low-power prayer, and they serve here as a perfect introduction and overview for the topic of prayer stumbling blocks. Here are the reasons Dee presents, along with some passages of Scripture for the believer to apply to combat some of them. (This material has been adapted from sermons written by Dee Duke, Senior Pastor of the Jefferson Baptist Chruch in Jefferson, Oregon. Dee is a long-time mentor of mine, and his material is used by permission.)

If you lack horsepower in your prayer life, it may be for one of these reasons.

Because You Are Not Actually a Follower of Christ

We know that we have come to know him if we obey his commands. The man who says, "I know him," but does not do what he commands is a liar, and the truth is not in him (1 John 2:2-4).

Because You Are Living with Unconfessed Sin

If we confess our sins, he is faithful and just and will forgive us our sins and purify us from all unrighteousness (1 John 1:9).

If I had cherished sin in my heart, the Lord would not have listened" (Psalm 66:18).

When you spread out your hands in prayer, I will hide my eyes from you;
    even if you offer many prayers, I will not listen.
Your hands are full of blood (Isaiah 1:15).

Each of us has an intuition about whether God is listening. If we feel as though God is not listening, we should go back to ask forgiveness for all known sins.

Because You Are Not Forgiving Others. Another word for this condition is *bitterness*.

For if you forgive men when they sin against you, your heavenly Father will also forgive you (Matthew 6:14).

Because You Are Not Reading Your Bible Enough

If you remain in me and my words remain in you, ask whatever you wish, and it will be given you (John 15:7).

If anyone turns a deaf ear to the law, even his prayers are detestable (Proverbs 28:9).

But they refused to pay attention; stubbornly they turned their backs and stopped up their ears (Zechariah 7:11).

Because You Are Not Being a Good Husband or Wife

Husbands, in the same way be considerate as you live with your wives, and treat them with respect as the weaker partner and as heirs with you of the gracious gift of life, so that nothing will hinder your prayers (1 Peter 3:7).

Because You Are Not Praying Enough. Most people pray only when they are in conflict or when they are uncomfortable. The Parable of the Persistent Widow proposes the opposite of this thinking; it is found in Luke 18:1-7. See also the previous chapter of this book for more on the topic of perseverance in prayer and on this parable.

Because You Are Not Appropriately Grateful for What God Has Already Given

I will praise God's name in song and glorify him with thanksgiving (Psalm 69:30).

Enter his gates with thanksgiving and his courts with praise; give thanks to him and praise his name (Psalm 100:4).

Because You Are Lacking in Faith

Jesus replied, "I tell you the truth, if you have faith and do not doubt, not only can you do what was done to the fig tree, but also you can say to this mountain, 'Go, throw yourself into the sea,' and it will be done" (Matthew 21:21).

Then Jesus began to denounce the cities in which most of his miracles had been performed, because they did not repent. "Woe to you, Korazin! Woe to you, Bethsaida! If the miracles that were performed in you had been performed in Tyre and Sidon, they would have repented long ago in sackcloth and ashes. But I tell you, it will be more bearable for Tyre and Sidon on the day of judgment than for you. And you, Capernaum, will you be lifted up to the skies? No, you will go down to the depths. If the miracles that were performed in you had been performed in Sodom, it would have remained to this day. But I tell you that it will be more bearable for Sodom on the day of judgment than for you (Matthew 11:20-24).

Then the disciples came to Jesus in private and asked, "Why couldn't we drive it out?"

He replied, "Because you have so little faith. I tell you the truth, if you have faith as small as a mustard seed, you can say to this mountain, 'Move from here to there,' and it will move. Nothing will be impossible for you" (Matthew 17:19-20).

Hindrances to Answered Prayer

Selfishness and Earthly Desire Hinder Prayer. James 4:3 says, "When you ask, you do not receive, because you ask with wrong motives, that you may spend what you get on your pleasures." God generally will not give us all the things that our sinful nature clamors for—any more than we would give our child the gleaming knife he or she sees on the kitchen counter. Some of our selfish desires would be more dangerous to us than the keen edge of the knife to that child. Many "good" things can be desired from an earthly and selfish motive and from a fleshly spirit.

We Are Afraid We Will Get It Wrong. One of the easiest ways to embarrass someone is to ask about his or her prayer life. In fact, I almost never run into someone who is comfortable answering. Many people did not grow up praying as a child, so prayer is a skill they are learning in adult life. Believers frequently feel they are behind in spiritual growth because of their lack of comfort with prayer.

I played football in high school in the holy land—Nebraska. I played for Bellevue High School, a real football powerhouse in the '70s. My favorite play was the 54 trap. It was an awesome play. The center would block the man over the right guard, and the right guard would block the man over the center. This left the linebacker uncovered, and he would sprint toward the quarterback expecting to make a big tackle in the backfield. But the left guard would pull from the left side of the line and would "exchange pleasantries" with the linebacker who would be one step or maybe two in the backfield. This would more often than not spring open the play for six to eight yards. I played tight end, and my job was to sprint down field and hit the left safety. The first time we ran this play each game, I lumbered off the line toward an unsuspecting safety, who would be looking at the play and not noticing that I was gunning for him. This allowed me to smack him hard.

We ran this play about ten to twelve times a game. The second time we ran the 54 trap, everything was the same. Everyone pulled and blocked just like the previous time, except this time the safety would remember me and be watching for me. Safeties are faster than tight ends, so when I attempted to block him, he would simply step out of the way.

Then, at some point in the game, we would run the 54 trap pass. This was the identical play, except by now the safety was wise to me, so when I got close, he was long gone. I would take one step past him and the quarterback would pass the ball in my direction, and I would be wide open.

Jerry Rice, the famed wide receiver for the San Francisco 49ers, once said, "There are only two reasons for missing a pass: taking your eyes off the ball or getting greedy." My problem was all of the above. I would look down field and see that there was nothing between me and the end zone, get greedy, and take my eyes off the ball. Paying attention to all the wrong things, I missed the pass every time.

As a matter of fact, I was so bad at catching passes that the coaches gave me a nickname, "Stone Hands." If the coach called a 54 trap pass, it was normal procedure for me to be pulled right away. He would put in the other tight end, Swenson, because he had hands. On a couple of occasions the coach called the play but forgot momentarily to replace me. I can still hear the coaches yelling as we approached the line of scrimmage. "It's a pass. Get Stone Hands out of there. Stone Hands, you're out. Swenson, you're in." There was no attempt to camouflage the play; the coaches just wanted me off the field. As you can see, my pride has still not completely recovered from the rejection.

This story transfers to the prayer world. People struggle in many ways with prayer. They are concerned about how they sound when they pray and about what they are saying. They compare themselves with others and feel insecure. But *the moment we begin to focus upon any of these worries we have in prayer, we have actually stopped praying.* The focus in prayer is to always be on God. When we begin to think about ourselves, the focus shifts to all kinds of other topics that have nothing to do with Him. Thinking about how we sound when we pray is not a part of a healthy prayer life.

Graciously, God has designed prayer so that you can hardly get it wrong. God is not interested in your grammar or pronunciation; on the most basic level, God is interested in your heart and in your dependence on Him. If those are in line, as soon as you say something to Him, you have a prayer.

If prayer is the channel through which power and provision move from heaven to earth, does it make any sense to think it would be so fragile that you and I could foul it up? No, of course not. Does it make any sense to think it would be so hard that only a few could figure it out? The sad truth is that this insecurity is quite successfully used by the evil one to prevent us from praying.

We Wrongly Believe Our Prayers to Be Unanswered. I maintain that God says yes to His promises and to our prayers that are prayed in His name, according to 2 Corinthians 1:18-20 and 1 John 5:14-15. But we have a preconceived notion about what yes looks like. We are convinced that when we pray for a new car, it looks like a shiny BMW roadster. When in reality the answer is yes to our need for transportation but that it's in the form of a Honda with a sunroof or a bus pass good for the entire month. His answers may look different from what we envision, and may also be on a different schedule from we like or expect.

We Are Afraid of Exposure. I can hide from you and not let you see what I am thinking or feeling. But I can't hide from God. The moment I begin to pray, I am undone and exposed. God knows my heart, motives, and feelings. He even knows my prayers before I pray them. But when I pray, my motives, feelings, and heart are exposed to me more clearly. There is a vulnerable, exposed intimacy in prayer that scares some people away, as it has me at times. If you persist in prayer, however, the closeness to God you experience will become your most prized possession.

Any relationship is established in communication and transparency. Relationships take time to mature. The beauty of a strong friendship is the familiarity and trust we develop with the other person. In time each of us begins to know what the other likes to drink. We know each other's favorite movie, and even some of the memories that we each find most encouraging. To have this level of closeness, exposure is required. We share likes and dislikes and stories that make us laugh. Time is invested and memories made.

Some are put off in a relationship with God because of the exposure required. As crazy as it sounds, there are those who don't think God is on to them yet. If they can keep God at arm's length, maybe He will never figure out what they are up to. This is so tragic because there is nothing better than being loved by someone who knows your faults and decides to love you anyway.

Prayer exposes motives, attitudes, and sinful thoughts and behaviors. Prayer and a real relationship with God have a wonderful way of putting things into perspective; as we pray we can see adjustments that need to be made in our speech and behavior, all at the hand of a loving, supportive friend.

A businessman who ran a budget-type motel occasionally had irate customers who yelled at him. One day he got tired of it and came up with an idea. He posted a mirror behind the counter so that when people started yelling, they could see how ridiculous they looked. The idea worked. Prayer similarly provides a mirror for our attitudes, thoughts, and motives, and it therefore changes our perspective on many things. Prayer time is when God places what is on His heart onto our hearts.

We Feel Time Pressure. Increasingly, time pressures have crowded out the intentional place that prayer seems to require. Much of communication keeps getting shorter and more cryptic: e-mail, instant messaging, text messages, and tweets are the order of the day. God has not fallen into this trap. He is deliberate, not in a hurry nor overwhelmed by life. He does not text. If we are to know His mind, there is no shortcut or speed dial. His mind is only plumbed by much unhurried contact.

When we moved to the house where we live in Arizona, I was excited about the patio. We have a fairly large patio on the west side of the house that is very inviting. I was looking forward to sitting with Annie on the patio as the sun went down. We have now lived there ten years and have only sat on the patio twice just to relax. There is no question that time is hard to come by, so we have to prioritize how we spend it, and with whom. But remember to firmly and decisively make time for prayer, and to leave all time concerns outside the scope of your attention as you begin to pray.

We Have Control Issues. We love to be in control, but prayer requires the obliteration of control. Prayer demands that we depend upon Another and set aside our wills for His will. So many just *don't want to go there.* We would rather do it on our own than give up our perceived power. I am a controller by nature; you can ask any of my friends or family. One of the things I have learned along the way is to give up control of my life to God every day. I do this in prayer, and it usually sounds like this, "God, I have my day all planned today. But if you need to take me in a different direction, I will willingly go. This day is yours, and I am your servant. Use me as you see best." That way I am not shaken when the day goes in a different direction from the one I planned. If I don't pray this way, I am not much fun to live with when my plans fall through.

We Allow Ourselves to Be Convinced That "Prayer Is Not My Thing." Prayer is not some kind of option. It is not as though you are at the Golden Corral of spiritual disciplines and you get to pick what you like from the buffet line. Prayer is vital communication with the Father and *must* be developed. A more accurate comparison would be to say that prayer is like walking; it is not automatic, but it must be developed for a healthy and full life. To determine not to pray is like deciding not to walk because it looks like you might break a small sweat on your way to the fridge, or not to talk because you have trouble mastering some of the more difficult words.

We're Not Sure What Prayer Will Accomplish Anyway. You may have heard the story of the small town church that prayed that the bar down the street would close. One day there was a lightning strike and the bar burned to the ground. The bar owner took the church to court for the loss of his business. He contended that it was the church's fault his business had burned. The church, on the other hand, defended itself, claiming it had nothing to do with the bar burning. The judge's insights on the case were most insightful. He said, "I have a bar owner who believes in God and the power of prayer and a church that believes its prayers had nothing to do with the demise of the bar." That church is not alone.

We struggle with prayer because we are not really sure it will do any good. We wonder in our secret heart of hearts if prayer is really just talking to the sky. This kind of doubt comes from not having a genuine relationship with Jesus. When our relationship with Jesus is questionable, our confidence in prayer will be shaky at best.

This is just another great reason to record prayers as I mentioned earlier. When you have a record of what you have prayed and how God worked, your confidence will increase and your questions will evaporate.

What Did Prayer Accomplish in the Bible? As part of the discussion of our troubling doubts, think about these occasions:

- After prayer, Jesus fed five thousand men from five loaves and two fish. (See Matthew 14:13-21.)
- Peter and John were released from jail when the church prayed. (See Acts 12:1-9.)
- Hezekiah prayed for his health to be restored, and he was given fifteen additional years of life. (See 2 Kings 20:1-11.)
- After the church had prayed, the place where they were meeting was shaken. (See Acts 4:31.)

There are hundreds of references to "prayer," "praying," and "prayed" in the Bible. At some point we have to decide if we believe them or not and settle the question, Will prayer do any good? for ourselves. Until we do, we will be only somewhat interested in, and in no way committed to, developing a prayer life.

We Don't Need Anything. People who have no felt needs are not drawn to prayer. I was in Uganda a couple of years ago, a delightful country that has undergone a radical transformation. Under the bloody rule of Idi Amin, the people had suffered greatly, and in that time, believers went out into the jungle at night to pray because they had great hardship. Their suffering taught them to pray.

As we traveled along in Kampala, Uganda's capital city, we witnessed something we have never seen before; many shops and businesses with Christian names. Not one or two but hundreds of them. Just for fun, my wife started to record them for us to enjoy. Here are some we were able to capture:

♦ Abraham's Kindergarten Day Care
♦ All Saints Primary School
♦ Angel High School
♦ Back to Eden Health Clinic
♦ Blessed Ladies and Gents Boutique
♦ Born Again Faith Foundation
♦ Christian Hardware
♦ Ebenezer Restaurant
♦ Glory Be to God Salon
♦ Glory Electronics
♦ Glory Guest House
♦ Glory Inn
♦ God Cares Salon
♦ God Is Able Shop
♦ God's Mercy Wholesale and Resale Shop
♦ God's Service Clinic
♦ His Grace Taxi
♦ Hosanna Restaurant
♦ Jesus Cares Mini Mart

- ♦ Joy Supermarket
- ♦ Lord Cares Metal Workshop
- ♦ Lord's Gift Cards
- ♦ Master Inn
- ♦ Miracles Shop
- ♦ Mount Sinai Medical Services
- ♦ Mulango Faith Beautiful Salon
- ♦ Nicodemus Pork Butcher
- ♦ Peace Beauty Salon
- ♦ Praise Supermarket
- ♦ Salon God's Love Electronics
- ♦ Trust Electronics
- ♦ Trust in God
- ♦ Victory Unisex Salon
- ♦ Yashua Enterprise

We even encountered this note on a trash bin: "If God is with us, who can be against us?"

Many Ugandans now know how to pray, primarily because they have been in great need. Maybe it is better to say that their physical needs have been very apparent to them, while ours are covered. But we do have genuine needs we are utterly powerless to meet, and if we are wise, those needs will drive us to concentrated prayer.

CHAPTER 12

Spiritual Warfare Prayer:
Fighting the Invisible

God shapes the world by prayer.
The more prayer there is in the world,
the better the world will be,
the mightier the forces against evil.
—E.M. Bounds

A pastor friend recently called me in a real panic. He told me his son, 20 years old, was experiencing some demonic activity. My friend has been a pastor for twenty or more years and leads a successful church of one thousand or so. He called me because I had preached for him in his Sunday morning services a few years ago and we had talked about spiritual warfare. He began texting me. Here are his unaltered text messages:

> Please pray for my youngest son and our family. We have been up for hours battling something demonic in him. I have never experienced anything like this . . . facial distortions and a weird evil voice that was not my son's voice.

Thx for asking. Pretty intense . . . all through the
night until about 11PM. Then son fell asleep. We all
stayed together in the living room and quietly prayed
through the night. This morning we made a decision
to ignore the voice and facial changes. I really believe
this is a time of renewing our minds.
My son is in my office at the church with me. He is
sleeping. I am trying to get him into normal
environments and back into a healthy mindset.

We are experiencing the strength of the Lord.
Thanks for your continued prayers. When there is a
manifestation I just tell my son to stop it and remind
him he has the ability to control. With God's help
we are not giving attention to evil—we are focusing
on God's power.

He is coming out of this. He is talking normally and
resting. Thanks for your love and support.

We are doing great and getting stronger each day.
Son is having fewer episodes and they are much
further apart. It is a battle of the mind—we are
pouring over the Word of God constantly and
praying without ceasing. There is renewal in our
family—cleansing and confession . . . the power of
God is undeniable.

Thanks for your diligent prayers. Tonight I'm
praying that son will sleep in his bed alone and
experience the peace of God.

Difficult night . . . appreciate your prayers. God is
doing something big in all of us. We will get thru

this. I was reading in Numbers 22-24 and it was confirmation that we are taking new territory for the Lord and the enemy is looking for a way to stop us.

Each day we see more improvement. We are thankful to God and to our friends for their prayer support.

Overall we know God is going to make something good out of this.

Paul, thanks for asking . . . Son is doing so much better. He is getting through the nights much better. We continue to pray for a complete recovery.

We have not had any episodes—it is now more a battle of the mind. We continue to pray and believe for complete victory. *I believe he is doing well because of answered prayers.*

Note: It is not wise to ignore anything you suspect to be demonic activity. My friend and his family had done significant spiritual warfare and praying. After they had completed this regimen, they felt it was acceptable to begin ignoring continued harassment. Thankfully, my friend's son has improved, but demonic activity is real and can be debilitating. Real action is required. (To help establish a battle plan, I recommend reading *The Bondage Breakers* and *Victory Over the Darkness: Realizing the Power of Your Identity in Christ* by Neil T. Anderson and these books by Mark I. Bubeck: *Raising Lambs Among Wolves, The Adversary: The Christian Versus Demon Activity, Overcoming the Adversary: Warfare Praying Against Demon Activity, Rise of Fallen Angel: Victory over the Adversary Through Spiritual Renewal,* and *Spiritual Warfare Prayers.*)

Satan's Mission

We may not like to think about it, but Satan has real goals with regard to us. He is also staggeringly intelligent, gifted with a wide array of abilities and an army of lower demonic beings, and he knows how to set about achieving those goals. In a sense, he is on a mission, and it looks something like this:

- ◆ He desires to prevent God from being glorified by keeping people from being saved.
- ◆ He purposes to make humans and human society as miserable as possible in this present life. "The thief comes only to steal and kill and destroy; I have come that they may have life, and have it to the full." John 10:10
- ◆ He wants to kill us. 1 Peter 5:8 says, "Be self-controlled and alert. Your enemy the devil prowls around like a roaring lion looking for someone to devour."
- ◆ If he cannot harm us any other way, sometimes he will work to make us comfortable and complacent in order to keep us from being effective in the kingdom.

Understanding the War

There is an *invisible world* that is very real. Ephesians 6:12 says:

> For our struggle is not against flesh and blood, but against the rulers, against the authorities, against the powers of this dark world and against the spiritual forces of evil in the heavenly realms.

We must use *invisible weapons.*

2 Corinthians 10:3-5 is one of the passages that most clearly speaks of spiritual warfare and weaponry:

> For though we live in the world, we do not wage war as the world does. The weapons we fight with are not

the weapons of the world. On the contrary, they have divine power to demolish strongholds. We demolish arguments and every pretension that sets itself up against the knowledge of God, and we take captive every thought to make it obedient to Christ.

We face an *invisible enemy*.

Jesus spoke frequently about Satan, and to him. A cursory reading of the New Testament will show that up to a quarter of all of Jesus' parables, miracles, and teachings are somehow related to Satan.

Our evil adversary is named in these descriptive terms in the Bible:

♦ Satan, which means "adversary"
♦ Devil, or "slanderer"
♦ The Father of Lies
♦ Tempter. He is out to satisfy your emotional needs in order to move you off what is good and toward what is evil.
♦ Accuser of the brethren. "You are no good," he tells you, "a terrible Christian/father/husband/person." His messages are usually in broad terms. By contrast, the Holy Spirit points out specific individual sins, such as, "You just lied to her."

Five of Satan's Favorite Tactics

In keeping with the names and character descriptions above, here are some of the things he does to set us back.

He Appeals to Our Flesh. He appeals to our own weakness and capacity for evil. We are already weak, and he works to exploit the weakness.

Watch and pray so that you will not fall into
temptation. The spirit is willing, but the body is
weak (Matthew 26:41).

Those who live according to the sinful nature have
their minds set on what that nature desires; but
those who live in accordance with the Spirit have
their minds set on what the Spirit desires. The mind
of sinful man is death, but the mind controlled by
the Spirit is life and peace; the sinful mind is hostile
to God. It does not submit to God's law, nor can it
do so (Romans 8:5-7).

Actions to Combat This Tactic. Surrender your life to Christ and
live in the Spirit. This will help hold the flesh in check.

He Feeds Us False Ideas. God has set the standard for morality
by His word, but Satan loves challenges, and he works to change
public opinion about sin. When I first began ministry over 30 years
ago, no one ever talked about homosexuality. I know it was out
there, but it was never discussed. Today, Satan has pushed hard to
plant the rationale and make it common thinking that
homosexuality is a genetic issue and not a sin. The Scriptures clearly
call homosexuality evil:

"Do not have sexual relations with a man as one
does with a woman; that is detestable" (Leviticus
18:22, NIV 2011[23])

We can observe a similar process in operation with regard to
alcoholism, living together before marriage, and pornography. Satan
has done his best to dispute the word of God, and to cause those
without knowledge of the Scriptures to believe the lie that these are
a disease, or that they are not as bad as they once seemed.

214

A little study of the word informs us that Satan is in the business of blinding the mind of humans to the truth.

> The god of this age has blinded the minds of unbelievers, so that they cannot see the light of the gospel of the glory of Christ, who is the image of God (2 Corinthians 4:4).

> Those who oppose him he must gently instruct, in the hope that God will grant them repentance leading them to a knowledge of the truth, and that they will come to their senses and escape from the trap of the devil, who has taken them captive to do his will (2 Timothy 2:25-26).

On a number of occasions I have counseled men who are involved in an affair, which the Bible calls adultery. Their story has become quite predictable. They did not mean to get entangled, but it just happened, generally from not protecting themselves from places and situations where they could be vulnerable. Their rhetoric is consistent. "I know this is not how it is supposed to happen, but we are so happy and we *believe God has put us together.*" This is classic speech for someone who has been deceived by the god of this age. When you try to bring a person in this state to the truth, it often feels like you are shooting a BB at a tank. They have completely lost their bearings; they cannot distinguish truth at all because they have been so thoroughly blinded.

Action to Combat This Tactic. Train your mind by the Word so that you cannot be fooled by popular opinion or misled "experts" with an agenda.

He Opposes Us Directly. He does so through harassment and illness.

Harassment. Paul mentions in 1 Thessalonians 2:18 that he wanted to visit the Thessalonians but Satan prevented him:

> For we wanted to come to you—certainly I, Paul, did, again and again—but Satan stopped us.

Paul also describes a thorn in his flesh that he calls a messenger of Satan:

> To keep me from becoming conceited because of these surpassingly great revelations, there was given me a thorn in my flesh, a messenger of Satan, to torment me" (2 Corinthians 12:7).

I have noticed when an individual or a family steps out in faith, the evil one frequently opposes them and attempts to discourage them directly. His goal is to make things so difficult that they step down from their advance in faith and retreat in fear.

We had this experience firsthand with our middle son, Joel. At first, we were not attuned to the actions of satanic beings, but the indications in his story are easier for me to read now.

Joel went to a Christian College in Chicago for his undergraduate work. This was a hard time for him and for his mom and me, because from the beginning there was trouble. Joel had difficulty sleeping. He would go multiple nights with only two or three hours of sleep. Extreme exhaustion began to set in. He developed neck problems that were excruciatingly painful, and the attacks kept coming.

Joel worked as a valet for a high-end restaurant in downtown Chicago, and he got off at two in the morning. On several occasions he was followed home. So he came to us one day and asked if he could buy a moped. But my wife is a nurse, and we had one rule in our house. No motorcycles! She had worked on a rehab floor and seen young people with horrendous injuries from motorcycle crashes.

As we talked about his request, however, we decided that it was safer for him to ride a moped in this major city at 2 a.m. than to ride public transportation with a pocket full of tips.

He ordered the moped over the Internet, and when it arrived, it was only partially assembled. Joel had no tools and the instructions were written in Chinese. He got it together with the help of a stranger, and he was off to a good start.

But only a few days later he was on his way to teach a Bible study to some other college kids when he remembered that he did not have his Bible. So he stopped by his apartment and ran up to the tenth floor to retrieve it. In the brief moments he was gone, someone stole the moped.

Joel was distraught, and I didn't blame him . . . he had not been sleeping, he was in constant pain, and now he had spent every dime he had on a moped and it was gone. To make matters worse, Joel had not had the cycle long enough to get the license plate mounted. So how do you find a stolen moped in Chicago among 100,000 homes, with no identification?

It should have been apparent to me earlier, but it hadn't been. There were too many bizarre things happening to Joel: "This must be spiritual warfare," I finally concluded. So my wife and I decided to fast and pray for him. She took the first day, Monday and I took the next, then we traded off every other day.

On Thursday, Joel called and told us something crazy had happened. Andrew, his roommate, was on his way to work on a bicycle, their only remaining means of personal transportation. For some reason, he decided to take a different route that day from his normal path. As he was riding along on the bicycle, he noticed a moped in the driveway of one of the houses about a quarter of a mile from their apartment. He thought, "No, it can't be." But he decided to go back and take a closer look. He parked the bike down the road and chained it to a chain-link fence. Then he snuck into the driveway and looked at the moped. He lifted the seat and there was Joel's license plate. So Andrew took out his key and stole Joel's moped back.

We believe this was a direct answer to prayer. What are the chances of finding a moped in downtown Chicago? We have found fasting and prayer is the best way to do battle with the evil one when the bizarre begins to occur.

Action to Combat the Tactic of Harassment. Pray and fast.

Illness. When Paul prayed for healing of the thorn in his flesh (we don't know what that thorn was), he was told, in 2 Corinthians 12:7-9a:

> To keep me from becoming conceited because of these surpassingly great revelations, there was given a thorn in my flesh, a messenger of Satan, to torment me. Three times I pleaded with the Lord to take it away from me. But he said to me, "My grace is sufficient for you, for my power is made perfect in weakness."

Please don't misunderstand me. Every cold or cough is not a demon, but at times there are evil spirits connected with some health issues.

Action to Combat the Tactic of Illness. Pray and fast.

He Misleads Us by Our Experiences. We all have experiences each day that form patterns of thinking for us. For example, most of us have a general idea what will happen when we drive on the freeway without securing the load in a pick-up, or what it feels like to drive on ice, because we have done these things. It is possible to be so conditioned by repeated outcomes that we question God's word when He calls us to a greater level of faith walk. This effect is magnified when we listen to Satan's input about our experiences.

So for example, you go on a global connection trip, begin tithing, start attending church weekly, or commit to a prayer time, and what happens? Bedlam breaks loose. Things begin to break at your house, you lose your job, and someone needs surgery, or any number of other setbacks may occur. Satan will bring all the harassment he can muster into your experiences to make us think that Christianity just doesn't work or is too costly. His goal is to discourage you from the commitments you have made and cause you to go back to your old ways. He will use your present realities and expected outcomes to dishearten you from following through, and from ever even trying to have victory in those areas again. He will use tough experiences or discouragements to stamp out the flame of faith that you stood on to take your initial step forward. He loves to cause us to think it is just too hard to follow God, or it is far too costly.

This happens to all of us if we are not vigilant. I remember listening to Bible stories in Sunday school as a kid. My teacher had a beautiful flannel graph board she used to bring the stories of the Bible alive. The lessons were so vivid that I wanted to be like one of the characters in her weekly teaching. I longed to be like Gideon and have the faith to take on a whole army with 300 men, or like Elijah, and have the kind of walk with God that would allow me to call down fire and consume a drench offering.

Recently my wife and I have been going through some difficult experiences. In fact, they have been so difficult that I have allowed myself to get discouraged with it all. And to be completely honest, I have been wrongly listening to Satan's rants through it all. "It will always be this way." "This may go on for years." As I was listening to Satan's interjections, he was beginning to achieve his intention of stealing what little faith I had left, based on the difficulty of my present experiences.

In the midst of it all, the Lord spoke to my heart: "Remember when you wanted to be Gideon or Elijah as a kid?" "Yes," I said, fearing where this was going. "Well, I am calling you to be Gideon in your present experiences for me. I am asking you to ignore the odds and what it looks like and trust me. I am asking you to be Gideon in your story and your struggles." This was a brand new thought for me. It was fun to go back and insert myself in a story that I knew the outcome of. But to face the army with three hundred men today, in my struggle, that was a lot to ask. And it required I ignore my experiences or perceived outcomes and trust Him.

In time, Satan will stop his attacks, but only when he has determined you are not going to cave in.

Action to Combat This Tactic. Expect and prepare your mind for pushback when you step out in faith to follow God. Satan will try various means to discourage you from maintaining your commitments of faith, so be alert to his scheme. Ask God for mercy as you step forward in faith to be able to keep your commitments.

He Rattles His Saber and Roars Like a Lion. As two armies size each other up, both may begin to flex their muscles to cause the other to back down. This age old practice is known as saber rattling. Satan is a master at it. He loves to put something out there for us to worry about or to fear. If we aren't careful, we will allow that seed of fear to become implanted, and it will produce a large crop. The truth is that God is in control and we have him as our defender. We have no reason to fear at all (Isaiah 41:10). Satan just loves to rattle the saber and watch us worry, but pay him no mind. Someone has said, "Fear is faith in the enemy." I love that line, and need to remind myself of it often.

1 Peter 5:8 reminds us of the spiritual field of battle on which we live out our Christian lives:

> Be self-controlled and alert. Your enemy the devil prowls around like a roaring lion looking for someone to devour.

Action to Combat This Tactic. Pray to hear God's voice, and learn to listen for *and to* what He says, and not to the noise of Satan's saber rattling.

Fight Back with These Actions

In 2 Corinthians 10:3-5, the Apostle Paul gives us these insights into the unseen:

> For though we live in the world, we do not wage war as the world does. The weapons we fight with are not the weapons of the world. On the contrary, they have divine power to demolish strongholds. We demolish arguments and every pretension that sets itself up against the knowledge of God, and we take captive every thought to make it obedient to Christ.

We can fight back against the schemes and strongholds of the evil one, and there are specific actions we can use as weapons in the fight:

- Discern the involvement of evil.
- Close all doorways.
- Break strongholds.

Discern the Direct Involvement of Evil. Americans don't give much thought at all to spiritual warfare, so it is usually not our first thought even when it is happening to us, staring us in the face. Often we will do everything else first, leaving the use of spiritual warfare tactics for the absolute last resort.

Several years ago a young couple sought me out. They had two small children, a girl, 5 years old and a boy, 2. The girl would not let the parents hold her, and the boy had many episodes during which he would see something frightening he called "monkeys." The sight of the "monkeys" would send the young boy into a panic and fits of terror. The parents had taken him to psychiatrists and doctors to no avail. By the time I met them they were worn out and very discouraged. Someone suggested they try a pastor instead of a doctor.

Their story sounded to me like spiritual warfare. You can often tell the work of the evil one by the bizarre nature his work displays. I quizzed them to see if they had any involvement with the occult, but they could not think of any. So I asked them to get Neil T. Anderson's book *The Bondage Breakers*, and to work through the pages in the back that outline all involvement with the occult. They said they would, and we set another meeting. This time they came back more tired than the week before, but they did find some items of concern. After going through Anderson's book, they remembered a grandma who had dabbled with witchcraft and spells. This was something they had forgotten until they went through Anderson's book.

Now that we had successfully applied the first tactic, we prayed to close that doorway into their lives, and each doorway like it, with the blood of Jesus. They went on their way and I saw them a couple of weeks later. I thought they were going to carry me around on campus on their shoulders. When they went home that very day their little girl ran up to them and hugged them, and the boy never had any more incidents with the "monkeys."

Not all spiritual warfare cases are this straightforward or improve this quickly. But determining doorways and praying spiritual warfare prayers over them is a simple first step for dealing with them.

To Discern Evil Influences. Research and consider the surroundings, the history, and the other sources that may represent an evil influence for the person or persons involved. (Then pray spiritual warfare prayers over the person, specifically asking for the destruction or removal of that evil influence and others.)

Firmly Close All Doorways. What we call a "doorway" is any access point, past or present, the evil one can use to gain entry into a life for doing his dirty work. Sins and situations like anger, bitterness, pride, worry, self-reliance, discouragement, lying, immorality, drug use, child abuse, abortion, unforgiveness, false thinking, and the occult are all potential doorways.

I have a friend I will call "Z," who works at a large plant here in Phoenix with a team of five others. He joined one of our service intercession teams and was participating well. But shortly after Z started joining us for intercession, he began to experience an intense attraction to a woman at work who was not his wife. He had worked with her for years, but after he joined our prayer team, this temptation manifested itself. He was not sleeping at night and was filled with guilt. The situation had become desperate. We met right away, and he told me his story. Again, it appeared to me to be spiritual warfare, mostly because of the timing of the outbreak. We walked through the concepts of spiritual warfare and prayed together. I pointed out the timing of the trial to Z so he could see the connection between his new role as a prayer warrior and the temptation. I forwarded him a spiritual warfare prayer that has proven most helpful to many in similar situations. He made the decision to pray that warfare prayer a couple times a day and promised to stay in touch.

Within a week, the problem had greatly diminished and he was doing much better. Within a month he was back to normal.

To Close Doorways for Evil. Ask the question, "How does Satan gain access to my life repeatedly?" Make a list of each way. Then choose to ask God close all doorways with an appropriate prayer. This is the prayer we use for this.

> God, I know _____ is wrong and it violates what you have taught me. I confess it as sin, and ask that you forgive me and close any access point that the enemy has into my life by this sin, in the name of Jesus Christ, and by the power of his blood.

Sometimes fasting is needed along with prayers for closing doorways.

Break Any Strongholds. You may be wondering, "If a doorway is an access point for evil in my life, then what can a stronghold be?"

And even more urgently, "Do I have any strongholds in my life?" A stronghold is an element of our lives we have allowed Satan or his minions to "occupy" (maintain a consistent, influential presence) through continual, repetitive sin.

If we sin once, we simply have a sin that needs to be repented of, and we move on. But if we commit a sin over and over, in time a stronghold can be built.

Let's take gluttony, the sin of over-eating regularly. Eventually, if repeated enough times, gluttony can become a way of life. Although the health effects of overeating are very real and dangerous, somehow we are blinded to its sinfulness and "carry on," almost as if gluttony were normal.

Lust, alcohol, anger . . . the list of strongholds is pretty long, and they all start the same. Un-bridled lust can quickly turn into uncontrollable sexual sin; un-hindered drunkenness becomes alcoholism; and poor anger-management can become full-on rage if Satan has his way.

In Romans 6:12-13 and 16, Paul addresses the problem matter-of-factly:

> Therefore do not let sin reign in your mortal body, so that you obey its evil desires. Do not offer the parts of your body to sin, as instruments of wickedness, but rather offer yourselves to God, as those who have been brought from death to life; and offer the parts of your body to him as instruments of righteousness.
>
> . . .
>
> Don't you know that when you offer yourselves to someone to obey him as slaves, you are slaves to the one whom you obey—whether you are slaves to sin, which leads to death, or to obedience, which leads to righteousness?

Whenever there is an evil stronghold, Satan is the *de facto* lord in that particular area. He is king, ruler, and the one who is being obeyed. The one being obeyed is the one we worship, intentionally or not. Let me restate that even more directly: *When we allow strongholds to remain, we pay homage to Satan and unintentionally worship him.* He desperately desires this honor and worship! Take a moment to consider why Satan is so determined to build strongholds in a person's life.

To Break Strongholds. Here are four recommendations:

♦ Make sure you have surrendered your life to Jesus Christ completely, with nothing held back.

♦ Pray this prayer or something like it:

> "God, I know I have given way to the sin of _____. I know that it is wrong and that it violates what you have taught me. God, I have committed this sin so many times that it has now become a stronghold in my life. Satan is using the stronghold of _____ to destroy me. I ask you, Lord Jesus Christ, to have mercy on me and break and drive out the stronghold of _____ in my life. You alone can do this and I am asking for your forgiveness, your grace, and your mercy.

♦ Enlist others to pray with you about a stronghold. Fasting is often necessary, along with prayer, to break a stronghold.

♦ Pray regularly one of the spiritual warfare prayers found at the end of the chapter daily to assist in breaking strongholds.

Stronghold Groupings Explain Sin Connections. Look at the two stronghold groupings below. (These are used by permission from Restoration Ministries; a more complete list of groupings may be found on their website, which is at restorationministries.org, and in the Appendix of this book.) The boldface words describe or name the general stronghold, while the items below are indications that, if common in the person's life, that stronghold is in place in that person. The symptoms are related and tend to appear together if this stronghold is in place.

CONFUSION
(DOUBT AND UNBELIEF)
Suspicious
Apprehensive
Indecisive/Double-Minded
Skeptical
Unsettled
Easily Distracted
Lack of Commitment
No Love of the Truth
Distorted Judgment

WITCHCRAFT/
FAMILIAR SPIRIT
Blasphemy
Preoccupied with Evil
Psychic Experiences
Rebellious
Devalues Life
Identifies with Sinful Nature
Fixated on the Future

Pray Them Out. The following prayer is a suggested "Roundup Prayer for the Eviction of Controlling Wicked Spirits" from *Spiritual Warfare Prayers* by Mark I. Bubeck, used by permission. This prayer can be used to do offensive battle against the enemy. I have suggested this prayer over and over again to people who have been struggling with evil.

> I worship and honor my heavenly Father, the Lord Jesus Christ and the Holy Spirit; the true and living God who promised, "I will never leave you or forsake you." I welcome and honor the unseen presence of my Lord Jesus Christ who promised always to be with us when we meet in His name. I honor and thank You, Lord Jesus Christ, for Your unseen presence in this very place with us. I ask You to be in charge and to effect only Your will and plan in our lives. I yield fully to Your will in the eviction of any and all wicked spirit control from my life. I desire the Holy Spirit to do the sanctifying work within my whole person and being that He is there to do. I ask You, Lord Jesus Christ, to assign Your holy angels to protect us from any strategies of darkness designed to oppose this prayer for freedom. Keep Satan and all his opposing hosts of evil away from us. I also ask You to insure that wicked spirits evicted from my presence will depart quickly and directly to the place where You consign them to go.
>
> In the name of my Lord Jesus Christ and by the power of His blood, I affirm my authority over all wicked spirits assigned to control me and hinder my life and witness for Christ. I now command all lingering wicked spirits assigned to harass, rule and control me to cease their work and be bound in the presence of the Lord Jesus Christ. I bind all backup systems and replace wicked spirits assigned to rebuild evicted strongholds. They may not do that! I command all those spirits assigned against me to be and remain whole spirits. I forbid any dividing,

restructuring or multiplying of wicked spirit activity against me. There is to be one way traffic of evil spirit activity out of my life and to the place the Lord Jesus Christ consigns them. I pull in from other family members all those wicked spirits working under the chain of authority established by the powers of darkness assigned to rule over me. I command them all to be bound together here in the presence of my Lord Jesus Christ in that spiritual realm where He dwells with me and they know His presence. I bind all of your wicked ears open and it is my will that you must hear and obey Him who is your Creator and Conqueror. I declare the Lord Jesus Christ to be my Redeemer and Lord. I affirm that God has seated me with Christ Jesus in the heavenly realms far above all principalities and supernatural powers of darkness and evil.

Lord Jesus Christ, I ask You to tell all of these powers of darkness assigned to afflict and rule over me where they must go. I want them out of my life and confined where they can never trouble me again. I yield fully to Your sovereign plan for my life and all of the purposes You have in this battle I have been facing. I ask You, Lord Jesus Christ, to tell them clearly where they must go.

(A brief pause is in order to honor the Lord Jesus Christ's work of addressing His authority and victory against those powers of darkness bound in accountability before Him.)

I now ask the Holy Spirit dwelling within my person to effect the will of the Lord Jesus Christ concerning these afflicting powers of darkness. Just as You forced them out of people's lives in response to Jesus' commands when he walked on this earth, I ask You to accomplish that for me now. I ask You, Spirit of the living God, to evict from my conscious, sub-conscious and unconscious mind all control of any wicked powers. Break all of their power and control over my thought processes. They must go where the Lord Jesus Christ sends them. Sweep them away and make my mind clear of any wicked spirit control. I now ask that the Holy Spirit would renew and sanctify my mind. Cleanse and take full control of my conscious, unconscious and sub-conscious mind, precious Holy Spirit. Set it totally apart for the Glory of God and the service of my Lord Jesus Christ. I deliberately yield my mind to the Lordship of Christ, the truth of God's Word and the will of my heavenly Father.

I now ask that the Holy Spirit would look all through my emotions on the conscious, sub-conscious and unconscious level. Evict any controlling powers of darkness and may the holy angels escort them to the place where the Lord Jesus Christ is commanding them to go. Clean them out and totally away from my person. I ask that the gracious Holy Spirit would take control of my emotions on every level of the function of my feelings. Sanctify my emotions. Fill my emotions with the Spirit's fruit of love, joy, peace, patience, gentleness, meekness, faithfulness and self-control. I welcome the Holy Spirit's internal control of my feelings. I look to the Spirit of God to sanctify and renew my emotions. I reach out to experience the Lord's plan for my emotional freedom and spiritual wellbeing. I now ask that the Holy Spirit would look all through my conscious, unconscious and sub-conscious will for any control of wicked powers.

Evict them now to where the Lord Jesus Christ is commanding them to go. Sweep my will totally clean from evil control and manipulation. May the Holy Spirit of the true and living God renew and sanctify my will fully for the glory of God. Will within me to do the will of God. May the Lordship of Jesus Christ be obediently lived out in my life by the Holy Spirit's full control of my will.

I offer my body in all of its parts and functions as an expression of my spiritual worship to my heavenly Father. I ask the Holy Spirit to look all through my body for any controlling activity of wicked spirits. Look all through my brain and central nervous system for any fallen spirit's affliction or control. Evict them totally away from this physical control center for the function of my mind and body. I offer my brain and its capacities for the quickening, renewing control of the Holy Spirit. Sanctify and refresh my brain so that it functions in spiritual harmony with Your control of my whole person. Look all through my body and sever any wicked spirit control of my senses of vision, hearing, smell, touch or taste. Look all through the organs of my body for any defiling work of the kingdom of darkness. Sanctify my body's organs and their function by the quickening work of the Holy Spirit.

I surrender all my physical appetites to Your lordship. I give to You my need and craving for food and drink. Examine and cleanse from demonic activity all the organs of my digestive system. Set apart my sexuality for the glory of God. Evict any work of the enemy in my sexual functions and organs. I surrender these to Your lordship, and I submit myself to Your holy plan for moral purity and sexual intimacy only in the bonds of marriage.

Evict any afflicting, evil powers totally away from every part of my body. Sanctify it in its entirety. I want my body to be a "holy body", not only in its standing in God's redemptive plan but also in its function. As a part of my spiritual worship to my Father in heaven, I offer my body as a living sacrifice to be used only for all that is acceptable in His sight.

I now yield up my whole person again to the true and living God and His full control. I ask the Father, Son and Holy Spirit to control me fully. I thank You for the freedom that You have effected within me during this time of prayer. I now look to the love of my heavenly Father, the lordship of Jesus Christ, and the ministry of the Holy Spirit to enable me to daily walk in the spiritual freedom promised me in God's holy Word. I reject, resist and refuse anything less. In the name and worthiness of my Lord Jesus Christ, I place these petitions before my Father in heaven. Amen.

A Daily Prayer for Freedom

Finally, as an example of the kind of prayer we can use on a regular basis for asking God's protection in our battle against evil, consider this wonderful one borrowed from *Waking the Dead*, by John Eldredge.[24]

My dear Lord Jesus, I come to you now to be restored in you—to renew my place in you, my allegiance to you, and to receive from you all the grace and mercy I so desperately need this day. I honor you as my sovereign Lord, and I surrender every aspect of my life totally and completely to you.

I give you my body as a living sacrifice; I give you my heart, soul, mind and strength; and I give you my spirit as well.

I cover myself with your blood—my spirit, my soul and my body. And I ask your Holy Spirit to restore my union with you, seal me in you, and guide me in this time of prayer. In all that I now pray, I include (my family - by name) Acting as their head, I bring them under my authority and covering, and I come under your authority and covering. Holy Spirit, apply to them all that I now pray on their behalf.

Dear God, holy and victorious Trinity, You alone are worthy of all my worship, my heart's devotion, all my praise and all my trust and all the glory of my life. I worship you, bow to you, and give myself over to you in my heart's search for life. You alone are Life, and you have become my life. I renounce all other gods. All idols, and I give you the place in my heart and in my life that you truly deserve. I confess here and now that it is all about you, God, and not about me. You are the Hero of this story, and I belong to you. Forgive me, God, for my every sin. Search me and know me and reveal to me any aspect of my life that is not pleasing to you, expose any agreements I have made, and grant me the grace of a deep and true repentance.

Heavenly Father, thank You for loving me and choosing me before You made the world, You are my true Father—my Creator, my Redeemer, my Sustainer, and the true end of all things, including my life. I love you; I trust You; I worship You. Thank You for proving Your love for me by sending Your only Son, Jesus, to be my substitute and representative. I receive him and all his life and all his work, which you ordained for me. Thank You for including me in Christ, for forgiving me my sins, for granting me his righteousness, for making me complete in him. Thank You for making me alive with Christ, raising me with him, seating me with him at your right hand, granting me his authority, and anointing me with your Holy Spirit. I receive it all with thanks and give it total claim to my life.

Jesus, thank You for coming for me, for ransoming me with Your own life. I honor You as my Lord; I love You, worship You, trust You. I sincerely receive You as my redemption, and I receive all the work and triumph of your crucifixion, whereby I am cleansed from all my sin through your shed blood, my old nature is removed, my heart is circumcised unto God, and every claim being made against me is disarmed. I take my place in your cross and death, whereby I have died with you to sin and to my flesh, to the world, and to the Evil One. I am crucified with Christ, and I have crucified my flesh with all its passions and desires. I take up my cross and crucify my flesh with all its pride, unbelief and idolatry. I put off the old man. I now bring the cross of Christ between me and all people, all spirits, all things. Holy Spirit, apply to me, (my family) the fullness of the work of crucifixion of Jesus Christ for us. I receive it with thanks and give it total claim to my life.

Jesus, I also sincerely receive You as my new life, my holiness and sanctification, and I receive all the work and triumph of your resurrection, whereby I have been raised with you to a new life, to walk in newness of life, dead to sin and alive to God. I am crucified with Christ, and it is no longer I who live but Christ who lives in me. I now take my place in your resurrection, whereby I have been made alive with you, I reign in life through you. I now put on the new man in all holiness and humility, in all righteousness and purity and truth. Christ is now my life, the one who strengthens me. Holy Spirit, apply to me, (my family) the fullness of the resurrection of Jesus Christ for us. I receive it with thanks and give it total claim to my life.

Jesus, I also sincerely receive You as my authority and rule, my everlasting victory over Satan and his kingdom, and I receive all the work and triumph of your ascension, whereby Satan has been judged and cast down, his rulers and authorities disarmed, all authority in heaven and on earth given to You, Jesus, and I have been given fullness in you, the Head over all. I take my place in your ascension, whereby I have been raised with you to the right hand of the Father and established with You in all authority. I bring Your authority and your kingdom rule over my life, my family, my household and my domain.

And now I bring the fullness of Your work—Your cross, resurrection, and ascension—against Satan, against his kingdom, and against all his emissaries and all their work warring against me and my domain. Greater is he who is in me that he who is in the world. Christ has given me authority to overcome all the power of the Evil One, and I claim that authority now over and against every enemy, and I banish them in the name of Jesus Christ. Holy Spirit, apply to me, (my family) the fullness of the work of the ascension of Jesus Christ for me. I receive it with thanks and give it total claim to my life.

Holy Spirit, I since rely receive you as my
Counselor, my Comforter, my Strength, and my
Guide. Thank you for sealing me in Christ. I honor
you as my Lord, and I ask you to lead me into all
truth, to anoint me for today. I fully open my life to
you in every dimension and aspect—my body, my
soul, and my spirit—choosing to be filled with you, to
walk in step with you in all things. Apply to me,
blessed Holy Spirit, all of the work and all of the gifts
of Pentecost. Fill me afresh, blessed Holy Spirit. I
receive you with thanks and give you total claim to
my life and to (my family) as well.

Heavenly Father, thank you for granting to me
every spiritual blessing in the heavens in Christ Jesus.
I receive those blessings into my life today, and I ask
the Holy Spirit to bring all those blessings into my
life this day. Thank you for the blood of Jesus. Wash
me once more with his blood from every sin and
stain and evil device. I put on your armor—the belt of
truth, the breastplate of righteousness, the shoes of
the readiness of the gospel of peace, the helmet of
salvation. I take up the shield of faith and the sword
of the Spirit, the Word of God, and I wield these
weapons against the Evil One in the power of God. I
choose to pray at all times in the Spirit, to be strong
in you, Lord, and in Your might. Father, thank you
for your angels. I summon them in the authority of
Jesus Christ and release them to war for me and my
household. May they guard me at all times this day.
Thank you for those who pray for me; I confess I
need their prayers, and I ask you to send forth your
Spirit and rouse them, unite them, raising up the full
canopy of prayer and intercession for me. I call forth
the kingdom of the Lord Jesus Christ this day

throughout my home, my family, my life, my church, my domain. I pray all of this in the name of Jesus Christ, with all glory and honor and thanks to him.

CHAPTER 13

Next Level Praying

There is no other activity in life so important as that of prayer.
Every other activity depends upon prayer for its best efficiency.
—M.E. Andross

The American church consistently downplays both the importance and the power of prayer, and, as we have already noted, it regularly pushes prayer ministry to the sidelines. But why should we settle for mediocrity in any ministry, and especially in this practice that so directly influences our lives and our churches with the power of God? Fortunately, some will persist in prayer, and some churches will gain those benefits. In a church that is truly crossing the threshold through transformational prayer, there will be increasing opportunity and plenty of need for the greater depth represented by the following prayer types and tasks.

Prayer Evangelism

This section is reprinted with permission from *Breaking Strongholds: How Spiritual Warfare Sets Captives Free* by Tom White.[25]

Any well-written evangelism material will teach important passages of Scripture to share with unbelievers to clarify who Jesus is and to explain what steps are to be taken to gain eternal life. *Apologetic facts* are taught to help persuade potential believers, and some emphasis is also placed upon the importance of *relationship-building* to open the door to evangelism. All these tools are important and should be applied to their fullest extent. But prayer is another essential tool, and a frequently underused one, in opening the hearts of people to hear the gospel.

Dave's life is a good example of what I'm talking about. Dave and I became friends because of our mutual interest in antique tools. He had been collecting these tools for thirty-five or forty years before I met him, and after we became acquainted he began mentoring me in the ins and outs of collecting. When I first began to pray for his salvation, he had no interest in any spiritual things, but our friendship was established. Eventually, Dave developed Guillain–Barré syndrome, which is a nerve disorder. It eventually took his life, but a few days before he died, he accepted Christ into his life on his hospital bed with his wife at his side. No one will ever be able to convince me that my prayers, along with the prayers of many other people, led to Dave's salvation. Don't forget to pray over those you are attempting to reach with the Gospel!

What follows is a list of some of the key elements of evangelistic prayer. As you begin to pray for an individual's salvation, look back at this list and re-read the passages listed with each point. Then pray!

Pray for Yourself. Begin by asking God for an infusion of Christ's love for the lost into your heart (see 2 Corinthians 5:14). Ask for a balance of fearlessness (see Ephesians 6:19), as well as for clarity and sensitivity (see Colossians 4:4–5), in presenting the gospel.

Believe That the Lord Is Able to Reach Even the Most Resistant People. Affirm Jesus' words: "With God all things are possible" (Matthew 19:26b).

Present the Names of Those Who Are Lost, or Who Have Backslid, Before the Throne. Stand on the Scriptures "one died for all" (from 2 Corinthians 5:14), God "wants all men to be saved" (from 1 Timothy 2:4), and "not wanting anyone to perish" (from 2 Peter 3:9). Though there is no guarantee that someone will say yes to

God's grace, God has said yes to all people in the atoning sacrifice of His Son.

Ask the Lord to Compel a Lost Soul to Seek Redemption. Jesus said clearly, "No one can come to me unless the Father who sent me draws him" (John 6:44a). Ask the Holy Spirit to allow the person to see their sin for what it is and desire to seek reconciliation with God. In light of eternal destiny, we can be bold in asking God to do whatever He needs to do to shake and wake a person to spiritual reality.

Ask the Spirit to Reveal the Reality of Sin. The requirement of righteousness to be reconciled to God, and the fearful inevitability of judgment (see John. 16:8) to lost souls.

Ask God to Reveal Supernaturally the Deity of His Son. (See Matthew 11:27.) Ask God to illuminate the mind of a lost person with the revelation of Jesus' sacrifice as the only hope for reconciliation (see 1 John 2:2).

Boldly Confront the Enemy. Pray with precision, faith, and authority to silence and subdue the influence of any evil spirit that devours the understanding of the Word of God. Pray that the strongholds spoken of by John will be bound: "the cravings of sinful man, the lust of his eyes and the boasting of what he has and does" (from 1 John 2:16). Satanic spirits energize and exploit these strongholds. If we first ask God to reveal Jesus to a person, then we can move on Jesus' authority to get right up in the enemy's face and break his blinding and binding grip.

Pray for Divine Openings or Clear Evidence of the Lord in a Person's Life. And co-labor with the Spirit to bring a lost sheep into the fold or a prodigal back home.

Ask the Lord Each Day for "Divine Appointments" with Unsaved Persons. An effective ambassador should be available to pray with authority and able to give answers that open a door to God's redeeming grace.

This is harvest time, and the devil surely knows it. Let's rise to the occasion and move on the commission our Lord gave to Paul:

> I am sending you to them to open their eyes and
> turn them from darkness to light, and from the
> power of Satan to God, so that they may receive
> forgiveness of sins and a place among those who are
> sanctified by faith in me (Acts 26:17b-18).

Prayer Journeys

A prayer journey to a mission field is an extremely effective way to combine your church's global outreach and prayer ministries, adding the joy of intercultural discovery and the passion of missions to the prayer lives of team members. Planning a trip for the purpose of prayer raises awareness of the importance of prayer to all who hear about it ("You mean you're going all the way over there to *pray?*") while blessing global workers with the encouragement of a dedicated prayer team ("You mean they're coming all the way over here to *pray for us?*").

Goals. The goals for a prayer journey are as follows:

- To pray for the global field worker, his local associates, and his project and also for the nation their work is benefiting.
- To soften spiritual resistance the missionary may be experiencing, and may have been facing for a long time.
- To grow and develop each team member's heart for the nations.
- To help all team members become stronger in their prayer lives.

Six Steps Toward a Team Prayer Journey

1. Select a destination and, even more important, a global field worker who is interested in having a prayer group come and pray over his or her work, host country, and local field.

2. Pick a date, and select some of the parameters of the trip (such as the length of the trip, the basic number of team members, expectations, and other basic trip details). It is important to do this in cooperation with the field worker.

3. Ask lots of questions of the field worker so that nothing is a surprise. (In the Appendix you will find the questionnaire we use for this purpose at Central.)

4. Begin to determine a budget and price for the trip on the basis of the information from the questionnaire.

5. Recruit team members. Look for people who are ready to take a bold step to improve their prayer lives, or who already show an interest in global ministry, and are willing to improve their prayer for it.

6. Begin team meetings for training and preparation. These meetings are vital for the achievement of the trip's purposes.

Be Sure to Partner with Your Church's Global Outreach Team Whenever Possible. At Central, we have a tremendous and very active Global Outreach team. They plan twenty-five or so trips a year to somewhere in the world, so they have extensive expertise in trip organization and administration. Our prayer ministry works with them to plan and execute the logistics of our prayer trips. But even if your church's global outreach efforts are somewhat less developed, it is important to cooperate with that team for the purpose of developing both ministries.

Our guidelines require each team member invest about twenty-six hours in pretrip preparation. Because they are training teams all the time, our Global Outreach department essentially does this part of the work for us. They help us to understand the culture where we are going and to learn some language basics. They book our flights and obtain our visas.

It is also important to invest in the trip through prayer preparation. Our teams depart on their trips ready to pray for long periods of time because we put in significant time praying together beforehand. For instance, we often prayer-walk a crowded area to help them get a feel for what it will be like to pray in a foreign country with lots of traffic and distractions.

We have found that many prayer journey participants come home and become committed prayer team members, assuming vital roles in the ministry, and we have built wonderful relationships with many others as well.

Prayer for Healing

The churches I've been involved with believe what Scripture says in James 5:14-15:

> Is any one of you sick? He should call the elders of
> the church to pray over him and anoint him with oil
> in the name of the Lord. And the prayer offered in
> faith will make the sick person well; the Lord will
> raise him up. If he has sinned, he will be forgiven.

Some ministries are afraid to pray for healing because they are not sure it is God's will. This is a paralyzing approach. Instead, we should boldly ask the Father in faith for healing, and then submit to whatever God chooses to do.

Anointing with Oil

While serving as senior pastor of a church, I frequently received calls requesting that our elders anoint a sick person with oil for their healing. This practice comes from the book of James chapter 5:14-15 (quoted above). We may easily grasp the concept of calling the elders of the church to pray over someone who is gravely ill, but we may just as easily miss the significance of the last verse's instructions to "confess your sins to one another so that you may be healed."

We decided to take this concept seriously and as literally as possible, so the elders of our church made it a habit to gather an hour before the time set for the anointing to confess our sins to each other. We did this out loud, and each man participated. At first this was difficult to do, no question about it. But soon it felt like the right thing and became very natural for us. Following the elders' confession time, we then used the remaining time until the church member arrived for prayer about other needs.

When a person first asked to be anointed with oil and prayed for about a sickness, we directed them to this passage and let them know the elders would be confessing their sins before praying. We also informed the person who was requesting the anointing that the elders would be asking them if there were any sins they would want to confess before we entered into the anointing.

Before praying, we listened to the sincere confession of any sins the person shared, and to those of the spouse if he or she was there, and then anointed the sick person with olive oil. This act was followed by a time of prayer for healing; normally each of us prayed.

We used olive oil, based on the practice of Moses described in Exodus 30:22-25:

> Then the Lord said to Moses, "Take the following fine spices: 500 shekels of liquid myrrh, half as much (that is, 250 shekels) of fragrant cinnamon, 250 shekels of fragrant cane, 500 shekels of cassia—all according to the sanctuary shekel—and a hin [that is, probably about a gallon] of olive oil. Make these into a sacred anointing oil, a fragrant blend, the work of a perfumer. It will be the sacred anointing oil."

The emphasis in our prayer times was always on God and His power and never on us. We knew and showed freely that we could not do anything other than simply call out to Him.

God provided many amazing results from those prayers for healing. One of these involved a woman, 40 years old, who asked us to pray for her ovaries because they were badly damaged. Her doctor had informed her they likely needed to be removed, based on scans that showed enormous cysts. So we prayed, and the day after the prayer time the doctor did the surgery, intending to remove the ovaries. But he found them to be like those of a teenager, with no malady at all. This healing was an enormous blessing for this woman, as she was newly married for the first time and hoped to have children someday soon.

Anointing a Home with Oil? Sometimes I am asked to pray over and anoint a new home for a believer. I have even seen nervous travelers anoint an airplane they are climbing into. This allows me to address the larger question of the applications of anointing with oil in the Bible. That phrase "anointing with oil" is, in fact, used more than fifty times in the English Standard Version of the Bible, and the anointing was done for a variety of different reasons.

People were anointed for the purpose of preforming a specific task or fulfilling a high role. In 1 Samuel 10:1 we see Samuel anointing Saul for his role as king:

> Then Samuel took a flask of oil and poured it on
> Saul's head and kissed him saying, "Has not the Lord
> anointed you ruler over his inheritance?"

Anointing was also done to set a particular place apart for God's use. For example, an oil anointing was used to set apart the tabernacle for God and His presence, as described in Exodus 40:9:

> Take the anointing oil and anoint the tabernacle and
> everything in it; consecrate it and all its furnishings,
> and it will be holy.

On the basis of these passages, I find it simply makes sense today to apply the same principle for anointing the home of believers, or for other similar purposes. For a home, I use simple olive oil and I start in the center of the house. My practice is to anoint the top of the doorjamb in the shape of a cross. I pray a prayer of blessing and protection over the home, beginning with that room specifically and all that takes place in it. Then we go to each additional room of the house and do the same thing. I always encourage the person whose room it is to say the prayer over their room. This gets the whole family involved in a meaningful way and makes for a very sweet time. I usually have the father close our prayer time to sort of symbolically cement him as the "pastor of his address."

Prayer times like this can be most helpful and encouraging to believers, and they are definitely worth the effort.

Use and Give Away These Scriptures About Healing

As the prayer pastor of a large multisite church, I frequently receive phone calls from people requesting prayer. And often the person on the other end has just learned he or she has a disease or other serious health concern. What can I do for them beyond simply assuring them I will pray, and then praying? There is something else we can all do to help people we know who are facing a health crisis. What follows is a list of scriptures on healing I like to send out to people to read over as they walk through their struggle. (I also arranged for someone to read each scripture on to a cd that I give out.) We have found that this scriptural "tool" works in very real and amazing ways to comfort and restore hope to hurting and desperate people, and I encourage you to use them as we are committed to using them.

John 8:31-32

> To the Jews who had believed him, Jesus said, "If you hold to my teaching, you are really my disciples. Then you will know the truth, and the truth will set you free."

Exodus 15:26

He said, "If you listen carefully to the voice of the LORD your God and do what is right in his eyes, if you pay attention to his commands and keep all his decrees, I will not bring on you any of the diseases I brought on the Egyptians, for I am the LORD, who heals you."

Exodus 23:25

Worship the LORD your God, and his blessing will be on your food and water. I will take away sickness from among you.

Deuteronomy 7:12-15

If you pay attention to these laws and are careful to follow them, then the LORD your God will keep his covenant of love with you, as he swore to your forefathers. He will love you and bless you and increase your numbers. He will bless the fruit of your womb, the crops of your land—your grain, new wine and oil—the calves of your herds and the lambs of your flocks in the land that he swore to your forefathers to give you. You will be blessed more than any other people; none of your men or women will be childless, nor any of your livestock without young. The LORD will keep you free from every disease. He will not inflict on you the horrible diseases you knew in Egypt, but he will inflict them on all who hate you.

Deuteronomy 28:1-4, 6-8, and 13

If you fully obey the LORD your God and carefully follow all his commands I give you today, the LORD your God will set you high above all the nations on earth. All these blessings will come upon you and accompany you if you obey the LORD your God: You will be blessed in the city and blessed in the country. The fruit of your womb will be blessed, and the crops of your land and the young of your livestock— the calves of your herds and the lambs of your flocks.

. . .

You will be blessed when you come in and blessed when you go out. The LORD will grant that the enemies who rise up against you will be defeated before you. They will come at you from one direction but flee from you in seven. The LORD will send a blessing on your barns and on everything you put your hand to. The LORD your God will bless you in the land he is giving you."

. . .

The LORD will make you the head, not the tail. If you pay attention to the commands of the LORD your God that I give you this day and carefully follow them, you will always be at the top, never at the bottom.

2 Kings 20:5

". . . 'This is what the LORD, the God of your father David, says: I have heard your prayer and seen your tears; I will heal you. . . .'"

2 Chronicles 7:14

"If my people, who are called by my name, will humble themselves and pray and seek my face and turn from their wicked ways, then will I hear from heaven and will forgive their sin and will heal their land."

Psalm 23

The LORD is my shepherd, I shall not be in want. He makes me lie down in green pastures, he leads me beside quiet waters, he restores my soul. He guides me in paths of righteousness for his name's sake. Even though I walk through the valley of the shadow of death, I will fear no evil, for you are with me; your rod and your staff, they comfort me. You prepare a table before me in the presence of my enemies. You anoint my head with oil; my cup overflows. Surely goodness and love will follow me all the days of my life, and I will dwell in the house of the LORD forever.

Psalm 30:2

O LORD my God, I called to you for help and you healed me.

Psalm 91:1-7, 10-11, and 14-16

He who dwells in the shelter of the Most High will rest in the shadow of the Almighty. I will say of the LORD, "He is my refuge and my fortress, my God, in whom I trust." Surely he will save you from the fowler's snare and from the deadly pestilence. He will cover you with his feathers, and under his wings you will find refuge; his faithfulness will be your shield and rampart. You will not fear the terror of night, nor the arrow that flies by day, nor the pestilence that stalks in the darkness, nor the plague that destroys at midday. A thousand may fall at your side, ten thousand at your right hand, but it will not come near you.

. . .

[T]hen no harm will befall you, no disaster will come near your tent. For he will command his angels concerning you to guard you in all your ways."

. . .

"Because he loves me," says the LORD, "I will rescue him; I will protect him, for he acknowledges my name. He will call upon me, and I will answer him; I will be with him in trouble, I will deliver him and honor him. With long life will I satisfy him and show him my salvation."

Psalm 103:2-5

Praise the LORD, O my soul, and forget not all his benefits— who forgives all your sins and heals all your diseases, who redeems your life from the pit and crowns you with love and compassion, who satisfies your desires with good things so that your youth is renewed like the eagle's.

Psalm 107:20

He sent forth his word and healed them; he rescued them from the grave.

Psalm 118:5-6, 14, and 17

In my anguish I cried to the LORD, and he answered by setting me free.

The LORD is with me; I will not be afraid. What can man do to me?

...

The LORD is my strength and my song; he has become my salvation.

. . .

I will not die but live, and will proclaim what the LORD has done.

Proverbs 3:2 and 5-8

. . . for they will prolong your life many years and bring you prosperity.

. . .

Trust in the LORD with all your heart and lean not on your own understanding; in all your ways acknowledge him, and he will make your paths straight. Do not be wise in your own eyes; fear the LORD and shun evil. This will bring health to your body and nourishment to your bones.

Proverbs 4:20-22

My son, pay attention to what I say; listen closely to my words. Do not let them out of your sight, keep them within your heart; for they are life to those who find them and health to a man's whole body.

Proverbs 12:18

Reckless words pierce like a sword, but the tongue of the wise brings healing.

Proverbs 14:30

A heart at peace gives life to the body, but envy rots the bones.

Proverbs 15:4

The tongue that brings healing is a tree of life, but a deceitful tongue crushes the spirit.

Proverbs 15:30

A cheerful look brings joy to the heart, and good news gives health to the bones.

Proverbs 16:24

Pleasant words are a honeycomb, sweet to the soul and healing to the bones.

Proverbs 17:22

A cheerful heart is good medicine, but a crushed spirit dries up the bones.

Isaiah 54:17

"[N]o weapon forged against you will prevail, and you will refute every tongue that accuses you. This is the heritage of the servants of the LORD, and this is their vindication from me," declares the LORD.

Isaiah 58:8

Then your light will break forth like the dawn, and your healing will quickly appear; then your righteousness will go before you, and the glory of the LORD will be your rear guard.

Jeremiah 30:17a

"'But I will restore you to health and heal your wounds,' declares the LORD."

Jeremiah 32:27

I am the LORD, the God of all mankind. Is anything too hard for me?

Malachi 4:2

But for you who revere my name, the sun of righteousness will rise with healing in its wings. And you will go out and leap like calves released from the stall.

Matthew 4:23-24

Jesus went throughout Galilee, teaching in their synagogues, preaching the good news of the kingdom, and healing every disease and sickness among the people. News about him spread all over Syria, and people brought to him all who were ill with various diseases, those suffering severe pain, the demon-possessed, those having seizures, and the paralyzed, and he healed them.

Matthew 8:2-3

A man with leprosy came and knelt before him and said, "Lord, if you are willing, you can make me clean." Jesus reached out his hand and touched the man. "I am willing," he said. "Be clean!" Immediately he was cured of his leprosy.

Matthew 8:16-17

When evening came, many who were demon-possessed were brought to him, and he drove out the spirits with a word and healed all the sick. This was to fulfill what was spoken through the prophet Isaiah: "He took up our infirmities and carried our diseases."

Matthew 9:35

Jesus went through all the towns and villages, teaching in their synagogues, preaching the good news of the kingdom and healing every disease and sickness.

Matthew 10:1 and 7-8

He called his twelve disciples to him and gave them authority to drive out evil spirits and to heal every disease and sickness.

. . .

"As you go, preach this message: 'The kingdom of heaven is near.' Heal the sick, raise the dead, cleanse those who have leprosy, drive out demons. Freely you have received, freely give."

Matthew 11:1-5

After Jesus had finished instructing his twelve disciples, he went on from there to teach and preach in the towns of Galilee. When John heard in prison what Christ was doing, he sent his disciples to ask him, "Are you the one who was to come, or should we expect someone else?" Jesus replied, "Go back and report to John what you hear and see: The blind receive sight, the lame walk, those who have leprosy are cured, the deaf hear, the dead are raised, and the good news is preached to the poor."

Matthew 14:14

When Jesus landed and saw a large crowd, he had compassion on them and healed their sick.

Matthew 14:35-36

And when the men of that place recognized Jesus, they sent word to all the surrounding country. People brought all their sick to him and begged him to let the sick just touch the edge of his cloak, and all who touched him were healed.

Matthew 15:30

Great crowds came to him, bringing the lame, the blind, the crippled, the mute and many others, and laid them at his feet; and he healed them.

Matthew 19:1-2

When Jesus had finished saying these things, he left Galilee and went into the region of Judea to the other side of the Jordan. Large crowds followed him, and he healed them there.

Matthew 20:30-34

Two blind men were sitting by the roadside, and when they heard that Jesus was going by, they shouted, "Lord, Son of David, have mercy on us!" The crowd rebuked them and told them to be quiet, but they shouted all the louder, "Lord, Son of David, have mercy on us!" Jesus stopped and called them. "What do you want me to do for you?" he asked. "Lord," they answered, "we want our sight." Jesus had compassion on them and touched their eyes. Immediately they received their sight and followed him.

Matthew 21:12 and 14

Jesus entered the temple area and drove out all who were buying and selling there. He overturned the tables of the money changers and the benches of those selling doves.

. . .

The blind and the lame came to him at the temple, and he healed them.

Mark 1:30 and 31

Simon's mother-in-law was in bed with a fever, and they told Jesus about her. So he went to her, took her hand and helped her up. The fever left her and she began to wait on them.

Mark 3:1 and 5

Another time he went into the synagogue, and a man with a shriveled hand was there.

. . .

He looked around at them in anger and, deeply distressed at their stubborn hearts, said to the man, "Stretch out your hand." He stretched it out, and his hand was completely restored.

Mark 6:56

And wherever he went—into villages, towns or countryside—they placed the sick in the marketplaces. They begged him to let them touch even the edge of his cloak, and all who touched him were healed.

Mark 9:23

"'If you can'?" said Jesus. "Everything is possible for him who believes."

Mark 16:15-18

He said to them, "Go into all the world and preach the good news to all creation. Whoever believes and is baptized will be saved, but whoever does not believe will be condemned. And these signs will accompany those who believe: In my name they will drive out demons; they will speak in new tongues; they will pick up snakes with their hands; and when they drink deadly poison, it will not hurt them at all; they will place their hands on sick people, and they will get well."

Luke 4:16-19

He went to Nazareth, where he had been brought up, and on the Sabbath day he went into the synagogue, as was his custom. And he stood up to read. The scroll of the prophet Isaiah was handed to him. Unrolling it, he found the place where it is written: "The Spirit of the Lord is on me, because he has anointed me to preach good news to the poor. He has sent me to proclaim freedom for the prisoners and recovery of sight for the blind, to release the oppressed, to proclaim the year of the Lord's favor."

Luke 4:40

When the sun was setting, the people brought to Jesus all who had various kinds of sickness, and laying his hands on each one, he healed them.

Luke 5:15

Yet the news about him spread all the more, so that crowds of people came to hear him and to be healed of their sicknesses.

Luke 6:17 and 19

He went down with them and stood on a level place. A large crowd of his disciples was there and a great number of people from all over Judea, from Jerusalem, and from the coast of Tyre and Sidon, . . . [A]nd the people all tried to touch him, because power was coming from him and healing them all.

Luke 7:21

At that very time Jesus cured many who had diseases, sicknesses and evil spirits, and gave sight to many who were blind.

Luke 9:1-2

When Jesus had called the Twelve together, he gave them power and authority to drive out all demons and to cure diseases, and he sent them out to preach the kingdom of God and to heal the sick.

Luke 9:11

[B]ut the crowds learned about it and followed him. He welcomed them and spoke to them about the kingdom of God, and healed those who needed healing.

Acts 4:29-30

"Now, Lord, consider their threats and enable your servants to speak your word with great boldness. Stretch out your hand to heal and perform miraculous signs and wonders through the name of your holy servant Jesus."

Acts 5:16

Crowds gathered also from the towns around Jerusalem, bringing their sick and those tormented by evil spirits, and all of them were healed.

Acts 10:38

. . .how God anointed Jesus of Nazareth with the Holy Spirit and power, and how he went around doing good and healing all who were under the power of the devil, because God was with him.

Acts 19:11-12

God did extraordinary miracles through Paul, so that even handkerchiefs and aprons that had touched him were taken to the sick, and their illnesses were cured and the evil spirits left them.

Romans 1:16

I am not ashamed of the gospel, because it is the power of God for the salvation of everyone who believes: first for the Jew, then for the Gentile.

Galatians 3:13

Christ redeemed us from the curse of the law by becoming a curse for us, for it is written: "Cursed is everyone who is hung on a tree."

James 5:14-16

Is any one of you sick? He should call the elders of the church to pray over him and anoint him with oil in the name of the Lord. And the prayer offered in faith will make the sick person well; the Lord will raise him up. If he has sinned, he will be forgiven. Therefore confess your sins to each other and pray for each other so that you may be healed. The prayer of a righteous man is powerful and effective.

1 Peter 2:24

He himself bore our sins in his body on the tree, so that we might die to sins and live for righteousness; by his wounds you have been healed.

3 John 2

Dear friend, I pray that you may enjoy good health and that all may go well with you, even as your soul is getting along well.

Prayer and Fasting

The phrase "prayer and fasting" is found both in Scripture and in the vocabulary of many who are serious about prayer today. Prayer and fasting may be defined as going without something (generally food) in order to focus on prayer and fellowship with

God. Prayer and fasting may go hand in hand, but this is not always the case. A person can legitimately pray without fasting or fast without prayer. But the two work very well together; when fasting and prayer are combined and dedicated to God's glory they reach their full effectiveness. It is important to note that a dedicated time of prayer and fasting must not be some kind of attempt to manipulate God into doing what we desire. Rather, it is simply a method of "forcing yourself to focus" and to rely on God for the strength, provision, and wisdom for your need.

The Bible Has Much to Say About Fasting. The Old Testament law specifically required prayer and fasting for only one occasion, which was the Day of Atonement. This custom became known as "the day of fasting" (Jeremiah 36:6) or "the Fast" (Acts 27:9). Moses fasted during the forty days and forty nights he was on Mount Sinai receiving the law from God (see Exodus 34:28). King Jehoshaphat called for a fast in all Israel when they were about to be attacked by the Moabites and Ammonites (see 2 Chronicles 20:3). In response to Jonah's preaching, the men of Nineveh fasted and put on sackcloth (see Jonah 3:5). Prayer and fasting was often done in times of distress or trouble. David fasted when he learned that Saul and Jonathan had been killed (see 2 Samuel 1:12). Nehemiah entered a time of prayer and fasting upon learning that Jerusalem was still in ruins (see Nehemiah 1:4).

We also find prayer and fasting in the New Testament. Anna "worshiped night and day, fasting and praying" at the Temple (Luke 2:37). John the Baptist taught his disciples to fast (see Mark 2:18). Jesus fasted for forty days and forty nights before His temptation by Satan (see Matthew 4:2). John the Baptist's disciples routinely fasted according to Jewish custom, but Jesus and His disciples did not. However, Jesus said His disciples would mourn and fast after He had left them (see Matthew 9:14-15, Mark 2:18-20, and Luke 5:33-35). The church of Antioch fasted (see Acts 13:2) and sent Paul and Barnabas off on their first missionary journey (see Acts 13:3). Paul and Barnabas spent time in prayer and fasting for the appointment of elders in the churches (see Acts 14:23). The early Christians practiced fasting at least occasionally (see Acts 13:3 and 14:23).

In both the Old and New Testaments, fasting is seen as useful for *humbling oneself* as a sign of commitment or repentance and for increasing faith, especially when accompanied by prayer. Fasting allows one to be devoted to spiritual matters without distraction from earthly things. However, fasting was not to be considered an end in itself, nor a substitute for obedience to God and doing good deeds (see Isaiah 58:3-10).

Required or Recommended? The Word of God expects believers to spend time in prayer and fasting. Matthew 6:16 says, "And *when* you fast . . ." (emphasis added). Jesus' wording indicates that we *will* fast, but gives little indication about how, or for what purpose, and certainly does not prescribe any particular frequency. The descriptions of fast types and the verses that follow will help us see how we might go about holding a fast according to one of six Biblical patterns.

There Are Six Different Types of Fasts in the Bible. They may be viewed as specific, or more applicable, to certain situations. All of them are useful when applied today, and when combined with intensely focused attention to prayer, each can lead to very effective communication with the Father.

1. **Normal.** This is abstaining from food for an unspecified length of time. Example: Jesus "ate nothing during those days, and at the end of them he was hungry" (Luke 4:2).
2. **Absolute.** This is abstaining from food and water; normally no more than three days. Examples: For three days Paul was blind, and did not eat or drink anything" (Acts 9:9); Moses (see Deuteronomy 9:9), Ezra (see Ezra 10:6), and Esther (see Esther 4:16) fasted as well.
3. **Partial.** This is restricting one's diet of certain foods for one meal a day. Examples: At Daniel's request, "the guard took

away their choice food and the wine they were to drink and gave them vegetables instead" (Daniel 1:16 and 10:3).

4. **Regular.** This is for fast days that commemorate an event, or weekly fasts on a regular day. Examples: the Day of Atonement (Leviticus 23:27; Psalm 35:13; Isaiah 58:5); a fast day (Jeremiah 36:6); four separate festivals (Zechariah 8:19); twice a week (Luke 18:11-12).

5. **Public.** These fasts are called in times of special need and emergency. Almost all regular fasts were public fasts, but all public fasts are not necessarily regular ones. Examples: King Jehoshaphat when Judah was invaded (2 Chronicles 20:1-4), Ezra returning the exiles (Ezra 8:21-23), Ninevah, as a result of Jonah's preaching (Jonah 3:5, 10).

6. **Private.** These are fasts done by an individual as decided by that individual. We are instructed not to let others know we are fasting. These fasts are to be private because the focus of the fast is to be God and not others (Matthew 6:16-17).

Why Fast? The immediate practical effect of fasting is the intensification of prayer. By entering a time of prayer with fasting, a believer essentially forces himself to pray more intensely by manipulating his own physical body. But there are other motivations beside prayer, including the following, which are also valid biblical reasons to fast.

To Humble Oneself. The purpose of Christian fasting should be to take our eyes off the things of this world and focus our thoughts on God. By taking our eyes off the things of this world through prayer and biblical fasting, we can focus better on Christ. Matthew 6:33 teaches, "But seek first his kingdom and his righteousness, and all these things will be given to you as well."

To Express Distress and Grief. Loss of appetite is a natural reaction in times of distress, grief and mourning, and fasting was considered appropriate at these times. David fasted as a sign of grief when Abner was murdered (see 2 Samuel 3:35). There was a seven-day fast at the death of Saul (see 1 Samuel 31:13).

To Accentuate Spiritual Preparation. Fasting is a self-sacrifice that makes one humble and more accepting of God's will. Moses fasted for forty days in preparation for receiving the Ten Commandments (see Exodus 34:28). Daniel fasted for three weeks before receiving his vision (see Daniel 10:2-6). Jesus fasted for forty days in preparation for His temptation by the devil (see Matthew 4:1-11 and Luke 4:1-13).

For Repentance and Atonement. When Jonah predicted the downfall of Nineveh, The Ninevites fasted as a sign of repentance in hopes God would spare their city (see Jonah 3:3-9). The Day of Atonement was an annual obligatory day of rest and fasting for the Israelites (see Numbers 29:7). When the Israelites sinned, they often humbled themselves and fasted in hopes of regaining God's favor (see Judges 20:26 and 1 Samuel 7:6).

Personal Experiences with Prayer and Fasting

Annie and I both became quite concerned when one of our grown sons began to smoke cigarettes. So we determined that we should fast and ask God to cause him to quit, and we began to do so. Just a few days later, we were talking in the family room and our son revealed that he had decided to quit. This happened with no discussion of the subject on our part; it was an entirely personal decision on his part. My position on this is that he did not quit only as a result of his parents' fast, but that our prayer and fasting were a part of "getting that ball rolling." After several more fasts and lots of prayer, he has now given up cigarettes for good.

Annie and I often fast one day a week for our children and for the ministry. We don't get it done each week, but we both see that it pays tremendous dividends.

Fasting has proven to be the strongest weapon in our (Annie's and my) armory for spiritual warfare purposes. As mentioned previously, this tool or weapon is something we use generously when we feel as though we are facing ongoing enemy attacks. Once we have recognized a danger, we take turns fasting (Annie will take one day and I will take the next) until the threat passes. Sometimes a situation has required extending the number of days, or God may resolve other situations much more quickly.

Once I felt called to an extended juice fast during which I drank only three large glasses of juice a day. The hunger passed after just a few days, and I found the juice gave me enough nourishment so that I could continue to work and actually felt quite well. I won't lie, though; when that fast ended, the hamburger tasted really good!

Plan Your Fast. It is important to think, plan and pray before beginning a fast. The many opportunities to slip up or give up are usually a problem if we fail to plan adequately. And the spiritual preparation also helps to maximize the prayer effects of the fast, so the benefit begins even before the first hunger pangs. I recommend the following preparatory thoughts and actions:

1. **Submit.** Ask God to lead you in all aspects of your fast from the very first time you begin thinking about it, intentionally making it all His, and for His glory.
2. **Plan.** Write out your plan for the day (or days) and times of the fast. The day that works best for practical reasons is probably the day you should choose for your fast. I like to fast from sundown to sundown, but other options are equally valid.
3. **Write Out Your Purpose for This Fast.** If there are specific requests you will be bringing to God, list them, along with other more general spiritual goals you may have.
4. **Plan and Time Your Last Meal.** Consider how you will break the fast. Be careful not to plan a huge meal as the last meal before the fast or the first meal afterward. The focus is not to be on the food, but upon God.

Here are two more considerations:

5. **Consider Fasting and Praying with Someone Else.** Fasting is usually considered to be an individual spiritual activity, but my wife and I have shared in some wonderful fasts together. Having someone else join you in the fast, if it is appropriate, may serve to help both (or all) of you stay accountable. We may also think of fasting as something we do in secret, but there is even a time and place for corporate fasting. A church might fast together for a very sick child or for God's direction on a given subject.

6. **Fasting Should Always Be Limited to a Set Time.** Limit fasting because there are serious health risks associated with not eating for extended periods. Fasting is not a method of punishing our bodies, and it is not to be used as a "dieting method with spiritual benefits," either. We should not spend time in prayer and fasting in order to lose weight, but rather to gain a deeper fellowship with God.

Important: Always consult your physician before beginning a fast.

Finally, if you are leading a church or group to fast and pray together, announce the goal of the fast early enough for others to plan and *invite* (not guilt or cajole) them to join in. Be especially careful not to make the people feel guilty who are unable or who choose not to fast, and do not leave them with the impression you believe they are less spiritual. Begin the fast together as a group and end it together at the appointed time. After the fast, it may be encouraging and informative to bring the group together to review the experience and to discuss what was gained or learned in prayer.

For additional reading on this subject, there is a great little pamphlet available called *Seven Steps to Successful Fasting and Prayer*, by Bill Bright. I have purchased hundreds of these to give out to believers as a primer on fasting. You can find the PDF of this work online at http://www.cru.org/training-and-growth/devotional-life/7-steps-to-fasting/index.htm.

Life Prayer

Let's think back to the topic of an earlier chapter, in which we discussed that prayer may be broken down into categories like *casual prayers*, *crisis prayers* and, best of all, *kingdom prayers*. Kingdom prayers are prayers of intercession that call upon God to advance His kingdom.

Here are a few examples of simple kingdom prayers:

- God, please end abortion in our land for good.
- Lord, please protect the work of my friends in Indonesia and cause it to flourish.
- Father, please bless our church's youth ministry with many new students for the coming school year.

Notice again that a kingdom prayer contains no requests for the person doing the praying. It is solely focused on extending and advancing God's work.

Probably everyone shares the tendency to pray far more casual prayers and crisis prayers than we do kingdom prayers. Again, praying casual and crisis prayers is not wrong, far from it. But these types should not be the only kinds of prayers we pray, and we should do what we can to move toward more kingdom prayers. In that vein, allow me to now move on to a category of kingdom prayers I have come to call "life prayers."

A life prayer is a kingdom prayer that has become an individual's constant and fervent intercessory plea to God. It comes from the heart of the believer, and the believer does not forget it from day to day. It becomes an important element of his or her relationship with the Lord, a topic they bring before Him frequently, even daily.

Imagine praying a kingdom prayer so long that it gets "buried in your soul." You pray it over and over, expressing the same request to God to the point that it becomes your heart's consistent cry for God's kingdom. Each time you pray, you are moved to pray that same kingdom prayer. It never grows old for you, and it is always filled with deep meaning and feeling for you. When you pray a kingdom prayer so long, and with such fervency, it can be said to become your life prayer.

There are a couple of good reasons I include teaching on life prayers in our church's prayer ministry, and why I encourage team members and other believers to create and adopt one.

- ♦ The creation (or discovery) of a life prayer, along with the commitment to begin praying it, helps a believer to grow in praying other kingdom prayers.
- ♦ The fervent praying of a life prayer may release important thoughts and feelings a believer has kept buried deep inside. These thoughts and feelings are central to that person, and frequently seem to have been placed there directly by God's Spirit.

Here is my life prayer: "That the American church will begin to value prayer more and become a house of prayer for the nations." Yours may express something that is very important to another area of ministry or that reflects a deep need you consistently notice in the world or community around you.

Maybe the best way to illustrate the concept of a life prayer is to tell about a woman I ran into in Albania one spring on a prayer journey. Suzanna Dabney and her husband, Jack, a pastor, lived in Virginia, and they took on the challenge to pray more strategically for the world. So they began to pray for Albania, not so long ago, when the dictator that ruled had effectively cut it off from the world.

As they prayed one day, God moved Suzanna to go to the store to buy black and white striped "prison cloth" to make curtains for her dining room. She hesitated at first and had many excuses. "God, that will not match what we have in the room." "God, no one carries 'prison cloth.' I could look for years before I'm able to find it."

But the Lord did not let up on Suzanna, and she finally went in search of the fabric that God told her to buy. Not so incredibly—God knows what He's doing—the first store had enough "prison cloth" for her to make curtains for all of the dining room windows! And she made the curtains. Because Suzanna had a heart for those Albanians imprisoned because of their faith, she felt she should keep the curtains drawn. When she heard of a Christian being released from prison in Albania, she would open the curtains for three days, but then close them again to remind her to pray. Suzanna and Jack have nine children, and her curtains attracted quite a bit of attention with all the people and activity around their house. This gave her the opportunity to share her story of prayer for Albania over and over again.

When Albania fell from communism in 1991, Suzanna and Jack were some of the first workers to move there to begin mission work. Now she and Jack are more than eighty years young and have been praying and serving for many, many years!

I love Suzanna's story and the stories of others like her because they teach us to pray the big prayers for others' needs instead of our own all the time. Her story models for us what it means to pray kingdom prayers instead of staying on Aunt Bessie's bunion or our own troubles.

If I were to stick a microphone in front of you and ask, "What are you praying for?" would you have a well thought-out answer? Most of us would likely stammer around a bit before finally saying something like, "I am praying for my wife and kids, for my raise this fall, and for our pastor." Let me be clear, yet again: there is nothing wrong with personal prayers or crisis prayers. However, they should not be the only prayers we pray. *Most of us need to ratchet up our kingdom praying to a higher level.*

Allow me to make a bold claim. I believe the effects on the world and on the church worldwide would be tremendous if every Christian were to discover and consistently pray a life prayer until death or the Lord's return. God's power would be released in all the arenas, transforming lives and communities. As I have been sharing this concept with our prayer team, the results have been exciting to watch. One man has begun praying for the men of our church to step up, and he has started to really lead in prayer. One woman has dedicated herself to pray for the believers in North Korea who are persecuted for their faith.

One way to begin to see some immediate change might be to challenge one entire congregation—your congregation, let's say—of believers to create, or discover, their individual life prayers, and then to watch as God takes the church across the threshold into transformed ministry. But allow me to start by challenging you personally: What are you praying? Are any of your prayers kingdom prayers, or are they mostly personal or crisis prayers? What is your life prayer? Wouldn't this be a good time for you to discover that prayer and begin praying it?

Jericho March

(This idea is adapted from *Jericho March Prayer* by Becky Cerling Powers.)

Many believers are very familiar with the story of Joshua's capture of Jericho in Joshua chapter six. You may recall that Joshua was instructed to march around the city once each day for six days. His men were to be fully armed, and the seven priests were to blow the trumpets of ram's horns in front of the Ark of the Covenant. Then, on the seventh day, Joshua and his men were to march around the city seven times, and again the priests were to blow the ram's horn trumpets before the Ark. When the people heard a long blast on the trumpets they were to give a loud shout, and the walls were to collapse. This event stands for us as a lesson in allowing the Lord to fight the battles for us that would otherwise be unwinnable.

This suggests for us a creative approach to prayer, but our creativity does not need to degenerate into the absurd. I once heard a story about a young man who wanted a certain young woman to marry him, so rather than win her heart the old fashioned way with conversation or even chocolate, he began marching around her once each day, making loud noises and praying for God to give her heart over to him! It didn't work.

But have you ever considered marching around an obstacle or conflict in the same manner as a means of increasing your own faith in prayer for something? For instance, march around a piece of property that you believe the Lord wants to build a sanctuary on and ask Him to give it to you, or march (very discretely!) around the office of a co-worker, the one you can't seem to avoid conflict with, and ask God to remove the tension.

Becky Cerling Powers suggests doing a Jericho march in this way:

1. Read Ephesians 6:10-18 and Joshua 6 every day and pray over what you have read.
2. Ask the Lord to reveal strongholds in your life and reveal their source.
3. On the seventh day, set the day aside and read the material seven times. Then claim victory and watch God work.

How we have applied the Jericho march idea at Central:

1. We read Joshua 6 and Ephesians 6:10-18 every day.
2. We watched for principles and truths we could practice.
3. We asked God to reveal strongholds in our lives.
4. On the seventh day we read those verses seven times, came together, and shared what we had learned.

5. Then we asked God to remove those strongholds and shouted in faith that God would break them down.

It just makes good sense to me to experiment with and apply creative prayer ideas. A Jericho march seems like an exciting way to learn to walk confidently with God in a difficulty.

Practical Techniques to Meditate on God's Word

It is very common to teach Bible study and it is becoming more common to teach prayer. In some circles even the importance of journaling and meditation may be taught, but not many seem to teach how to tie this all together.

The connection and the process seem straightforward enough. We read and study the word to gain insights that point out areas in our lives we need to change. We ponder or meditate on what we have gleaned. We then use the insights from our study and meditation to direct our times of prayer. Our time in Bible study, meditation and journaling produces the words and topics for our prayer time. To study, meditate and journal but not pray over our insights is to miss the most important step, and our quiet time is reduced to a simply academic pursuit.

This material on meditation forms one part of the larger picture of a complete spiritual life, and is offered in hopes it will help you to glean the nuggets of gold that God wants to teach you in your time with Him. I have used each of the methods discussed below in my study and find them all to be helpful. I don't use all of them on each passage, usually only one.

Meditation in Scripture. The word *meditation* is found twenty-two times in our Old Testament and is connected to two root words in the Hebrew language. In those verses, the word has several different shades of meaning, as we can see in these examples:

- Psalm 1:2 says, "But his delight is in the law of the LORD, and on his law he meditates day and night." The meaning is "to murmur" (in pleasure) or "to ponder."
- Psalm 119:99 says, "I have more insight than all my teachers, for I meditate on your statutes." The meaning here is "to contemplate" or "reflect upon something with deep devotion."
- Psalm 19:14 says, "May the words of my mouth and the meditation of my heart . . ." Here the word indicates a musical repetition of God's words.
- Psalm 119:48 says, "I lift up my hands to your commands, which I love, and I meditate on your decrees." In this usage it means "to commune with God in worship."

In summary, for the Christian, meditation is the exercising of the mind that brings us into communion with God that results in choosing to obey His pondered truths. Meditation is being willing to graft God's Word into the way we think, which will produce spiritual fruit in our lives.

Relatively little is written about meditation except from an Eastern tradition. I've never heard a Christian class, session, or seminar on the subject. As we study the people of the Bible, they seemed to have incorporated meditation into their daily lives. We must rediscover the value of meditation. As indicated in Joshua 1:8, God's promise trusted and obeyed leads to God's blessings.

Meditation is so very important because the mind is the battlefield of life. We tend to think that the way to change a habit or sin is to stop the action. Really, though, all actions are the results of thought. The real battle takes place in the mind and our thoughts, long before we ever act. "Nearly ten thousand thoughts pass in and out of our minds daily. God wants as many of these as possible to be spiritually nourishing," Jim Downing writes in Meditation.[26]

Meditation unlocks God's words in our lives. Bill Gothard writes in *Training Faithful Women:*

> The words of Scripture are living words. They are
> eternal wisdom within the shell of human words.
> God wants us to "break open" these human words
> and begin to discover the rich wealth of personal
> application and understanding which are in them.
> This is done through meditation and the teaching
> ministry of the Holy Spirit in us.[27]

A friend of mine once called me out to his house because he had some small pecan tree sprouts to give away. They were still in the ground, growing under his large pecan tree. The sprouts were only six inches tall, so I was convinced that one shovel would dig one up. But to my surprise the taproot was three and a half feet deep. The roots of a tree are vital for nourishment, so they go deep and are strong. Roots secure the tree and carry the food and water that sustain the tree. This system parallels the root system of a human being's spiritual life. The root system needs to be strong and healthy to have a growing spiritual life.

Spiritual Roots. The spiritual roots of a person are nourished in the following activities:

- ◆ Prayer
- ◆ Bible study
- ◆ Memorizing scripture
- ◆ Meditation
- ◆ Service

Each of these, especially in combination with the others, feeds the spiritual life of the believer, steadily propelling him or her upward toward maturity in Christ.

Jim Downing writes in *Meditation*:

> The Christian who knows how to meditate in the
> Word of God has learned the first secret of sinking

that taproot of the soul into the living resources of Christ and drawing from Him the spiritual inflow needed in any time, place, or circumstance. The second clue for the soul's exercise is again Christ, God waters us with divine life. His promise to make our souls a watered garden becomes a reality.[28]

Meditate: Ponder and Pray the Truth You Learned Today. One summer, a fence went down on the family farm where I grew up. In this minor emergency, I was needed to count the cows, make sure they were all accounted for, and keep them from escaping through the downed fence. So I drove out into the pasture in the old farm truck and positioned it between the cows and the downed section of fence. I quickly got bored guarding cows. I became so bored, in fact, that I started counting the number of times a cow ruminated on its cud. I counted the number of times the first cow ruminated, and it was eighty-six times. I counted again and then again, and each time she chewed her cud exactly eighty-six times. Moving over to the next cow, I noted that she chewed her cud ninety-two times. Again I counted her chewing motion over and over and, sure enough, ninety-two times. Every cow I watched did the same thing. They each chewed their cud an exact number of times, and the range was between eighty-five and ninety-five times.

As I pondered my astounding findings, I reflected on our need to ruminate on Scripture. We move too fast and don't get all the nourishment God intended out of our spiritual food. We would be much better off if we would just slow down and regularly pull the richest nutrients from the word by meditation on it. Deepen and enrich this activity even more by praying before and after, and by saturating the entire experience in a prayerful state of attention to God's voice.

Set the Scene to Meditate. If you have just finished working in the yard and are still covered with grass and smell like gasoline and sweat, that's not the time to sit down with your wife for a nice romantic dinner. A little personal prep-work is needed, or the date is not going to have the intended effect. The same goes for meditation; with a little preparation, it all works much better.

Settle Your Life Down. Of course, this requirement for good meditation runs completely contrary to the way we live our lives. We normally live out fractured, fragmented schedules full of appointments and responsibilities we always seem to be just a little behind on. But deliberately set some time apart, blocking it out in red on the daily plan, and then carefully release all your tension, anxiety, and distractions. Meditation is not wasting time. Your time is a love offering to God.

Plan Your Meditation. A process like the following one works well for thorough meditation, but it will require some time. Be ready for the entire process before you begin to read, making sure you have reserved enough time to complete it.

- Read the text, and then write a paraphrase of what you have read.
- Ask and answer questions about the text to be sure you're getting it right.
  For example, read 2 Peter 1:1-4 and answer the following questions:

  ◊ Who is writing?
  ◊ What is the location of the writing and of the recipient?
  ◊ When was it written?
  ◊ How is God pictured in the text?
  ◊ How is Jesus pictured in the text?
  ◊ How is the Holy Spirit pictured in the text?
  ◊ What does this text teach me for my personal life?

♦ Pray the passage in this way:

   ◊ Agree with God's word (the passage you just read).

   ◊ See yourself as God sees you in the passage.

   ◊ Realize and express back to God the integrity of His word.

   ◊ Ask Him if there's something you should stop doing according to this passage.

   ◊ Ask Him if there's something you should change on the basis of the passage.

   ◊ Ask if there's a habit you ought to begin according to this passage.

   ◊ Praise Him for what he reveals to you about Himself from this passage.

   ◊ Thank Him for what he reveals to you and gives you in this passage.

   ◊ Ask yourself, "What can I ask Him for, based on this passage?"

   ◊ Ask yourself, "How can I intercede for someone else based on this passage?"

♦ **Reread It.** This time try emphasizing different words or phrases in prayerful attention to differences in meaning. Isaiah 26:3, for instance:

"*You* will keep in perfect peace him whose mind is steadfast, because he trusts in you."

"You *will keep* in perfect peace him whose mind is steadfast, because he trusts in you."

"You will keep *in perfect peace* him whose mind is steadfast, because he trusts in you."

"You will keep in perfect peace *him whose mind* is steadfast, because he trusts in you."

"You will keep in perfect peace him whose mind *is steadfast*, because he trusts in you."

"You will keep in perfect peace him whose mind is steadfast, *because he trusts* in you."

"You will keep in perfect peace him whose mind is steadfast, because he trusts *in you*."

- ◆ **Cross-Reference.** For more clarity, look up any cross-references you can find for the verse you are meditating on. This is especially helpful in reading the gospels. There is material in John that is not in the three synoptic gospels.
- ◆ **Ponder the Writer.** Picture him expressing this message. Visualize the scene. Assume the role of the character. Use your senses—smell, touch, hearing, sight, and taste—to understand better.
- ◆ **Read the Text from Another Translation.** Here's Romans 12:1-2, for example:

Therefore, I urge you, brothers, in view of God's mercy, to offer your bodies as living sacrifices, holy and pleasing to God—this is your spiritual act of worship. Do not conform any longer to the pattern of this world, but be transformed by the renewing of your mind. Then you will be able to test and approve what God's will is—his good, pleasing and perfect will (NIV).

With eyes wide open to the mercies of God, I beg
you, my brothers, as an act of intelligent worship, to
give him your bodies, as a living sacrifice,
consecrated to him and acceptable by him. Don't let
the world around you squeeze you into its own
mould, but let God re-mould your minds from
within, so that you may prove in practice that the
plan of God for you is good, meets all his demands
and moves towards the goal of true maturity (Phillips[29])

·

- ♦ **Personalize It.** Use the words "I," "my," and "me" in the
  passage so that the verse becomes more personal. For
  example, try using this method with a verse you have read
  many times to bring new life to the ideas. John 3:16 gains
  personal meaning: "For God so loved the world (me) that he
  gave his one and only Son, that whoever (even me) believes
  in him shall not perish (I shall not perish) but have
  eternal life."
- ♦ **Express the Opposite.** Again, John 3:16 is a very familiar
  verse, but if we reflect on the opposite of this verse we may
  get a greatly improved idea of the depth of the meaning.
  "For God so hated the world that he did not send his son
  and we were not eligible for eternal life."
- ♦ **Get Creative.** Write a poem or song based on the truths
  you've learned.
- ♦ **Memorize Scripture.** Memorization is an excellent way to
  internalize the meaning of God's word.
- ♦ **Listen to God.** Just sit quietly, intently listening for what He
  has to say to you.

Discern God's Voice

When He speaks to us directly, God's voice is unusual in
content. By this I mean its messages are better than and different

from my own private thoughts, my internal voice. Occasionally, a thought will pop into my head that is obviously not from me. It will be noticeably kinder than I usually am. It will be wiser than I am naturally, and often it will prompt me do something for someone that will both stretch me and turn out to be an unimaginably great blessing for them and for me. I have come to believe these prompts are from the Lord. If you invest significant time in prayerful meditation, you may begin to recognize His prompts very clearly. It is wonderful to know that the Spirit of God is communicating so clearly and directly with you, and to realize that you understand what He's saying.

Another identifying characteristic of God's voice is that it may come to you very clearly in the first person ("I"), speaking to you as the other person. "I want you to speak my truth to the man next door today."

Be sure to measure any thoughts or impressions by the Word of God. God's voice will be completely consistent with His word; if they are not consistent with His word, they are not from Him at all. For example, several times I have spoken at some length with people who have become involved in an extramarital affair. They say things like, "I know this is not how it is normally supposed to happen, but God has put us together and we are perfect for each other." Sometimes they even say, "I've prayed about this a lot, and that has only confirmed, it's definitely from God." When this happens I struggle to contain my reaction, because we know that God will not lead us in ways that are contrary to His revealed will in Scripture.

Just a Thought Before Bedtime

One of my greatest heroes is Dawson Trotman, who was the founder of The Navigators. If you haven't read his biography, *Daws: The Story of Dawson Trotman, Founder of the Navigators*, by Betty Lee Skinner[30], I highly recommend it. One of the ways Trotman used to meditate on Scripture was to think of a passage right before he went to sleep, and then fall asleep with that verse in his mind. All night long his subconscious mind would work on that verse. Trotman believed this method helped him gain some great insights, not to mention some very peaceful sleep. He taught his disciples these letters, H.W.L.W., which stood for "His Word the Last Word" on my mind. Give Trotman's method a try tonight, and give God the night key to your heart.

THRESHOLD

Multisite Prayer Ministry and Other Trends

*One should never initiate anything
that he cannot saturate with prayer.*
—Samuel Dickey Gordon

Let's be unflinchingly honest. Despite positive trends in some areas of ministry around the country, and despite the growth of megachurches and effective multisite ministries, it appears to me that the most important trends to report with regard to the topic of this book are all negative: the American church is losing prayer. Prayer meetings are sparsely attended, and teaching about prayer seldom reaches the preaching rotation. The message of prayer is buried behind leadership lessons and building campaigns. More attention is given to the lights and sound systems in many churches than to praying. In some churches, what little prayer there is seems more concerned with providing a good transition from one service element to another than it is about talking to God.

Andrew Murray in his book, *With Christ in the School of Prayer,* points out that Jesus spent time teaching us to pray, but no time teaching us to preach. Yet in most Bible colleges and seminaries not even one class on prayer is offered. Prayer may be included in some other class, but a full semester class on prayer is seldom taught. Something is wrong with this picture.

And *consequently* (please don't miss the weight of that word) our people are very weak in prayer. Most don't like to pray out loud, and too many prayer ministries have a hard time bringing men in to their ranks. If people can't pray, important communication with God simply is not happening. Who, do you suppose, wants it that way?

All of this leads us to ask the question, Why? Part of the answer lies in our vision of success. When we think of success, we may think of megachurches and lots of people. Megachurches like the one I serve are obviously playing an important role in American Christianity. But what does *success* in ministry really look like? Is it the number of people filling the seats, or are there other areas that need to be measured for a more complete picture of "success?"

Consider the countercultural thought that *equipping people to pray and teaching them to feed themselves is a path to the kind of success Jesus appreciates.* Success is not found in the drawing of crowds, and certainly not in drawing great crowds at any price. Jesus described His church as a house of prayer for the nations, not as a Mecca for entertainment, and not even as a place to hear our favorite speakers. Now, please don't think I am not in favor of good music and good preaching and teaching. I am! But I'm in favor of using those good, God-given tools to draw people to genuine worship and prayer and spiritual depth, not just to repeatedly lure weak believers to keep showing up at the building.

What the church in America needs is an awakening like we saw in the Fulton Street Revival described in Chapter 1. But awakenings usually seem to come out of hard times, and we are still too affluent to truly feel our need for God. We also need a challenge. Men pray like warriors and need something to kill or a mountain to scale when they pray. Most prayer meetings are not taking or killing anything, and men are bored.

Everywhere we look, it appears that programs and events are losing spiritual steam. But there are, in fact, places where transformation is occurring. Those are the places where we are seeing growth in prayer ministry, men praying, and new models of success. These are the ministries we need to examine closely to discover what they have discovered.

What Is Working in Prayer in America Today?

Focus on Repentance. God seems to always bless where there is genuine repentance. Preaching of truth under the leading of the Spirit leads to conviction of sin and realization of wrong thinking and wrong directions. Churches and individuals who turn to God dramatically and radically are seeing growth.

Following God's Agenda Instead of Ours. When people are willing to set aside personal goals and wishes, and especially their own comfort, and instead take on a mandate from God, the blessing will not be far behind. God's agenda is discovered through intensive prayer and searching of the word by God-focused, not self-focused, individuals and churches.

Uniting the Brothers. You can bet you will find the hand of God where you find people in unity. Psalm 133:1 says, "How good and pleasant it is when brothers live together in unity!" But how do we achieve it, when we all come from such different backgrounds and have such widely divergent interests? Not surprisingly, perhaps, the answer is to be found in times of praying together.

> Five times in the first five chapters of Acts, Scripture records that the disciples were in one accord. In each instance the Greek word *homothumadon* is used. The word is a compound from *homs* meaning 'same or together' and *thumos* meaning 'passion, anger, fierceness, wrath, indignation, heat, or glow.' Joining

these concepts together, the word can be understood as the same burning of heart, or same heart passion.[31]

Principles That Lead to Trends and Movements

Community Prayer Meetings Work Well. One of the best opportunities for adding momentum lies in community-wide and multichurch prayer events. Frequently there is not enough interest or not enough room in the budget at a single church to administrate, advertise and host a larger event. Yet the larger events are exactly what is needed to raise interest in prayer. Small events can unfortunately give the impression that the topic is unimportant, or not of general interest. It is helpful in prayer promotion at a large church to announce that a large regional event will be held nearby.

But Community Prayer Meetings Will Not Work Well at One Church's Location. Pastors are very protective of their flock, so to hold the prayer meeting or event at "the big church down the street" is threatening to some pastors. Prayer meetings seem to work best at neutral sites so that no one feels threatened, or that others are unfairly advantaged. I have seen this principle play out in a number of settings.

Senior Leadership Is Critical to Effective Prayer Ministries. Dee Duke, senior pastor of the Jefferson Baptist Church, is leading the way in this area. There are twenty prayer meetings each week at their church, and he also puts together three week-long prayer events each year. One week focuses on prayer for the ministry there in Jefferson, another one focuses on their Easter services and the people who will attend, and one is specifically for missions. These prayer focus events run for five days and are designed for fifty hours of prayer per week. Each hour starts promptly on time, beginning with a small devotion on the value of prayer; then they pray for forty-five minutes. They take a fifteen-minute break, and then begin again on the hour. The prayer weeks at Jefferson average fifty people praying per hour.

The secret lies with Dee. Because Dee is the senior pastor, he can exert tremendous influence on the direction of the church. Because he has a heart for prayer, his church has more prayer ministry—and *more prayer*—than most. There is no getting around it: senior leadership plays a significant role in establishing the value placed on prayer ministry in the church.

Juan Ramos, an inner-city preacher here in Phoenix, also understands this concept. He has a midweek prayer meeting with over a thousand attending each week. One week he brought all the men forward for prayer, and he prayed over them. Then they encircled the worship center and prayed for the women and children in the audience that night. This kind of powerful prayer experience for the whole church is really only possible in the context of a senior pastor who is completely committed to prayer and prayer ministry.

Understand What Moves Men to Pray. If you have been reading straight through this book, you already know that I believe deeply in the necessity of getting *men* to pray. The thing is, most men seem to pray out of a sense of *brotherhood* more than as a result of any program we might start up. When men feel like they belong to a brotherhood, they'll do what it takes to learn to pray. Creating that kind of environment for men is the trick, and therefore it is an essential short-term goal to be achieved in reaching the long-term goals of creating a house of prayer and crossing the threshold with the entire church.

Beyond a sense of brotherhood, men also need to be *inspired by the vision* of your prayer ministry *and by you or another leader* who is seeing results in prayer. For this reason, give books away and put quotes on prayer up on your door. And make them look masculine, not frilly and soft. Tell inspiring stories about prayer and your prayer ministry, and about God conquering problems through it, making a real difference. *Stories and testimonies* about answered prayer and changed lives can capture men's hearts.

Tell about *other men praying*. There is a simple story I like to tell to encourage men to pray. Several of us were in the prayer room when a women and her husband came in. They looked a little confused, so I began to explain our prayer room and how it works. My words seemed to satisfy her, but he looked uncomfortable. Eventually he whispered something to her and then left. About ten minutes later he returned and said, "I wasn't sure I wanted to pray for an hour, but God told me to get back in here." And he loved it.

Every story you can find about men praying should be told many times, put in the prayer newsletter, and leveraged for all it is worth. All this storytelling is part of the prayer leader's job, if he or she wants men to learn the benefits of praying.

Go Organic. Understand that *prayer works best when it is organic*, not in a program. I will discuss organic prayer again in some detail below as a goal of multisite prayer ministry, but here it is important to just establish the principle. Organic (or natural) prayer is something that leads naturally to movements and positive trends in prayer, and organic prayer is always better.

It's also true, and it just stands to reason, that *programs for prayer are always better when they lead to organic prayer*. Building easy-access prayer into each ministry, small group, and campus is the best way to put organic prayer opportunities in everyone's path. But you will "naturally" find when you allow prayer to be organic that some ministries, groups, and campus prayer leaders will capture the vision better than others, so there will be more and better prayer at some venues or in some groups than in others.

Prayer Ministry for the Multisite Church

Multisite or multicampus churches are probably the most important trend in the American church today. But if you are not a member of one of these large, multisite churches, even the very concept of a church with multiple locations - but sharing one preaching pastor and one leadership - may seem a bit alien. The campuses themselves may even be spread across a broad geographical area; in fact, some multisite churches have campuses so far apart they can no longer be said to be in the same area at all. It only makes sense to ask the question, "How can we even *begin* to envision an effective prayer ministry at six or eight campuses?"

But there can be no doubt that the trend of multisite ministries is already well established and growing dramatically, and this can only mean that an effective solution for multisite prayer ministry *must* be identified. The following statements by some of the leading thinkers in the field of multiple-campus churches begin to answer our prayer ministry question by shedding some light on the purpose of multisite ministry in general:

> The multisite movement is a strategic response to the question of how to maintain momentum and growth while not being limited to the monolithic structure of a mega church.[32]

And the following is from the Multisite Solutions website (http://multisitesolutions.com/), which is probably the primary source and hub for multisite ministry ideas. It describes the situation clearly:

> The multisite church models continue to grow in acceptance as legitimate, effective vehicles for outreach, volunteer mobilization, leadership development and regional impact. There are over 3,000 expressions of multisite church across North America. Fifty percent of mega churches have multiple campuses and another 20 percent are thinking about it. The multisite movement has grown so rapidly that it has outgrown the mega church movement in size. Each multisite church is unique, but there are some common trends emerging we can learn from.

Since this movement began in the mid-1990s, over 3,000 churches have embraced the multi church model and their number is growing daily. *Outreach Magazine* declared in 2007 that the multisite model is no longer a trend, but the "new normal." A survey by Lifeway Research in 2008 revealed that 45,000 churches "are seriously considering adding a worship service at one or more new locations or campuses in the next two years." In 2009, an estimated 5 million people, 10% of Protestant church-goers, attend a multisite church on Sunday across North America.

As people of prayer who believe in the ministry of the church, we must find and champion effective means to create models for prayer ministry that will have applications for multisite church models. In fact, on the basis of the statistics mentioned above, we might even say we *especially need to focus on prayer ministry models suitable for multisite churches.*

The wonderful news is that there is a very bright positive side of the multisite trend for prayer in America. If *Outreach Magazine*'s assertion that nine of the ten largest churches in America are multisite churches[33] is correct, this means that *an effective model for prayer ministry can quickly and conveniently affect the prayer practices of a large percentage of the potential praying believers in the country.* And those believers will already attend the *de facto* trend-setting churches for the country and the world. Things can change.

Let's go back and look again briefly at the basics of how multisite churches work. This is from the Multisite Solutions website:

> Multisite churches are just that: one church on multiple locations, all under one leadership and doing the same basic ministry. There are two characteristics that distinguish multisite campuses

from local churches: multisite campuses are centrally governed and centrally-budgeted (as opposed to self-governed and self-budgeted locally)" (emphasis added).

Since the multisite ministry style this describes is identical to that of Central, where I serve, we needed to look for answers to practical prayer ministry questions for a bigger picture than just the main campus of Central. And the answer seemed obvious to me: Build a prayer ministry model that will work in one church, ideally the main campus you attend, and that is transferable to your satellite campuses.

No matter what your multisite church's growth model is, you must determine leadership structure. There are essentially two options for this:

♦ **Localized Model.** Each church site makes its own decisions.
♦ **Centralized Model.** Decisions come from the main church.

The good news is that the answer is essentially the same for both. With either model, to do multisite prayer ministry well you must master prayer ministry on a single location first. Then it is a matter of multiplying what you do to the multiple sites. Once you have it figured out for one location you can begin to export the ministry to other locations.

Again, the Absolute Best Prayer Is Organic Prayer. It is important to pause here to emphasize a couple points about organic prayer, understanding that it may seem out-of-place in a discussion about big-program, multisite churches. You will see why it is so important.

By "organic prayer," I mean prayer that happens spontaneously and naturally, such as in small groups when a need is made known, at the end of a service when people are moved to pray by what they've just heard, or over the phone when we are talking together about everyday life. These prayer times are not on the tech-team's service planner or the church calendar. Un-programmed, natural prayer that takes place in the life of the local church is organic prayer. It does not appear to me that there was a "prayer ministry" in the New Testament church. The believers simply prayed organically - in great abundance - and the church flourished, *living* across the threshold.

Because this is not happening today in most churches, *we must intentionally build systems to encourage prayer that will lead to organic prayer in every fiber of every local church,* multisite or not. And this principle will also, to a great extent, need to dictate how we structure our multisite prayer ministry, because it dictates how we begin, from the first day on, to make prayer organic at the *first* campus.

If we need to build an entire system to encourage organic prayer on multiple campuses, we find the system that works best is to have *centralized direction* in prayer ministry and general *campus-specific freedom of expression* of the prayer ministry. In other words, the Prayer Pastor and leadership set the vision and course for prayer in the church at large (for all campuses), and each campus prayer leader oversees the prayer ministry on that campus. The result will be that prayer ministry will look similar on each location, but it will not be identical.

This is because each Campus Prayer Leader has different gifts and different strengths, and because "organic" ministry of any kind is an outgrowth of the people involved and their God-given gifts. We want to allow for these differences within accepted parameters, and without damaging the work in total. The prayer ministry will take on the strengths of the Campus Prayer Leader and the church, just as a church often takes on the emphasis of the senior pastor.

When we began to develop our prayer ministry at Central, Cathy and I spent almost all our time getting prayer ministry right on just one location. Now we spend our time working with the campus prayer leaders. Each Campus Prayer Leader reports to the Prayer Pastor for direction and input.

Org Chart

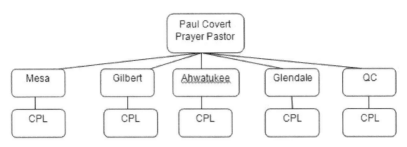

*CPL = Campus Prayer Leader

The keys to multisite prayer ministry are the Campus Prayer Leader and the leadership of the team of those leaders by the Prayer Pastor. This is his highest work priority.

At Central, for example, we have Campus Prayer Leaders, all of whom are volunteers (see the organizational chart above). It is their job to encourage prayer, build leaders, and facilitate the prayer on their particular campus, and to specifically pray for their campus pastor. Again, not all campuses' prayer ministries look completely alike, but they are similar. The Prayer Pastor meets at least monthly with the Campus Prayer Leaders. As of this writing, Central has five campuses and five Campus Prayer Leaders.

Our goal at Central is to put a leader on each campus who "owns" that campus's prayer ministry, and then to work with him or her to make sure that ministry is successful. They lead their ministry on their respective campuses, while I rotate between campuses to encourage, cheer them on, and help recruit.

I also meet with the Campus Prayer Leaders quarterly in a large team meeting. We pray for Cal (our senior pastor) and for the chairman of our elders, and then we spend some time talking about upcoming events, needs, and churchwide directional shifts they need to be aware of.

Profile of a Campus Prayer Leader. He or she:

♦ Is a team player.
♦ Has strong relational skills.
♦ Buys into the church's vision.
♦ Is loyal to the church's leadership.
♦ Is able to build a team.
♦ Is able to reproduce vision in others.
♦ Is able to shepherd others.
♦ Is flexible.
♦ Has an entrepreneurial mindset. [34]

Here are other characteristics by which to recognize good new leaders in general. He or she:

♦ Is a respectful discontent with the status quo.
♦ Is a practical thinker.
♦ Has others following his or her leadership.
♦ Is thick-skinned.
♦ Is respected by others.
♦ Can catch vision and pass it on.
♦ Is not afraid of responsibility or work.
♦ Completes jobs on time.
♦ Ability to confront well (when necessary). [35]

It is important, as we have discussed before, to be purposeful in the gender of the person you select for a Campus Prayer Leader position. Remember, most prayer ministries are led by women. If you select a woman, many of your men will migrate to another ministry. That does not mean that you should not select a woman, but this is a decision that will require much prayer and wisdom. We are, in fact, considering a woman for one of our campuses.

More Notes from Central's Example. We organize some events and projects for all campuses as all-church prayer initiatives, while others involve only one campus. It is important to note that our campuses are not very geographically close to each other. From Mesa to Gilbert is only ten miles, but from the Mesa campus to the Glendale campus is ninety miles or so round trip, right across the heart of the Phoenix metropolitan area. This consideration determines in very practical ways how we do ministry.

For example, we do 24-7 (see chapter 7) each year in November. This is a major event that takes months to put together, and about six to eight hours to set up. This year, we will do the 24-7 on the Mesa campus and ask all the other campuses to participate at Mesa this time. Again this year, we will continue to experiment with putting the 24-7 completely online so people can participate from anywhere in the valley and even around the world. We call it a *Virtual 24-7*. Originally we tried picking up the 24-7 and moving it whole from one campus to the next. This worked well enough with only two or three campuses, but now that we have five it is no longer practical. This is the kind of decision and the kind of change that multisite churches face continually.

Another example of an all-church prayer event is the School of Prayer. Our next SOP will be held on the Mesa Campus live, but we will also be videotaping it for showing by the Campus Prayer Leader on two, or maybe three, other campuses. The logistics are always complicated, because some of our campuses meet in schools and we only have a small window for showing the SOP material, which is four hours long. So we will need to find a creative solution, such as showing it in a home over a couple of nights.

We did the same thing with the National Day of Prayer. We put together an online version of the NDP events, so that no matter where you live in the Phoenix valley you could take part. We called this online version *2013*. We asked each small group or family to carve out thirteen minutes to pray for our nation. That may not seem like a long enough time, but it was the hook to get them started. Then we provided twenty specific prayer requests for the nation. (See the Appendix for the list). We also allowed the campus prayer leaders to determine what their campuses would do for this special day. Three campuses did a Thursday evening prayer meeting, using the material we provided. One campus did a come-and-go prayer time from noon to 7 p.m., during which people could come individually to the church for prayer. Each campus' effort was effective, and each reflected the church's overall prayer ministry vision, as well as the DNA of the respective Campus Prayer Leader.

We have a midweek prayer meeting on the Mesa campus called *Lift*. We tried it at the Gilbert campus, but it never took hold, so we don't do it there anymore. It is only offered at the Mesa campus for now. The Gilbert campus has more new believers than the Mesa campus, so it is possible we attempted that midweek meeting too soon for that campus. As the Gilbert campus's believers continue to mature we will look again at offering it there.

Many prayer events are suitable for all campuses. For example, we pray during every service on every campus. This is a high priority ministry, so we do it at all five campuses.

Prayer Ministry Elements for All Campuses. The elements are part of the ministry on all campuses:

- Prayer Partners
- Service Intercession
- Prayer Room
- Prayer Journeys
- Prayer Initiatives
- Entry of prayer requests from weekend services

Internet-Based Ministries. These are suitable for all campuses and members.

- Web Prayer
- UpTeam
- Daily Prayer Devotional

- Podcasts
- E-accountability group s

Ministries We Do on One or More Campuses. These depend on the gifts of the Campus Prayer Pastor, venue availability, maturity of the congregation, and expense.

- Prayer Garden
- School of Prayer
- Prayer Conference
- 24-7
- Lift (midweek event)
- Half Day in Prayer

When planning events, make sure you ask yourself the question, "Can we sustain this event for the long haul, and will it work when our church is larger than it is now?" I learned this lesson the hard way. When Annie and I started the church we planted in 1984, we used to invite the new people to our home for dinner. This worked well until we outgrew the nights we had available for it. Eventually we began hearing remarks like these, "You wanted to be our friends until we joined the church, but after we did, you moved on." In some ways that was true, because we were trying to reach as many people as possible. The idea was intended to help people get plugged in to the church and then help them begin to serve in some of the same ways we were serving. But we started something we could not sustain, and it ended up backfiring on us, even though our hearts were completely in the right place. Always think carefully before starting something.

Questions. There are still many questions to be answered concerning multisite prayer ministry around the country:

1. Which multisite models are working best for prayer in multisite ministries?

2. Is one multisite model actually more effective than the others, or does the effectiveness rest with the leadership abilities of the champion who oversees the work?
3. Who is doing a great job with innovation and leadership in multisite prayer right now? What new ideas are out there waiting to be shared?
4. Why is so little written on this subject?
5. Are all multisite churches working on implementing a model for prayer? If not, why not? Shouldn't this be included in the overall multisite plan?

Probably Any Model Will Work, If . . . If there is *enough effort*, if the *right leader* is in place, and if *God is getting the glory*, success in crossing the threshold is likely for various groups and ministries of even the largest church. The DNA carrier must be a strong leader who can lead the others who work at the different campuses and help the team to think of the multisite needs and opportunities that might be unmet or underutilized. The church leadership will need to plan into their calendar some all-church prayer initiatives to keep prayer in front of the people. These will help the whole church focus on prayer.

Joel Schmidgall, the executive pastor who oversees the prayer work at Mark Batterson's theater church in Washington, DC, shared an easy-to-implement good idea from their church's experience. It's an unusual method, used to raise the value of prayer among all their people at once: they put *nothing but prayer information* in their church bulletin for one Sunday, for all campuses. This bulletin includes information on prayer gatherings, all-church prayer needs, the prayer leadership's vision, and upcoming initiatives.

Fresh ideas like these are needed to unify large and multisite churches around prayer, and to move them across the threshold. It is important that innovators not keep their ideas to themselves because other leaders are out there seeking creative solutions to real problems.

CHAPTER 15

Prayer Help for Life Groups

There has never been a spiritual awakening in any country or locality that did not begin in united prayer.
—A.T. Pierson

Much of what has already been written in this book, maybe most of it, has some potential for application to small group ministry. But it just makes good sense to very specifically and intentionally make use of the many opportunities for organic prayer that small groups provide. Again, *the very best kind of prayer is organic prayer.* Small groups are the most organic (and most organic-prayer-friendly) groups in most churches. In this chapter, we will look at some creative approaches to getting a life group praying together to maximize organic prayer.

Specific Suggestions for Prayer in a Life Group

Prayer in a group can get stale, no matter who is leading it. One of the best things you can do to keep it fresh is to mix up the way you pray in your group. Here are several ideas to experiment with in your groups. Enjoy!

For Beginning Groups: Get Them Started. It's important to keep the goal in mind and to plan activities accordingly. In the case of new groups or groups that haven't yet learned to pray well together, the goal is simply to get them started. Try some of these activities:

- **Silent Intercessions.** The leader reads a general concern, and is then silent. Time is then taken to silently pray for specific people, actions, and ministries involved with that general concern. Then, after a short while, the leader speaks a word of the Bible relating to that concern, and prays briefly about it.
- **Learn to Pray Sentence Prayers.** "God, give Mary the wisdom she needs to deal with this _____." This is a simple way to get inexperienced pray-ers started. All they have to do is repeat the sentence and add in the one thing they want to pray for Mary. Everyone can do this one.
- **Focus Sentence Prayers for the Evening.** Themes might include the following:

  ◊ World missions
  ◊ The lost and unchurched
  ◊ Christian leaders
  ◊ Local church staff and ministries

  This is basically the same method previously described except that a theme is provided instead of a person. "God, help our global workers to _____."

- **Read Your Prayers.** Have each group member take the time to write out a prayer in class time and read it out loud as a prayer. Open and close the session as leader by asking God to "hear these written prayers of Your people."
- **Written Responsorial Prayers.** Those in liturgical churches know these from worship services. A petition is offered, then ended with a clear "ending tag," such as, "O Lord" or "in Jesus' name," followed by a standard response spoken by all, such as "hear our prayer" or "let it happen, Lord". Then the next written petition is spoken, and so on. (The tags and

responses can be more complex or specific than these, but simple often works best.)

For Groups That Are Farther Along, Add Content and Creativity

- **Pray in Groups of Two.** Pair men with men and women with women. Prayer needs are discussed briefly, then each person prays for the other's requests.
- **Use a Model.** Try the ACTS model, or one of the other patterns shared in Chapter 9 of this book, for prayer in your group.
- **Pray Through a Psalm.** Do so out loud together, expressing thanks, personal requests or intercessory requests based on the thoughts of the Psalm. You will probably need to help a group with this method at first, but most will catch on and love praying this way.
- **Thank God for His Promises.** Each group member thanks God in a short prayer for one promise in His word that is particularly important to him or her, expressing to Him why this promise is so personally meaningful.
- **Pray the Promises of God.** An extension of thanking God for His promises as above, in this kind of prayer the group expands on His promises, praying for needs that require specific, real-life answers on the basis of those promises.
- **Pray Your Favorite Verse.** Each group member is given the opportunity to express thoughts from his or her favorite passage of Scripture as thanks to God or as a personal request or even as an intercessory prayer.
- **Basket of Prayer.** Each person writes on a slip of paper one request that is on his or her heart. The papers are gathered in a basket and read aloud, and the group prays over them. This can be done by reading each one or leaving them unread all together in the basket. This method is especially

suitable for those rare cases for which it may be best to keep requests anonymous.

♦ **Targeted Evangelism Praying.** Each person in the group names *one* person that they most want to see turn to Christ, someone from work, a sports or hobby group, family, or other non-religious activities. It should be someone they know personally, and someone they meet in the course of their daily lives. After each one is spoken, the group then prays for an opportunity for the person who made the request to witness to this person, and also for other believers to have opportunities to speak to him or her.

♦ **Echoes.** Someone speaks a phrase of Psalm or hymn or a very specific prayer. Then each person repeats the phrase, with short breaks in between each time it is spoken. This gives everyone time to think on the phrase, or to silently let it sink in, listening for some stirrings within.

♦ **Group Confession and Sin Destruction.** One creative approach is for a leader to speak briefly about a general category of sin to awake a sense of conviction about this sin. Everyone then writes, on small slips of paper, a few words to express a specific instance of committing that kind of sin. These confessions are *not* to be read by anyone; this is between them and God. The papers are then collected in a cooking container. The group gathers around it and read aloud together a printed prayer of confession and sorrowful repentance for that kind of sin, expressing sincere determination to cease committing it. Then all go with the container to a *safe* place for a fire, and then someone sets the slips of paper on fire, allowing them to burn completely to ash. (Be sure to have something on hand to douse or smother it with in case of flare-up!) Once this is done, someone expresses thanks to God on behalf of the group that these sins are forgiven through Christ's work on the cross.

- **Personal Prayer for Strong Personal Needs ("Hot Seat" Prayer).** Sometimes, in a group setting, someone will be so hurt by life or so moved by the group or its actions that they will break down in tears. Other times the composure may hold, but the need for prayer is acute, and prayer is requested. Either way, ask that person to take a seat in the middle of the group. (This seat is known in some circles as the "hot seat.") Then ask him or her to begin praying, preferably aloud, about the specific need that is creating the burden. While he or she is praying, the others gather around, laying their hands on him or her and praying until a sense of comfort about the matter is given, or until that person brings the session to an end by saying an "amen."

- **"Jackson-Style" Prayer.** In this form of group prayer, everyone prays out loud at the same time. Experience has shown this to be a wonderful way to help people get comfortable with praying out loud, because it takes away the self-consciousness that comes from being the only one speaking.

- Don't forget the "Two Men in the Middle" and "Distilling God's Direction" exercises for group prayer, described in Chapter 9.

Small Group Prayer Request List Recommendations

If we are not careful and thoughtful, our prayer list for small groups will become unmanageably large, not to mention very "me" or "us" focused. The following guidelines will help to keep your group on track and your list under control.

Only Pray for People Who Are Close Family Members in a Small Group Setting. It is harder for people to pray with passion for requests when they don't know the people involved. By limiting requests, the leader helps ensure pray-ers will respond energetically and frequently to the needs that are presented.

Emphasize the Importance of Sharing "Acute" Situations. Encouraging your group to intercede for common requests makes the list much longer and keeps the focus on us. Asking group members for acute needs will limit the number of "Aunt Bertha's big toe" requests and allow the group to focus on the most important needs of the group.

Challenge the Group to Share at Least as Many "Kingdom Prayer Requests" as Requests for Themselves. Most American believers seem to have a tendency to share many prayer requests that make our lives better. Kingdom requests are for needs such as these:

- Requests for the people in our Crossroads (addiction recovery) ministry program who are struggling with addictions.
- For the church members who lead this program, that they will be effective and motivating to those who are trying to get free.
- That the Acts Ministry outreach to the homeless each month be effective in getting people back on their feet.

Use Index Cards for Personal Prayer Requests. We have probably all been in groups in which someone went on and on with their personal prayer request. By handing out cards as people come in and asking them to write out their prayer requests, you can limit the amount of information that can be shared. This way no request can be too long.

Important! Get Permission to Post a Request from the Person Involved. It would be very bad and maybe damaging to someone to read their name and need on a Small Group Prayer List for which they did not give their permission. Before you share a request with the group, ask the person if they mind you including them in your small group prayer list.

Be Very Cautious About Putting Sensitive and Specific Information on a Public Prayer List. At Central, we often sanitize a list so that the need is mentioned but the details are concealed. The following "unsanitized" request would not be a good one to publish: "Pray for no good husband and Betty Sue. They are, right now, down at the Hoot Owl bar. She says, 'Her ex-husband will kill my husband if he . . .'" We might record this in the following fashion. "Pray for Mary and her husband as they work on some marriage issues."

Avoid Including Unspoken or Anonymous Requests. Reserve the list for requests that can be prayed for knowledgably. While God will know whom you are praying for, only the most dedicated intercessors will venture prayer for unknown needs.

Purge the List Every Two Weeks. Doing so helps to keep it fresh. Some items will be ongoing and will need to be added again, but for most issues two weeks will be enough time.

Pick Out Something Your Group Can Pray for Together. This topic could be a ministry your group will continually pray for to help keep you others-focused—the student ministry or a global ministry worker, for example.

What You, the Leader, Need to Do

As a group leader, your role in helping your group pray together is essential. For instance, you must actively pray for your small group members to learn to pray. This both models the prayerfulness you want to teach and brings God's power into the project. You will also need to inform the group that you will be teaching them to pray during this session of small groups. Then you must effectively lead them to begin praying in a manner that will allow even the beginners to feel comfortable.

You will also want to explain the benefits of praying together as a group:

- ◆ Awareness of needs
- ◆ Meeting of needs
- ◆ Answered prayer
- ◆ Resistance to Satan's attacks

- ♦ Overcoming self-consciousness
- ♦ Growing closer to each other
- ♦ Sharing joy and pain together

Make sure to keep a prayer journal so you can point out answered prayers and thank the Lord for them together. This will reinforce the effectiveness of prayer.

As a final suggestion, at Central we determined we needed to write a Bible study on prayer for small groups, and such a study is something I recommend for any group that is intent on becoming adept at prayer. Our study was designed to give our small group leaders a break from teaching, while at the same time allowing the group to learn to love to pray. Cathy and I gave some input for our study material, and Andrew E. Moore, one of our prayer leaders at Central, wrote it up for us. We hope to make this material available soon.

Conclusion

"With man this is impossible, but with God all things are possible."
(Matthew 19:26b)

The "Even If" Principle

2 Kings 7:2 describes a desperate scene. The Arameans had laid siege to the city of Samaria. There was a famine in the land, and conditions in the city were truly hopeless from any normal human perspective.

In the midst of this darkness, the prophet Elisha matter-of-factly predicts one day that by the same time the next day food would be abundant. At this, the officer who attended to the king states his incredulity at Elisha's audacious prediction, saying, "*Even if* the Lord should open the windows of heaven, this prediction couldn't come to pass" (my paraphrase). The story's action continues at twilight, with four lepers making a decision to go over to the Aramean camp out of desperation. They thought, "If we stay here we will die of starvation. If we go over there and they spare us, we live, and if they kill us we have lost nothing."

But when they got to the Arameans' camp, what they saw was beyond belief. The Lord had caused the Arameans to hear the sound of chariots, horses and a great army. They had become so afraid that they dropped everything and fled for their homeland. So the lepers ate and drank and looted some tents of valuable items.

They hid some of the spoils, but then decided to tell the others in the city about their good fortune.

So they went back and called out to the gatekeeper all that had transpired. He relayed the message to the king, but the King was convinced it was a trap. So he sent out a few soldiers to investigate. They returned with news that verified what the lepers had said. Pandemonium broke out among the starving people as each hurried out of the city to get his share of the plunder from the Aramean camp. The king had assigned his officer to the gate (the same officer that had said, "even if the Lord should open the windows of heaven, this could not happen"). He was trampled to death when the people ran out to get their share of the bounty. He had exactly the wrong kind of "even if" faith.

I have thought about this passage many times, and I believe it teaches us a number of lessons. For one, we must have the other, right kind of "even if" faith, the kind Elisha must have had. This is the kind of faith that says from the heart, "Even if I can see no hope in my surroundings, I will trust in God, and I will pray to Him for what I need." And, "Even if everyone else is faithless and against me, I will have faith."

This story also teaches that we should never doubt God's provision for life or ministry. Those times when it looks like it is all completely impossible are the times when God will do His greatest work. Learn to love these times, because they are the occasions that force us to trust God in all new ways, to all new heights, and for the deepest of life's needs.

We find the right kind of "even if" faith in Shadrach, Meshach and Abednego as they are facing down the remarkable faith challenge of the blazing furnace. They said, *"But even if He does not (even if God does not save us from the furnace), we want you to know, Your Majesty, that we will not serve your gods or worship the image of gold you have set up."* Queen Esther made the choice to have faith as her people were about to be destroyed by the wicked Haman. She was willing to move forward even if it cost her very life. Mary was willing to surrender to God unconditionally when she became aware of His plan to have her bear the Son of God, even though she was unwed and would experience ridicule. "I am the Lord's slave," she said to the angel. "May it be done to me according to your word."

You Can Be Effective in Prayer Ministry. But it will take the right kind of "even if" faith, and an "even if" kind of prayer ministry. And prayer ministry will have its detractors, even in the church, and even among believers. There will unfortunately be those who say, "Even if God were to open the flood gates of blessing, this could not happen," or, bringing it a little closer to home, "Even if God does answer your prayers and bless your prayer ministry, this church won't change enough to cross that threshold you're talking about." But it can, because God is the One who can do it.

Pray. Pray by yourself. Pray together with others who will pray with you. Teach and lead others to pray. Then stand back in faith and enjoy being a part of what God will do.

You read in the Introduction about Samson Dunn and the Phoenix church he pastors called Catalyst Church. Samson wrote the following words after he and his church got serious about prayer:

> Last year (2012) it became apparent that after two years with no noticeable growth in attendance something needed to change. After meeting with the leadership team, we decided to begin to fervently seek God for direction. The result was the impression from God that we had reached capacity unless we began to teach our church to pray. The fact is that the campus we have is designed to accommodate 500 to 700 people and we were already running an average of 850 to 900 weekly

attendees. Not to mention the previous leadership had linked the property responsibilities together with a charter school that we had decided needed to go. The problem here is that the income from the school covered over a third of our annual budget. So needless to say, we were in a pickle: no extra finances, no growth in over two years and no idea which way to go. So we began to pray, nothing else, just pray.

During this time my good friend and longtime mentor Paul Covert shared with me that he was about to go on a study (sabbatical) for several months. I immediately got the idea of having him come over and teach our church how to implement a prayer ministry at Catalyst. Not that we were not a praying church already (largely as a result of the mentoring of a prayer pastor for years), but there was nothing organized, nothing that taught people to pray effectively. My friend Paul countered with the idea of having me and a team come over to Central for a prayer conference to learn the process. We of course were all over it, and that is where it all began.

Before we ever made it to the first day of the weeklong conference (which consisted of learning all day and visiting other churches all night), my associate called and said he had to rush his wife to the hospital the night before. Turns out she had a brain aneurism and was also 6 months pregnant. My potential leader for the prayer ministry had his home broken into the day before in broad daylight, and another leader was informed that her son had been admitted into the hospital and was about to have his foot amputated. (If you think I am making this up, believe me, I'm not this creative).

As we finally got a team of three of us together we headed off. As we began to learn how to make prayer a major part of our church, God began to change me. Now I know what you're thinking, ("sure, that's the point") but it was more than that, it was a different change. The change God began to facilitate was in my definition of success as a church. You see, all along I would look at what I considered to be successful churches, (you know, thousands of people) and think to myself, if I want to be successful I should do what they do. Now I began to see that success was not having all the big stuff but it was doing the big stuff, God was calling our church to put prayer at the top of our list of priorities.

After the conference, I and the leadership team agreed to pray for the next 30 days to allow God to give us clear direction as we moved forward. Once the thirty days were ended we began two ministries. One was what we call "Ignite Prayer Gathering," the other was "Prayer Intercessory." The Ignite Gathering meets on Wednesday nights and consists of worship, a short message on prayer, and an extended time of corporate prayer. The Prayer Intercessory is a gathering of individuals to pray during our Sunday services. Our church has never been the same. Our attendance grew by almost 50% in the first month, not to mention every ministry in our church has a sense of excitement that is obviously supernatural.

It would be impossible to put into words the amazing transformation our church has undergone over these past seven - eight months, but it is nothing short of miraculous. During all this, I also began to hear God impress on me this passage from Scripture,

"What must we do to be saved?" At first I did not understand, but then I realized that there were people in our church every week that leave with that question burning in their hearts, just like at Pentecost. You see, in our zeal to be like churches we deemed successful we did not offer an invitation at our church, but God made it clear that He was changing things in a major way. As a result, we began what we call the Gospel Presentation at the end of each service and allow people to receive Christ; the first week we did this almost 100 people publicly accepted Christ and it has been an average of 10-15 each week since. God is so amazing.

To sum this up, I think the biggest difference in what we do is that before we would spend time planning and then asking God to bless our efforts and help us reach our community, and He did. Now it seems more and more we are spending time being sensitive to what God is doing and the direction He is going and getting on board with Him. As a result, we are currently (after eight months) approaching 1500 weekly attendance. Not only that, but giving is up. We have more than compensated for the income from the school, every ministry in our church is flourishing, and there is an excitement that is too wonderful for words.

Central's Programs and Ministries

UpTeam Book

Here are sample entries from an UpTeam book. Each entry looks the same; we use a template. Each staff member can share one praise, three ministry needs, and two personal needs. Each person is limited to 255 characters so that no one's entries are too lengthy.

Paul Covert   Spouse: Annie
Team: Family Prayer

Praise and Thanksgiving

It looks like we have someone to join our prayer team. We are thanking the Lord for His favor on this need.

Ministry Need(s)

- Please pray for those who attended the School of Prayer. Since we talked about infusing life into our prayer times at life group, pray that people will try and have success with some of the new things they learned.
- I have been asked to lead some city-wide prayer efforts... Pray that I have lots of wisdom for these tasks.
- Pray for Cathy as she transitions from staff to volunteer staff. She has done a wonderful job and we are praying that her transition will go very smoothly.

Personal Request(s)

- Pray that I can serve my family well.

Pastor   Spouse:
Team: Connect   Role:

Praise and Thanksgiving

I want to praise God that I'm serving at a great church with a great team and seeing God do great things in our midst. We are seeing numerical growth on our campus which is an indicator of outreach and financial growth which is an indicator of maturity.

Ministry Needs

Pray for our Servant Minister initiative in November. We are hoping to involve 200 new people in First Impressions, Starting Point, Central Cafe and Bookstore. Pray for our planning and that God would be preparing the hearts of our campus to respond. Pray for the hiring of a new Inside First impressions Director.
_____ _____ is transitioning to Girlfriends. We are interviewing now. Pray for God to provide an inspiring team builder to lead this critical area of ministry.

Pray for our Thousand Bites Connection Event on the weekend of September 21-22. We are trying to connect 400 people into Life Groups. Pray for God to raise up the additional leaders we need (40 in all) to make this possible.

Personal Requests

Pray for me to be humble, patient and gentle. I want this to be a year where I invest heavily in relationship. Pray that God will keep this before me and grant me success in building relational capital with leaders and leading through my care for people.

Sample Small Group Prayer Card

Small Group Prayer Card

How can I pray for you this week?

Pray that I can listen to the Lord better in dealing with my teenage

son. _____

_____

_____

Please keep this card where you will see it, and pray for your prayer partner this week.

Pictures of Prayer Walls from Events

Prayer walls are large, approximately 20 feet long and 8 feet tall.

Individuals commit themselves to prayer by signing the prayer wall for a specific time.

Staff Prayer Card

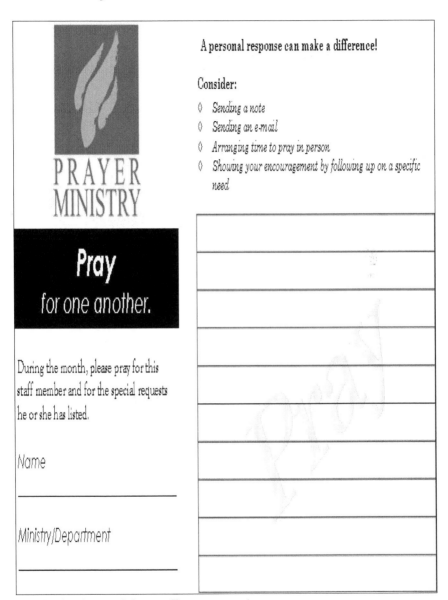

A personal response can make a difference!

Consider:
◊ Sending a note
◊ Sending an e-mail
◊ Arranging time to pray in person
◊ Showing your encouragement by following up on a specific need

PRAYER MINISTRY

Pray
for one another.

During the month, please pray for this staff member and for the special requests he or she has listed.

Name

Ministry/Department

This is the front of the staff prayer card.

PRAYER WORKS!

Upcoming Prayer Events

Lift—Prayer at Central
7 p.m. in the Starting Point Room
Wednesdays: Gilbert Campus
Thursdays: Mesa Campus

PrayerQuake 2008
June 18-20, 2008
City of Grace Church (formerly Word of Grace)
Register online at www.prayerquake.org

Half Day in Prayer
Second Saturday of the Month in the fall
and spring –watch for upcoming dates!
7 a.m. to noon (Vanpool from Mesa campus)

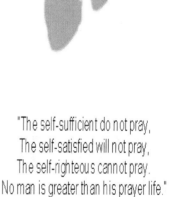

"The self-sufficient do not pray,
The self-satisfied will not pray,
The self-righteous cannot pray.
No man is greater than his prayer life."

Leonard Ravenhill

The back of the staff prayer card highlights upcoming events.

2013 Virtual National Day of Prayer Effort

What: 20 Prayers in 13 Minutes

When: Thursday, May 2, 2013, The National Day of Prayer

Where: By yourself, with your family, or with your Life Group.
Or attend a prayer gathering at one of these locations:

- Glendale Campus 11 a.m. through 7 p.m. in the Worship Center (a come-and-go opportunity)
- Mesa Campus, 11 a.m. through 7 p.m. in the Worship Center (a come-andgo opportunity)

As a nation, we seek forgiveness for . . .

- We have forgotten God and acted on our own power.
- We have gone our own way and chosen things above Him.
- We have given in morally to the influence of media, movies, and TV. (Romans 12:2)
- We have forgotten the fatherless and widowed of society. (James 1:27)
- We have become an angry and violent people.
- We have fostered racial tensions and prejudice.

As a nation, we give thanks for . . .

- The many blessings we enjoy as a nation. Speak these out loud and give thanks for them.

As a nation, we ask for . . .

♦ Pray for President Obama and our national leaders.
Pray specifically for:

◊ Wisdom and insight
◊ Character
◊ Policy
◊ Their families
◊ If any don't yet know Christ, to come to faith in Him
◊ Pray for the protection of the sanctity of marriage
◊ The US economy and national debt
◊ Our troops, their families, their faith, and their safety

As your people, we pray for the State of Arizona . . ..

♦ Governor Brewer and key State leaders.

◊ Wisdom and Insight
◊ Character
◊ Policy
◊ Family
◊ If any don't yet know Christ, to come to faith in Him.

♦ Immigration and a realistic resolution to this issue.

As your people, we seek first the Kingdom of God . . .

♦ We pray for the families of Central and our family to put God first.
♦ We pray for the marriages of Central and our marriage to remain strong.
♦ We pray that as parents we can raise our children to know and love God.

We pray for Central Christian Church that . . .

- ♦ We would have an increasing hunger for God's word.
- ♦ We would be passionate worshippers as we gather together weekly.
- ♦ We would live out authentic community in Life Groups.
- ♦ We would give ourselves in service to one another and the world.

Job Descriptions

For Campus Prayer Leaders

- Oversee all the prayer and prayer events at your given campus, touching base with Paul or Cathy for details.
- Work with Paul and Cathy to accomplish the goals of the Prayer Ministry.
- Recruit as you have the opportunity for prayer needs on your campus.
- Champion and demonstrate a prayerful presence on your campus.
- When possible, be the go-to person on your campus in Paul or Cathy's absence.

Facebook Coordinator

- Keep prayer requests, events, testimonies, and other creative material on the Web about prayer

Half Day in Prayer Leader

- Prepare and lead a Half Day in Prayer each month.
- Secure and be cleared to drive a Central van if leaving campus to pray.
- Make sure publicity is up on the Central Web site, on Central Worship Center slides, and Facebook.
- Check to see how many have registered midweek before a Half Day.
- Have copies of materials for each participant (e-mail to participants ahead of time, if possible).
- Lead the debriefing time.

Life Coaching Coordinator

- Keep a list of the men and women who want to be coached.
- Keep a current list of those who are coaching.
- Match the people who want to be coached with those who want to be coaches.
- Connect with all coaches on a regular basis to see how their coaching is going.

Lift Leader

- Lead and/or facilitate prayer in the midweek prayer gatherings at Central.
- Provide a small group feel to the prayer times.
- Recruit people to come and pray.
- Set up the room. Put it back into order after prayer time.
- Set the air to a comfortable temperature.

E-Accountability Team Leader

- Report in each week yourself, setting a good example.
- Respond to each team member's report.
- Pray for each team member and encourage team members to do the same.
- Develop a small group feel to your team.
- Let Paul or Cathy know of any problems with participants.

E-Accountability Team Member

- Report each week.
- Show care for the others on your team, by responding with prayer and e-mails after receiving their reports.

Newsletter Coordinator

♦ Assign articles to writers.

♦ Follow up on articles to make sure make deadline.

♦ Provide first layer of editing for the stories.

♦ Get material to Jayne, and see that it is proofed.

♦ Update the lists of newsletter recipients from time to time.

Newsletter Editor

♦ Take all copy and arrange into attractive, appealing, read-able, prayer-promoting newsletter.

♦ Be one layer of editing the copy.

♦ Find appropriate graphics or art to go with stories.

♦ Check all links to be sure they work in conjunction with the stories.

♦ Get the newsletter out as close to the first of each month as possible.

♦ Updates and manages contact list to ensure it is correct.

Newsletter Writer

♦ Receive an assignment from the coordinator with a target date for completion.

♦ Complete the writing assignment by the target date.

♦ Get your assignment to the editor by target date.

Office Help

♦ Come to the Mesa office at assigned times.

♦ Dress appropriately.

♦ Complete the tasks you are assigned.

Prayer Garden Leader

◆ Change Prayer Garden Station prayer copy once a month.
◆ Report to Paul or Cathy if anything needs repair in the garden.

Prayer Partner Leader

◆ Recruit and train prayer partners.
◆ Schedule the prayer partners at least three months out.
◆ Stay in contact with prayer partners, especially before scheduling, checking in to see if they would like to switch campus or the worship service time when they serve, and how their prayer partner experience is going.

Prayer Partner

◆ Take training to become a prayer partner.
◆ Pray before coming to serve.
◆ Be faithful to serving at the worship service where you are scheduled.
◆ Dress appropriately and use breath mints.
◆ Fill out legibly a Prayer Response Card for those you pray for and turn it in to Paul or Cathy or put it on the Web Prayer Page yourself if they want it listed there.
◆ Get Paul or Cathy involved if the person you pray with includes homicide, suicide or abuse in the request for prayer. Also involve them if the person is in precarious condition (for example, living out of their car).
◆ Watch for other prayer partners to see if they need assistance if you are not praying with anyone.
◆ Stay, or be sure someone else will, until the last prayer partner concludes with his or her prayer requester. No prayer partner should be left in the Worship Center alone.

Prayer Teacher for Small Groups

- Use agreed upon material.
- Teach small groups when asked on the subject of prayer.
- Recruit from the small group for prayer ministry needs.
- Keep Paul or Cathy informed on how it is going

School of Prayer Leader

- Secure someone to provide food and servers, speaker(s), and topics.
- Recruit people to greet, welcome, sign people up if they have interest in Prayer Team.
- Prepare room, and sound, with help from a team you recruit.
- Clean up afterward.
- Make sure the publicity is done on Central's website, Facebook, Worship Center slides, and any other suitable locations.

Service Intercession Captain

- Lead the prayer time for the service they direct.
- Each prayer time should have the following phases: confession, praise, prayer for the service, and prayer for the theme for that service.
- Bring and refer to Bible for prayer direction.
- View Intercession times as a small group.
- Take prayer requests from participating pray-ers. (All participants are encouraged to pray for one another, though it may not be during Service Intercession because our focus is prayers for others. But their requests should be taken and prayed for if time permits.)

♦ Contact members who are absent to check on them. This is to be done in a way that does not make them feel guilty, but lets them know they are missed and gives an opportunity to discover if there is something they need prayer for from us.

Service Intercession Member

♦ Attend the Service Intercession session you committed to as much as possible.
♦ Bring a Bible.
♦ Just come. If you can't, there is no need to call the captain.

UpTeam Leader

♦ Schedule people who want to pray one hour on the UpTeam schedule, and keep the schedule up to date.
♦ Help recruit people to join the UpTeam.
♦ Recruit captains for each day on the UpTeam schedule.
♦ Have the captains call and/or e-mail their day of pray-ers occasionally to stay in touch.

UpTeam Members

♦ Pray during your one hour a week.
♦ Pray for the requests listed in either the internet version of the UpTeam Book or the printed booklet.

Web Prayer Editor

♦ Enter prayer requests on Central's Web Prayer Page as needed.
♦ Sterilize or edit prayer requests and/or responses that are not appropriate before they go on the Web Prayer Page.

- Make Paul or Cathy aware of any prayer requests that have homicidal, suicidal, or abuse issues in them so that they can handle those situations appropriately.
- Make Paul or Cathy aware of any issues with this team or the Web Prayer Page.

Web Prayer Team Members

- Pray through the prayer requests on the Web Prayer Page at least one time a week.
- Respond now and then to those prayer requests open to a response, not giving advice, but briefly saying you are praying for the request.

24-7 Hosting Coordinator

- Recruit one man or woman (or a couple if they would like to do host together) to greet and welcome all who come to pray.
- Create a schedule of two-hour shifts throughout the time the prayer room is on the campus you are serving.
- Instruct them to help people understand what to do if they've never attended before.
- Instruct them to clean up stations and put materials in order a time or two during their shift.
- Contact the hosts to remind them when they are to come and serve.
- Be the contact person if they cannot make it when they agreed to come.
- Get Cathy or an alternate person to fill in.

24-7 Sign Up Coordinator

♦ Schedule one or two people to be in the lobby or courtyard (depending on what set up is available on your campus) to sign people up to come and pray one hour during the 24-7 Prayer Time on your campus.
♦ Schedule people to be available immediately after every worship service on your campus.
♦ Tell the person they will have to get material from somewhere on the campus they serve (to be determined on each campus) and arrange it on a sign-up table.
♦ Train them to welcome and encourage people to try praying one hour, and also see if anyone would like to help with hosting or security as well.
♦ Assure them materials will be provided.

24-7 Security Coordinator

♦ Recruit men to serve in three-hour shifts from 6 p.m. to 6 a.m. each night for the campus you are coordinating.
♦ Create a schedule for the days on your campus.
♦ Contact the men to remind them what to bring and when to come.
♦ Be the contact person if they cannot make it when they agreed to come.
♦ Get Paul or an alternate person to fill in.

24-7 Station Creator

♦ Attend planning sessions to coordinate all stations.
♦ Clear ideas and costs for display and other materials with Paul or Cathy.
♦ Gather a team to help set up and take down station.

Prayer Conference Food Coordinator

- ◆ Think of the food and drinks needed to welcome guests as they arrive and enjoy breaks.
- ◆ Clear costs and ideas with Paul and Cathy.
- ◆ Order and arrange the food in an appealing way.
- ◆ Recruit people to help serve, set up, and clean up

Prayer Conference Greeting Coordinator

- ◆ Recruit and schedule people to meet and greet guests as they arrive on campus.
- ◆ Train them to take people to where they need to be if they are lost or confused.

Prayer Conference Speaker Welcome Coordinator

- ◆ Contact the speaker to see what food or drinks would be conducive at welcoming and making his or her appearance optimum.
- ◆ Get what it takes for the speaker to be well cared for.
- ◆ Create a gift to send home with him or her.

Prayer Conference Ushering Coordinator

- ◆ Recruit and train people to welcome people inside the Worship Center.
- ◆ Help them know what to hand out or how to be ready to be helpful to the speaker (stay in contact via walkie-talkie with Paul or Cathy).
- ◆ Schedule them to cover all before and after sessions, and break times, if needed.
- ◆ Schedule usually will include a Friday night and Saturday morning time frame.

Prayer E-mail Series for Forty Days of Prayer and Fasting
for the Nation Campaign

Refer to Chapter 8 for this series of e-mail messages.

Prayer Budget for Central

The Prayer Budget at Central is $14,000 to $16,000 for expenses and ministry.

Here is a copy of the lines from the spreadsheet we use, to give you some idea of the categories.

Revenue Accounts

General Contributions
Event Revenue
Resource Revenue

Total Revenue

Expense Accounts

Expense General and Administrative Accounts

Servant Minister Encouragement
Staff Appreciation
Meals
Copy Costs
Cell Phone
Travel/Mileage
Continuing Education
Office Supplies
Office Equipment
Fees

Expense General and Administrative Accounts

Expense General and Administrative Accounts (Labor)

Contract Labor/Consulting

Total Expense General and Administrative Accounts (Labor)

Expense Services and Marketing Accounts

Printing
Postage
Publicity/Marketing

Total Expense Services and Marketing Accounts

Expense Ops Accounts

Ministry Cost of Goods (Resale)
Ministry Supplies (Consumables)
Equipment Rental

Total Expense Ops Accounts

Total Expense

Arena Web-Based Software for Churches

We use Arena at this point but are planning to move to Rock in the future. If you have questions about how we have used Arena, send e-mail to me at Paul.Covert@centralaz.com, and I can help you get connected to our Information Technology staff.

Personal Prayer Tools

Prayer Log. This is a model of the Prayer Log form I use for recording my prayer. I maintain this information on my computer.

Date Prayer Request	Encouragement			Answered
2/10/13 Nonbelieving neighbors	2/13/13			
2/12/13 Difficult coworker				
2/12/13 Wife's illness				2/12/13 recovered

Who I Am in Christ

These are biblical truths to "practice believing." Most people have no idea who they are in Christ. They have believed less about themselves. I will often ask people who struggle with low self-esteem to read this daily and begin to replace their thoughts about themselves with what God says.

I am God's:

♦ possession
♦ child
♦ workmanship
♦ friend
♦ temple
♦ vessel
♦ colaborer
♦ witness
♦ soldier
♦ ambassador
♦ building
♦ instrument
♦ chosen
♦ beloved
♦ precious jewel
♦ candle in a dark place
♦ city set on a hill
♦ salt of the earth

I have been:

♦ redeemed by the blood
♦ set free from sin and condemnation
♦ set free from Satan's control
♦ set free from Satan's kingdom
♦ chosen before the foundation of the world

- forgiven of all my trespasses
- cleansed by the blood of the lamb
- given a sound mind
- given the Holy Spirit
- adopted into God's family
- justified freely by His grace
- given all things pertaining to life and godliness
- given great and precious promises
- given authority over all the power of the enemy
- given access to God
- given wisdom

I have:

- access to the Father
- a home in heaven waiting for me
- all things in Christ
- a living hope
- an anchor to my soul
- a hope that is steadfast and unmovable
- authority to tread on serpents
- power to witness
- the tongue of the learned
- the mind of Christ
- boldness and access
- peace with God
- faith as a grain of mustard seed

I am:

- complete in Him
- free forever from sin's power
- sanctified and meet for the Master's use
- loved eternally

- eternally kept in the palm of his hand
- kept by the power of God
- not condemned
- one with the Lord
- on my way to heaven
- alive, quickened by is mighty power
- seated with Christ in heavenly places
- the head and not the tail
- light in the darkness/His sheep
- a citizen of heaven
- hidden with Christ in God
- protected from the evil one
- kept by the power of God
- secure in Christ
- set on a rock
- more than a conqueror
- born again
- a victor
- healed by His stripes
- covered by the blood of Jesus
- sheltered under His wing
- hidden in the secret place of the Almighty

I can:

- do all things through Christ who strengthens me
- find mercy and grace to help in needs
- come boldly to the throne of grace
- quench all the fiery darts of the wicked one
- tread on the serpent
- defeat the enemy
- declare God's truth
- pray always and everywhere
- chase a thousand

I cannot:

- be separated from God's love
- be lost
- be removed from His grasp
- taken out of the Father's hand

Promises to Use in Prayer

Prayer

♦ Isaiah 65:24: "Before they call I will answer . . . ."
♦ Psalm 37:4: "Delight yourself in the LORD and he will give you the desires of your heart."
♦ Psalm 37:5-6: "Commit your way to LORD, trust in him and he will do this: He will make your righteousness shine like the dawn, the justice of your cause like the noonday sun."
♦ Jeremiah 32:17: "'. . . You have made the heavens. Nothing is too hard for you.'"
♦ Jeremiah 33:3: "'Call to me and I will answer you and tell you great and unsearchable things you do not know.'"
♦ Matthew 18:19: "'Again, I tell you that if two of you on earth agree about anything you ask for, it will be done for you by my Father in heaven.'"

Peace

♦ Isaiah 26:3: ". . . keep in perfect peace . . ."
♦ Isaiah 32:17: ". . . fruit of righteousness will be peace . . ."
♦ Jeremiah 29:11: "'. . . plans to prosper you and not harm you, plans to give you hope and a future.'"
♦ Psalm 37:37: ". . . there is a future for the man of peace . . ."

Protection

♦ Psalm 5:11-12: "But let all who take refuge in you be glad; let them ever sing for joy. Spread your protection over them. . . . For surely, O LORD, . . . you surround them with your favor as with a shield."
♦ Psalm 91:3: ". . . he shall save you from the fowler's snare and from the deadly pestilence."

- Isaiah 43:2: "When you pass through the waters, I will be with you. . . ."
- Isaiah 54:17: "no weapon forged against you will prevail . . ."
- Jeremiah 15:20: "'I will make you a wall to this people, a fortified wall of bronze . . . .'"

Supply

- Psalm 34:10: "The lions may grow weak and hungry, but those who seek the LORD lack no good thing."
- Psalm 37:25: " . . . I have never seen the righteous forsaken or their children begging. . . ."
- 2 Corinthians 9:8: ". . . God is able to make all grace abound to you . . . ."
- Philippians 4:19: ". . . my God will meet all your needs . . . ."

Success

- Joshua 1:8: ". . . Then you will be prosperous and successful."
- Psalm 1:3: "Whatever he does prospers . . . ."
- Romans 8:28: ". . . all things God works for the good of those who love him. . . ."

Strength

- Isaiah 40:29: ". . . increases the power of the weak . . ."
- Isaiah 40:31: ". . . who hope in the Lord will renew their strength . . . ."
- Isaiah 41:10: ". . . do not fear, for I am with you. . . . I will strengthen you . . . ."
- Isaiah 41:13: ". . . the LORD, your God, who takes hold of your right hand . . . ."
- 2 Corinthians 12:9: "'My grace is sufficient for you . . . .'"

Deliverance

- Psalm 34:7-8: "The angel of the LORD encamps around those who fear him . . ."
- Psalm 34:17: "The righteous cry out, and the LORD hears them; he delivers them from all their troubles."
- Isaiah 59:19: ". . . For he will come like a pent-up flood that the breath of the LORD drives along . . . ."

Direction and Leading

- Psalm 37:23: "The LORD delights in the way of the man whose steps he has made firm. . . ."
- Psalm 32:8: "I will will instruct you and teach you in the way you should go. . . ."
- Proverbs 3:6: "in all your ways acknowledge him, and he will make your your paths straight."
- Proverbs 16:3: "Commit to the LORD whatever you do, and your plans will succeed."
- Isaiah 30:21: ". . . your ears will hear a voice behind you saying, 'This is the way; walk in it.'"
- Isaiah 58:11: "The the LORD will guide you always. . . ."

Fears

- Psalm 34:4: "I sought the LORD, and he answered me; he delivered me from all my fears."
- Isaiah 41:10: ". . . do not fear for I am with you, . . . and help you. . . ."
- Isaiah 41:13: "'. . . Do not fear; I will help you. . . .'"
- 2 Timothy 1:7: "God did not give us a spirit of timidity, but of power. . . ."

Souls

- ◆ Psalm 2:8: "Ask of me, and I will make the nations your inheritance. . . ."
- ◆ Psalm 126:6: "He who goes out weeping, carrying seed to sow, will return with songs of joy, carrying sheaves with him."
- ◆ 2 Peter 3:9: ". . . Lord is not slow . . . not wanting anyone to perish . . ."

Your Children

- ◆ Psalm 127:3: "Sons are a heritage from the LORD, children a reward."
- ◆ Proverbs 22:6: "Train a child . . . when he is old he will not turn from it."
- ◆ Isaiah 44:3: "I will pour out my Spirit on your offspring. . . ."
- ◆ Isaiah 54:13: "All your sons will be taught by the LORD . . . ."
- ◆ Isaiah 59:21: "'My Spirit . . . and my words that I have put in your mouth will not depart from your mouth, or from the mouths of your children, or from the mouths of their descendents from this time on and forever,' . . ."

Wisdom

- ◆ Psalm 19:7: "The law . . . is perfect . . . making wise the simple."
- ◆ Proverbs 1:7: "The fear of the Lord is the beginning of knowledge. . . ."
- ◆ Isaiah 50:4: ". . . LORD has given me an instructed tongue, to know the word. . . ."
- ◆ James 1:5: ". . . lacks wisdom, he should ask God, who gives generously to all. . . ."

Forgiveness

- Psalm 86:5: "You are forgiving and good . . . ."
- Isaiah 1:18: "Though your sins are like scarlet, they shall be as white as snow. . . ."
- Isaiah 43:25: "I am he who blots out your transgressions. . . ."
- 1 John 1:9: "If we confess our sins, he is faithful . . . and will forgive. . . ."

Ability Above Impossibility

- Jeremiah 32:17, 27: "Ah, Sovereign Lord, . . . Nothing is too hard for you."
- Philippians 1:6: ". . . he who began a good work in you will carry it on. . . ."
- Acts 20:32: ". . . the word of his grace, which can build you up. . . ."
- Ephesians 3:20: "Now to him who is able to do immeasurably more than all we ask or imagine, according to his power that is at work within us. . . ."
- Jude 24: "To him who is able to keep you from falling and to present you before his glorious presence without fault and with great joy. . . ."

Healing

- Exodus 15:26: "'. . . I am the LORD, who heals you.'"
- Psalm 103:3: "He . . . heals all my diseases."
- James 5:15: ". . . the prayer offered in faith will make the sick person well. . . ."
- Matthew 8:17: "He took up our infirmities and carried our diseases."

Sleep

- Psalm 4:8: "I will . . . sleep in peace for you alone, O LORD, make me dwell in safety."
- Psalm 127:2: " . . . for he grants sleep to those he loves."
- Proverbs 3:24: ". . . when you lie down, your sleep will be sweet."

Word of God

- Isaiah 55:11: "so is my word that goes out from my mouth: It will not return to me empty, but will accomplish what I desire and achieve the purpose for which I sent it."
- Jeremiah 23:29: " 'Is not my word like fire,' . . . 'like a hammer . . . ?'"
- Acts 20:32: ". . . which can build you up and give you an inheritance . . ."
- Hebrews 4:12: "For the word of God is living and active. Sharper than any double-edged sword, it penetrates even to dividing soul and spirit, joints and marrow. . . ."
- 2 Timothy 2:9: "God's word is not chained."
- 2 Timothy 3:16: ". . . is useful for teaching, rebuking, correcting and training . . ."

Stronghold Groupings

Restoration Ministries International provides a PDF of *Demolishing Strongholds: God's Way to Spiritual Freedom* by Mike and Sue Dowgiewicz at this website: http://www.restorationministries.org/HtmlFiles/HTMLBooks /DemolishingStrongholdsR.htm. Chapter 4 is "Steps to Identify and Demolish Strongholds."

Book List

As mentioned in Chapter 5, here is a list of some favorite books on prayer:

- *And the Place Was Shaken: How to Lead a Powerful Prayer Meeting* by John Franklin
- *Andrew Murray on Prayer* by Andrew Murray
- *Back to Jerusalem: Three Chinese House Church Leaders Share Their Vision to Complete the Great Commission* by Brother Yun, Peter Xu Yongze, Enoch Wang, and Paul Hattaway
- *The Christian in Complete Armour* by William Gurnall
- *The Circle Maker: Praying Circles Around Your Biggest Dreams and Greatest Fears* by Mark Batterson
- *Draw the Circle: The Forty-Day Prayer Challenge* by Mark Batterson. This is an exciting devotional on prayer.
- *Experiencing God: Knowing and Doing the Will of God* by Henry Blackaby, Richard Blackaby, and Claude King. This is an excellent book on walking in hearing and acting in obedience, with practical advice for daily application.
- *Fresh Wind, Fresh Fire: What Happens When God's Spirit Invades the Hearts of His People* by Jim Cymbala and Dean Merrill
- *God Guides* by Mary Geegh. In this book, the author shares stories of how God worked in India via listening prayer.
- *God on Mute: Engaging the Silence of Unanswered Prayer* by Pete Greig
- *Grace for the Moment* by Max Lucado
- *Handle with Prayer: How to Turn Your World Around While on Your Knees* by Charles F. Stanley
- *How to Listen to God* by Charles F. Stanley. This book details hearing from a Baptist perspective.
- *In a Pit with a Lion on a Snowy Day: How to Survive and Thrive When Opportunity Roars* by Mark Batterson

- *In Search of Guidance: Developing a Conversational Relationship with God* by Dallas Willard. Anything by Willard is well worth the effort.
- *Intercession, Thrilling and Fulfilling* by Joy Dawson
- *Love to Pray: A Forty-Day Devotional for Deepening Your Prayer Life* (with Study Guide) by Alvin VanderGriend
- *Magnificent Prayer* by Nick Harrison. This is a 365-day devotional, and it's excellent.
- *The Power of a Praying Husband* by Stormie Omartian
- *The Power of a Praying Parent* by Stormie Omartian
- *The Power of a Praying Wife* by Stormie Omartian
- *Power Through Prayer* by E.M. Bounds
- *Practicing God's Presence: Brother Lawrence for Today's Reader (Quiet Times for the Heart)* by Robert Elmer. The author updates letters and sermons from Brother Lawrence, a monk from the 1600s. It is an excellent depiction of the conversational walk with God in the smallest details of life.
- *Prayer* by Ole Hallesby
- *Prayer Is Invading the Impossible* Jack W. Hayford
- *Prayer Quest: Breaking Through to Your God-Given Dreams and Destiny* by Dee Duke
- *The Prayer-Saturated Church* by Cheryl Sacks
- *Prayer, the Great Adventure* by David Jeremiah
- *Prayer: Does It Make Any Difference?* by Philip Yancey
- *Prayer: Finding the Heart's True Home* by Richard J. Foster
- *Praying God's Word: Breaking Free from Spiritual Strongholds* by Beth Moore
- *Praying Life* by Jennifer Kennedy Dean and Becky Nelson
- *A Praying Life: Connecting with God in a Distracting World* by Paul E. Miller and David Powlison
- *Praying with Power* by Lloyd John Ogilvie. The author is a Presbyterian pastor in California who gives stirring examples of hearing and obeying and seeing miracles as a result. The book is balanced and well-written.

- *The Pursuit of God* by A.W. Tozer. Tozer was a well-known and respected theologian. Chapter 6 of this book discusses God's "speaking voice."
- *Red Moon Rising: How 24-7 Prayer Is Awakening a Generation* by Pete Greig and Dave Roberts
- *Rees Howells: Intercessor* by Norman Percy Grubb
- *The Secret of Guidance* by F.B. Meyer. This is an excellent book on praying and hearing.
- *Sensitivity of the Holy Spirit: Learning to Stay in the Flow of God's Direction* by R.T. Kendall
- *The Spirit of the Disciplines: Understanding How God Changes Lives* by Dallas Willard
- *Too Busy Not to Pray* by Bill Hybels
- *The Way of the Heart* by Henri J. M. Nouwen. This book is based on the teachings of the "desert Fathers" from the early church, 251 AD. Nouwen has written for *Leadership* magazine and is quoted often by other authors on listening prayer. I have benefited from every book I have read by Nouwen.
- *The Weapon of Prayer* by E.M. Bounds

Prayer Journey Planning Questionnaire

Questions to Ask the Field Worker

Travel

1. Please confirm with us the dates that you have on your calendar for this trip?
2. Where will we fly to? Is there a domestic flight, bus, or train from there to your location? If yes, which method and how much will it likely cost?
3. Is there a visa fee to visit your country? If yes, how much is it? Can the visa be obtained at the airport or does it need to be obtained before arriving?
4. Is there an airport fee to enter or leave your country? If yes, how much is it?
5. When we arrive in the airport where should we go to meet you?
6. Are there any other thoughts or tips we should know about getting to and from your country?

In-Country Logistics and Finances

7. Where will we be staying (hotels, with families, guest houses, combination, etc.)? How much will a room cost a night? Is that one or two people a room? We would like to stay in houses with families if possible, but a hotel/dorm/guest house is fine. If we are staying in hotels, how does that work? Do you help us find a hotel or do we try to find a hotel from here? If we stay in a hotel, we don't need to stay in a fancy one. We would prefer to stay in more of a modest one that reflects more of the local culture.
8. How many times a day do the people eat there? What does a typical meal consist of?

9. How much should we budget a day per person for food and water?

10. What does the average person use for transportation there? Will we be using that? Will we be walking much?

11. How much should we budget a day per person for transportation (buses, taxis, rickshaws, whatever)?

12. Not counting our day-to-day local transportation in country, are there any other big travel expenses once we are there?

13. Are there any other big expenses during the trip that we should plan for?

14. Are there any guide or translator expenses that we should expect?

15. How should we go about exchanging money?

In-Country Purpose and Schedule

16. Not in great detail, but roughly what do you envision us doing while we are there? What might a rough schedule look like? (In considering this question, please don't feel like you need to be our caretaker the whole time. We are fine with being passed around to different ministries/expatriots/ nationals. We are fine with and actually enjoy being exposed to multiple areas while we are there. A day or two to prayer-walk and to learn about the people and culture is also fine. Again, we don't want to be a burden to you while there, so feel free to come up with a creative schedule for us.)

Culture

17. Would it be possible to get a list (a few pages long) of cultural things to avoid and cultural things to do? We will train the team to be wise and culturally sensitive by principle, but a few cultural specifics would be helpful.

Please include any specific contextualization practices that we should be aware of.

18. While we are there are there any cultural festivals or holidays going on that we should be aware of? If yes, could you tell us a little about the event/holiday?

19. As we prepare the group to visit, we like to show them a movie/film/documentary that really helps them understand and learn about the culture and the people there. Have you seen any movie or film inside or outside of the country that would be good for the group to watch? If yes, which one?

Miscellaneous

20. What is the weather like during the time of year that we will be visiting?

21. What type of clothing do the men wear there during that time of year? Is that the same thing we should wear? What type of clothing do the women wear there during that time of year? Is that the same thing we should wear?

22. Are there any ministry or personal supplies you would like us to bring with us? If yes, what? We will try to have the team voluntarily get/gather these supplies. (In considering this question, also know that when we come to visit you, we will also try to bring a small financial gift for you. If there are many items on your list for personal and ministry supplies and our team is unable to get/gather all of them, would you like us to use some of that financial gift to purchase any of those remaining ministry or personal supplies?)

Impactful Locations to Visit

IHOP. Here is what the International House of Prayer in Kansas City, Missouri, has to say say about their own ministry:

Central to the programs, activities, and outreach of the International House of Prayer is our 24/7 prayer room, which is open to the public around the clock, day and night. The prayer room has been designed to reflect the tabernacle of David 1 Chronicles 22-24; it is a place where we never cease worshiping the Lord and interceding for our world. Each twenty-four-hour period is divided into twelve two-hour prayer sessions, each led by a full worship team.

All are welcome to come and go freely and to stay in the prayer room as long as they like. While in the prayer room, feel free to join in with the corporate worship and prayer, read your Bible, study a favorite commentary, write in your journal, or engage in private prayer. You may sit, stand, or pace up and down the aisles. Whatever you do, we ask that you do it in a manner that honors and serves the other people in the room."

Our prayer format is based on the heavenly picture that we see in Revelation 5, which speaks of the harp and the bowl—worship and prayer. Within the harp and bowl prayer model, we use two basic worship and prayer formats. Each twenty-four-hour period is divided into six two-hour intercession sessions (or sets, as we call them) and six two-hour worship with the Word sessions, which are more devotional in nature.

Intercession sessions are usually energetic, as the room is invited to engage in corporate prayer. There is generally a specific prayer focus, and individuals in the room are welcome to pray on the microphone for a corporate burden, which may involve the Kansas City region or believers worldwide. There are also cycles of "rapid fire prayer" when intercessors go to the microphone to pray a succession of 15-second prayers on a specific theme, as well as times of small group prayer for any who wish to participate.

Worship with the Word is a prayer format in which we agree with God's heart as we sing the biblical truths of who God is and what His promises are. These sessions are more devotional in nature, providing an atmosphere conducive to reading the Bible and entering into contemplative or devotional prayer. The current link is: http://www.ihopkc.org/prayerroom

The Brooklyn Tabernacle Prayer Meeting. I have taken my prayer teams to this church a couple times to see their Tuesday evening prayer meeting. The Brooklyn Tab meets in a renovated theater and draws people from all over the New York Area. The demographics are marvelous. Every race and ethnicity is present. Jim Cymbla leads the meeting, which features many different methods of prayer. Some would include: Praying in triads, pastoral prayer, and a myriad of other creative approaches. You should visit this church and just soak in what they are doing. We fly out on Sat and attend their Sunday services on that morning. Sunday afternoon we visit the city and have some fun. Sunday night we have visited a couple of other key churches like the Times Square church where David Wilkerson worked. On Monday we try to meet with one of the BT leaders who helps us understand their prayer ministry. That night the guys go to a ball game and the gals go to a play. Tuesday we see more of the city and Tuesday night we go to the prayer meeting. Wed morning we fly out and get back to work. Trips like this paint the picture of what prayer could look like in our church if we were willing to put out the effort.

Jefferson Baptist Church. This church in Jefferson, Oregon, is another must-see for prayer leaders. The church is about 2,500 on a given Sunday, but the town is only 1,800. So there are more people in church on a Sunday morning than in the whole town. The pastor Dee Duke is a friend of mine and one of my heroes. He prays three hours a day and has created a scrapbook that he has kept for years of the members of his church. He has graduation pictures, wedding picture, baby pictures that help remind him what to pray for each of his families.

Dee leads three prayer weeks a year. Each week has a specific area the congregation is covering in prayer like evangelism, world missions or their ministry. Each day has 10 hours of prayer. The early session is from 5 to 10 AM and the later session is from 5 to 10 PM. Dee leads these and they are in 45 minute segments. He starts with a small devotion on prayer and then reminds people of prayer etiquette. ("Pray loud, pray short" and so on). Then they pray corporately for 45 minutes. Then there is a 15 minute break, and they start again right at the top of the hour. They average 50 people per hour in their prayer events and it is powerful.

A couple of items worth noting:

♦ Dee leads a Prayer Conference in January each year that I have attended. It is very good, something you should consider taking your leaders to.
♦ He also has twenty prayer meetings a week that go on at his church. Of those he leads seven. This is truly a praying church.

DVDs

George Otis Junior has done a series of DVDs called *Transformation*. They are a bit dated now, but I have used them several times to build the vision of what could happen when a church gets serious about prayer.

Ed Silvoso has also created some wonderful DVDs on transformation, and these are newer and more up to date. I would recommend you purchase some of these.

Finally, Jim Cymbala has done a DVD series on prayer for small groups that works well. Give it a try.

Seminars

Billy Graham has a conference center in Asheville, North Carolina, called The Cove. Each year they put on a conference called Heart Cry for Revival. This is a magnificent conference. The atmosphere is outstanding and the teaching is even better. Put this on your list as a "for sure."

Our conference at Central is called Elevate, and we do it once every three years. We bring a couple of top-notch speakers and spend a Friday night and Sat morning together learning about prayer. You can check for our upcoming conferences on Central's website www.centralaz.com.

Consulting and Conference Speaking

If it would be helpful to you to have Paul Covert or someone from the ministry at Central coach you in prayer ministry, please do not hesitate to contact us. Paul travels and speaks all over the United States and Internationally. His easy-going style is perfect for helping churches get started and grow in prayer and prayer ministry.

You can reach Paul directly at Paul.Covert@centralaz.com

E-mail us if we can help!

Notes

[1] *The Holy Bible, New International Version* (Grand Rapids, MI: The Zondervan Corporation). Copyright 1978 by New York International Society. Unless otherwise indicated, this version of the Bible was used for all quotations.

[2] C.S. Lewis, *Letters to Malcolm: Chiefly on Prayer* (San Diego: Harcourt, 1992).

[3] From J. Edwin Orr's *The Light of the Nations*, pages 103-105, as presented on http://www.intheworkplace.com/apps/articles /default.asp?articleid=51927&columnid=1935 on October 13, 2013.

[4] Posted by Greene Street Letters on November 18, 2009, http://rapha2911.blogspot.com/2009_11_01_archive.html.

[5] Mahesh Chavda, *Watch of the Lord: Secret Weapon of the Last-Day Church* (Lake Mary, FL: Charisma House, 1999), page 117.

[6] George H Gallup Jr. *Religion in America* (Princeton, NJ: The Princeton Religion Research Center, 1996), pages 4, 12, 19.

[7] Philip Yancey, *Prayer: Does It Make Any Difference?* (Grand Rapids, MI: Zondervan, 2006), page 13.

[8] C. Peter Wagner, *The Prayer Shield* (Ventura, CA: Regal Books, 1992), pages 78-79.

[9] Paul and Tracey McManus, *The Seven Great Prayers*.

[10] The Navigators, *Eighty Days of Discipleship*. In the devotional thought for Day 8, "Communion with God," by Rusty Rustenbach.

[11] Dan R. Crawford, *Disciplines of Personal Prayer* (2009). In Chapter 25, the author gives the source of this information as Evangelical Missions Quarterly.

[12] Eric Foley, *These Are The Generations: The Story of How One North Korean Family Lived Out the Great Commission for More Than Fifty Years in the Most Christian-Hostile Nation in Human History* (Colorado Springs, CO: W Publishing, 2012), page 7.

---

13   Alistair Begg, senior pastor of the Parkside Church in Chagrin Falls, OH, from http://www.conversationsalongtheway.com/2010_01_01_archive.html.

14 This material has been adapted from sermons written by Dee Duke, Senior Pastor of the Jefferson Baptist Chruch in Jefferson, Oregon. Dee is a long-time mentor of mine, and his material is used by permission.

15 Cheryl Sacks, *Prayer Saturated Church.*

16 The USS *Constitution* is the "world's oldest commissioned warship afloat" according to http://www.history.navy.mil/ussconstitution/).

17 *Constitution* has continued to sail occasionally under her own power, as recently as August 2012 according to http://boston.cbslocal.com/2012/08/19/uss-constitution-sails-under-own-power-for-first-time-in-15-years/).

18 Dale Stohre, *Soundings: Exploring the Depths of Your Life* (Pilot Press, 1988), page 17.

19 William Gurnall, *The Christian in Complete Armour*. This is Volume 2 of a twelve-volume set, *Fifty Greatest Christian Classics*, Lafayette, IN: Sovereign Grace Publishers, 1990) by J.P. Green Jr., page 397.

20 Charles M. Olsen, Transforming Church Boards into Communities of Spiritual Leaders (Alban Institute, 1995).

21 Adapted from an article on William Carey from myshekinah.org.

22 From a reprint of *An Hour with George Mueller: The Man of Faith to Whom God Gave Millions*, Edited by A. Sims, Chicago: Moody Press, 1939), page 13.

23 *Holy Bible, New International Version,* Copyright 1973, 1978, 1984, 2011 by Biblica, Inc. Used by permission.

24 John Eldredge, *Waking the Dead* (Thomas Nelson Publishers, 2003).

25 *Breaking Strongholds: How Spiritual Warfare Sets Captives Free* by Tom White (Servant Books, 1993).

26 Jim Downing, *Meditation.*

27 Bill Gothard, Training Faithful Women.

28 Jim Downing, *Meditation.*

29 J. B. Phillips, The New Testament in Modern English (HarperCollins, 1962).

30 Betty Lee Skinner, *Daws: The Story of Dawson Trotman, Founder of the Navigators* (Grand Rapids, MI: Zondervan, 1974).

31 John Franklin, *And the Place Was Shaken: How to Lead a Powerful*

Prayer Meeting.

[32] Geoff Surratt, Greg Ligon, and Warren Bird, *The Multisite Church Revolution* (Zondervan, 2006).

[33] *Outreach Magazine*, October 2007.

[34] Geoff Surratt, Greg Ligon, and Warren Bird, *The Multisite Church Revolution* (Zondervan, 2006).

[35] Fred Smith, *Breakfast with Fred Smith: Mentoring a Generation of Leaders.*

Made in the USA
San Bernardino, CA
07 October 2017